Burt's Ode to Tammy

I once knew a lady named Tammy
Who had an old-fashioned daddy and mammy
At one time she had to pick cotton
For which she has long since forgotten
Now she's grown up with kids of her own
Got a big shining bus, two houses, twelve phones
She's pretty and smart, can even write charts
But what's best is this beauty's big heart
Sometimes she's sick and she stumbles
Sometimes she's mad and she grumbles
Nobody loves what's perfect ————
This don't rhyme, but who gives a @!&*#.

Burt Reynolds

STAND BY YOUR MAN
TAMMY WYNETTE

An Autobiography
with Joan Dew

PUBLISHED BY POCKET BOOKS NEW YORK

Cover photograph by Norman Seeff

All record covers and portraits of Tammy Wynette
courtesy CBS Records, copyright © CBS, Inc.

POCKET BOOKS, a Simon & Schuster division of
GULF & WESTERN CORPORATION
1230 Avenue of the Americas, New York, N.Y. 10020

For my father,
Bernie, and
Carolyn
With my love

Chapter 1

*T*HE sign in the emergency room of Children's Hospital in Birmingham, Alabama, read "This room is for waiting only, not for sleeping." I must have looked at it a thousand times that night in 1965 as I paced the floor waiting for someone to come back and tell me what was wrong with my baby. I remember wondering why they had found it necessary to put such a sign there. I didn't see how any parent could relax enough to sleep while waiting for news of a sick or injured child.

My own baby, Tina, had been taken from me hours earlier by a nurse who disappeared through swinging doors, leaving me alone and frantic with worry. I had come home that afternoon from the beauty parlor where I worked as a hairdresser to find my aunt, Princie Hamby, waiting for me at the door. "There's something wrong with the baby," she said. "Every time I try to pick her up she screams in pain, and I think it's her back."

My third daughter had been born prematurely less

than four months before, but she had been at home with me for only three weeks. Tina had spent the first three months of her life in an incubator. The doctors had told me she might not survive because her weight was only an estimated two pounds at birth, and she wasn't fully developed. She had no fingernails, eyebrows, or eyelashes, but she had a head full of black hair. She still weighed less than five pounds when they let me bring her home. She was so small that my uncle's size 12 wedding ring would slip over her little hand right up to her shoulder. The idea of such a tiny thing coming down with any illness scared me to death, so when my aunt said something was wrong I didn't wait to call a doctor. I wrapped Tina in a blanket, laid her on the front seat of the car, and drove right to Children's Hospital. That was at 6 P.M. By dawn the next morning I still hadn't heard a word. It was as though the hospital had swallowed up my baby through those swinging doors. Just when I thought I couldn't take another minute of not knowing her condition or her whereabouts, a fair-haired young doctor stepped into the waiting room and called my name. Something about his manner—his expression, his tone of voice—made me afraid to hear what he had to say, and my legs were trembling as I stood up. He was blunt and to the point. "Mrs. Byrd, your baby has spinal meningitis. Her chances of surviving are very slim because she's so small and weak. If there's anyone you want to call, you'd better do it now. We'll keep you posted on her condition."

A day and a half passed before I heard anything more. My uncle, Harrod Pugh, and my grandmother had come to sit with me. When the doctor returned to the waiting room, he walked over and put his hand on my shoulder. His face was pale and drawn. "I'm sorry," he told me, "she's not going to make it. She's having one convulsion after another, and her spinal fluid is as black as coal soot when it should be milky white."

I collapsed in tears. When you've just been told your baby is dying, there are no words of comfort, and the young doctor didn't try to find any, but he looked so distraught when he left the room, my heart went out to him. Uncle Harrod pulled me close to his chest, trying to soothe my sobbing. I was still crying an hour later when the doctor appeared again. I thought he had come to tell me Tina was dead, and I braced myself. Instead he was shaking his head in disbelief. "She's still hanging on," he said. "But I don't want you to take this as a sign of hope. It simply means that she's stronger than we thought, and she may live a few more hours or even a few days." I had been begging to see her, somehow thinking that if I could just touch her, hold her, everything would be all right. But I had been told that the disease was so contagious that they had put her in isolation, and no one could see her. Now the doctor was saying I could go to her. "I'm going to let you go into isolation with her if you want to, but you must understand that once in the room you cannot come out until it's over. We can't take a chance on spreading the disease." I didn't care how long I had to stay, as long as they'd let me be with Tina.

I followed the doctor through the swinging doors, down a long corridor to a door that had a small glass partition at eye level. In the days that followed I came to think of that foot-square piece of glass as my only contact with the outside world. Before going into the room I was given a hospital gown and told to remove the white uniform I had worn from the beauty shop. My purse was enclosed in a plastic bag, and I was given an operating room cap to cover my hair and a mask to wear near Tina. When I was ready the doctor opened the door, closing it quickly behind us. My eyes fixed on the incubator in the center of the room, but I was afraid to walk over and look inside it. What I could see from where I stood brought a new flood of tears, and I was sure the doctor would make me leave if he thought I was on the verge of hysterics. So I took a deep breath and walked to the incubator, determined to hold back my tears until I was alone.

The treatment appeared to be as terrible as the disease. Tina's little nude body was strapped to a thin mattress attached to a board. They had shaved her head. There were needles stuck in her stomach, her feet, the back of her head, even the soft spot in the top of her head where they were draining fluid off her brain. Except for her mouth, which had remained a rosy pink, her entire body was a blackish color. Her neck was swollen as wide as her head, which was drawn back in an arch. She lay as still as death. The doctor showed me two holes in the end of the incubator where I could put my hands through and touch her. He told me to try to massage her back, if I could get to it, and to ring for the nurse at the first sign of another convulsion. She had several that afternoon and evening—horrible spasms that shook her little body, jerking her like a dog that's been hit in the road, drawing her torso backward until it was bent like a horseshoe. Then she would lapse again into a deathlike unconsciousness, lying for hours without moving a muscle.

The isolation room had no windows, except the glass partition in the door, and no furniture except the incubator and a chair. There were a closet and a bathroom on one wall, the hall door on another, and the other two were bare. The room was painted a pale hospital green, a color I hate to this day, and the iridescent light reflecting off the walls gave everything a greenish cast. No daylight penetrated the room and no sounds except my own breathing. I remember thinking that this must be what it's like in prison, in solitary confinement.

I had never felt so alone in my life. My husband had left me. I had no idea where he'd gone or if he was coming back. My mother and grandparents were back home in Mississippi. My father's sister, Aunt Princie, was taking care of my older daughters, Gwen and Jackie, who were four and three, and I didn't know how long it would be before I could see them again. I was making only $45 per week at the beauty shop, trying to support myself and my children on that, and living in a $23-a-month government housing project apartment with bare concrete floors and a few scarred pieces of old furniture. I was also in debt several thousand dollars to my uncle who had paid the hospital bill when we brought Tina home after three months in an incubator.

I was twenty-three years old and I had reached the lowest point of my life. If someone had told me at that moment that the next ten years would bring fame and wealth, I would have said they were completely crazy. All I kept thinking was, I'm sitting here with my life in shambles around me, and if Tina dies I know I can't take it, but I don't know how I'll take care of her if she lives. There was no doubt in the doctor's mind that Tina would be mentally retarded if through some miracle she lived.

After a few days the family got word to me that my mother had come up from Mississippi to take care of Gwen and Jackie. I also learned that my husband Euple Byrd had come back for a few days but had left again even though he'd been told of Tina's condition. For two-and-a-half weeks I didn't leave the isolation room once. Meals were brought to me but I could eat very little, and my weight dropped from 112 to 90 pounds. I massaged Tina's little body until my arms ached. I prayed. I waited. Finally, on the seventeenth day, the doctors took her off the quarantine list, and I was allowed to go home to get a hot bath. It was the most wonderful bath I've ever had. All that time I'd had on the same clothes and the same tennis shoes I'd worn to the beauty shop. My feet were so swollen that when I took my shoes off the strings had left deep imprints in my skin.

I continued to spend most of my days and every night at the hospital, but there was no change in her condition until the end of the fifth week. I was standing beside the incubator massaging her little legs when I saw her move her lips in a sucking motion. That was the closest she'd come to showing any sign of life since her convulsions weeks earlier, and I was overjoyed. I quickly ran to my purse and dug out a new pacifier that had been in there since the day I took her to the hospital. I stuck it in her mouth, but for a minute or so nothing happened. Then suddenly she began pulling on it, sucking away, and I was so excited I ran down the hall to tell the doctor. He came back to look at her, but he wouldn't give me any encouragement whatsoever. "Don't let this get your hopes up, because I still don't believe she can make it," he said. Somehow I knew he was wrong. I knew she would live. A week later he said that she had improved so much she *might* have a fifty-fifty chance. And within another week she had recovered completely. When they released her from the hospital after seven weeks, they called her their "miracle baby."

During the long days and nights I sat in isolation with Tina while she fought for her life, I spent a lot of time wondering about my own. I had never had big dreams for myself, never longed for things that seemed unreasonable or out of reach. I had wanted to get off the farm, I had wanted to get married. I had wanted to raise a family, I had wanted a happy home. Surely that wasn't asking for too much. Where had I failed? Where had I gone wrong? Was God now punishing me because I wanted a divorce from a man I should never have married in the first place? No one in my family had ever been divorced, and it was clear to me that my efforts in that direction were considered a disgrace. My mother was so strongly opposed to the idea, and my husband had convinced her I should be committed to a sanatorium! Maybe I *was* crazy. I had been through enough since my marriage six years earlier to make me wonder at times myself. But I did know one thing. There *had* to be more to life than picking cotton and doing housework. Even when I was a little kid who'd never been off the farm. I knew that.

Sometimes the waiting and the worry made me wish I could go back to those days on my grandfather's farm in Mississippi when life was simple and no problem was so difficult my grandfather couldn't handle it. But then I would remember that, even at best, life on a cotton farm is backbreaking work. I have great respect for farmers and their families because I know what they have to go through to dig a living out of the land. I hated every minute I spent picking cotton, and even today I get a backache just driving past a cotton field. I had made up my mind that I'd do anything before I'd go back to that life, but I never dreamed then that "anything" would turn out to be the one thing I loved doing most of all—singing. Singing was something you did for *fun,* and work was something you did because you *had* to. The idea of getting paid to sing, making a career out of it, was only a fantasy. To me a career meant getting my state beautician's license. That was my security because I knew as long as I had it, I could always get a job. I'm still proud of that license, and I continue to keep it renewed and up to date after all these years. I guess I still think getting paid to sing is too good to be true, and if it ends tomorrow I can always go back to doing hair.

I come from solid English-Irish stock, generations of hardworking, practical people who put their faith in God and their sweat in the land. The land represented more than a living. It was the only security they had. Even when a crop failed a man could get a loan from the bank to tide him over if he owned his own piece of ground. My maternal grandfather, Chester Russell, took great pride in his 600 acres of good Mississippi bottom land. He had worked hard from the time he was a young man to buy it up, little by little, for a few dollars an acre, and he's held onto it all these years. His farm is located in Itawamba County, a section of Mississippi known as "Tornado Alley," very close to the Alabama line. I was born there on the afternoon of May 5, 1942, in the house my grandfather built with lumber he cut from his own land.

Under normal circumstances the birth of their first

baby would have certainly been a happy occasion for my young parents, but I'm sure the grief they faced at the time cast a shadow on my arrival. My father was dying, and he knew it. Five months earlier he had undergone brain surgery in Memphis only to be told his tumor was inoperable. He had suffered terrible headaches since adolescence, but nobody thought much about things like that back in those days in the country. He had fallen off a horse and hit his head on a rock when he was thirteen, and doctors believed the tumor had developed then. But it wasn't discovered until after he had been married more than a year and my mother knew she was pregnant.

After his surgery, doctors warned him that he would go blind before he died. He prayed to God to let him hold onto his eyesight long enough to see his baby. I don't remember him, but I've heard so many stories about the nine short months he lived after I was born that I feel like I knew him. His name was William Hollice Pugh, and like my mother Mildred he came from a family of farmers. But his dream had been to become a professional musician. Before he became ill he often played at local functions with his two brothers, his cousin Dan Hall, a friend, G. B. Grissom and Leland Jackson. He wasn't a trained musician, but music was his hobby and he could play any instrument he picked up. He played tenor guitar, bass, mandolin, accordion, and piano—and he sang, too. My mother says having me around brought him his only real happiness during those last months. After he started going blind he would sit at the piano with me on his lap and place my hands on the keys and pick out a song. Mother says she recalls coming into the room and finding us like that many times, banging on the piano, laughing. He seemed to be the happiest then. He had resigned himself to death, but watching him slowly slip away was horrible for my mother. He was from a religious family, so he believed in a life hereafter. But not long before he died a country preacher came to visit him and told him that believing wasn't enough.

He said, "Hollice, if you don't accept the Lord as your Savior right now and get baptized, you'll go straight to hell when you die." That was a cruel thing to say to a dying man, and it upset my grandparents, but my father apparently didn't want to take any chances, so he was baptized by that old preacher.

Christmas of 1942 was a sad time for my mother. She couldn't have had much holiday spirit celebrating her baby's first Christmas when she knew it was also her husband's last. He was in a great deal of pain. His headaches had become more frequent and intense, and he was already totally blind. The tumor was affecting his personality, too. He had always been a very calm and gentle man, but toward the last he began having violent outbursts of temper. He died in his sleep on February 13, 1943. He was just twenty-six years old.

The only legacy my father left me was his love of music. He made my mother promise him over and over again that she would encourage me to take an interest in music if I had any talent at all. She kept her promise —until I wanted to make a career of it—then she (along with almost everyone else in my family) thought I'd lost my mind! I began taking piano lessons when I was eight, but by that time I could already pick out simple little songs or church hymns by ear. This eventually caused my piano teacher Phelam Ganus to give up on me. I wasn't interested in learning his old notes, since I could already pick out all the tunes I wanted to play, so when he'd give me a new piece to learn, I'd persuade him to play it for me before I left his house. Then I'd go home and play it the same way I'd heard him do it. At the next lesson I'd play the song as though I'd learned it note by note, but he caught on to my trick very quickly. After a few years he refused to teach me any longer because I could play much better than I could read notes. I saw him shortly before he died in 1975. I was visiting my grandfather in the hospital near home, and someone told me Mr. Ganus was there also. When I walked into his room he recognized me immediately, but I was still just little Wynette to him. He said, "I knew someday you'd make something of yourself, but I don't like the color of your hair. It used to be brown." And then he dropped off to sleep.

I played flute in the high school band and I played guitar and accordion, but I still do best on piano and organ, and I still play mostly by ear. My father's brother, Uncle Harrod, taught me to pick guitar when I was twelve. He had lost his arm working for the railroad by then, but he could still play chords, so he would sit with me and place my fingers on the right strings with his one hand. He taught me every chord I know.

After my father died my mother moved to Memphis to work in an airplane factory. Those were the war years and defense plants offered good money and jobs around the clock. She needed the income, but I've always thought she probably also wanted to get away from home for awhile and all the unhappy memories of my father's long illness and death. I stayed behind with my grandparents. Their other daughter, my Aunt Carolyn, was just five years old when I was born, so we were raised like sisters. When mother came back from Memphis, she moved in with us and helped out on the farm. I grew up calling my grandparents Mama and Daddy just like my mother did. They were more like my parents than my grandparents. Mama took charge of everything, including me. I can remember my mother saying, "Mama, she needs a whipping." She'd be telling on me for something I'd done as though I were her little sister instead of her daughter. My grandmother was a big, happy, robust woman. I don't think I ever saw her cry over anything. If you did wrong, you got spanked and it was over. But she never yelled or nagged. I never heard one argument between my grandparents, although I know they must have had their ups and downs. They were affectionate with one another, and my grandfather loved to tease her. She made fresh biscuits every morning for breakfast, and he'd wait until she had her hands in the dough; then he'd walk by and pinch her on her fanny. She'd pretend to fume, but I suspect she really liked it. I remember one morning when she got him back. I was sitting at the kitchen table watching Daddy. As usual he waited until she had dough up to her elbows; then he slipped up behind her and gave her a big pinch on the rear. She whirled around with a handful of dough and plopped it right in his face. He just stood there with dough stuck to his mouth and nose and hanging from his eyebrows, wearing this surprised expression as though he couldn't believe what she'd done. She got the biggest kick out of that.

My grandfather has been incapacitated from hardening of the arteries of the brain for more than a year now. Mama died in 1976 and he just seemed to go downhill after that. It's heartbreaking to see a man who led such an active life bedridden and unable to communicate. It's all I can do to go and visit him because it hurts me so to see him that way. Before he got sick I loved going to the old homeplace because there are so many warm childhood memories there. The house is almost exactly the same as it was when I was growing up. It's a three-bedroom frame house with big front and back porches. In the summer we'd sit in the front porch swing at night and look at the stars and watch the fireflies flickering in the yard. Outside there's a barn and the old sawmill where Daddy cut the lumber to build the house in 1928. There was always a huge sawdust pile there when I was little, and Daddy had told me and Carolyn not to play in it because of the danger of falling in it and suffocating. But of course we did it anyway. It was one of our favorite places to play. Everyone in the area had a storm cellar and ours was right outside the back door. We headed there immediately every time we saw signs of a tornado. Once a big blow lifted the whole barn and blew it away. And another time we watched the roof sail off a neighbor's house and break into a million pieces. Daddy made a point about his attitude toward religion that day.

The neighbors, Luther Anderson and his wife and daughter, lived in a log cabin on Daddy's property. They were at our house when the sky went dark and the storm began gathering overhead. Daddy told them to come on to the storm cellar with us. But Luther said, "Chester, you don't have enough faith. You ought to know the Lord will take care of you. We're going on home." Daddy said, "Okay, but the Lord has given me the good sense to do some things on my own, and I wouldn't expect him to save me if I stood out in the middle of the road and let a car hit me." The Andersons went on home anyway. Not ten minutes later we were looking out the narrow storm cellar window that Daddy had put in at ground level and we heard this awful noise that sounded like a freight train coming down on us. There's no sound in the world as frightening as an approaching tornado. Once you hear it, it's too late to get away. Then we saw the roof fly off the Anderson cabin like a piece of cardboard. Within two minutes Luther was banging on the storm cellar door for us to let him in. Daddy laughed and said, "Well, the Lord took care of you all right. But he also taught you not to tell me I shouldn't go to my storm cellar!"

My favorite place to play was the washhouse just outside the back door. Mama kept a wringer washing machine in there and the old wood-burning stove they'd used before they got electricity when I was about three years old. We used that stove when we had power failures, which was often in Tornado Alley. There was a little upstairs to the washhouse where we kept army cots so guests could sleep there when we had a lot of company staying over. All the children who visited loved sleeping in the washhouse because it was like camping out. Since Mama washed every day, I could play there and be near her but still have a place to make playhouses and army forts. I was too tomboyish to play with dolls. Cowboys and Indians and cars and trucks were my games. I used to hate it when it was time to slaughter livestock because Mama used the stove in the washhouse to can her meats, and the smell of fresh-killed beef or pork made me sick to my stomach. I'm not too fond of meat even now. I much prefer fresh vegetables and homemade biscuits and cornbread.

There are trees all around the house that Daddy planted as saplings, and Mama grew honeysuckle and hyacinths that smelled wonderful in the spring and summer. When the weather was warm Daddy would fix gnat pots—smoke pots made from used motor oil to keep the insects away—and we'd sit outdoors under the trees, snapping beans and shelling peas from our garden so Mama could can them for the winter.

Daddy called me Nettiebelle. When I was born my mother had wanted to name me Gloria, but my grandmother told her that everyone would call me "Glory, Glory," so she decided on Virginia Wynette. The Wynette was my father's nurse who took care of him when he had brain surgery, and she had been so kind to him he wanted to show his appreciation. Everyone in the family still calls me Wynette, but my grandfather never did. It was always Nettiebelle. Whenever company came to the house he would say, "This is Nettiebelle. I raised her. She's mine. Her daddy died when she was nine months old, and I've been her daddy ever since." That was always my introduction. And he was a daddy to me, and I was a daddy's girl. I slept in bed with him until I was thirteen years old, and it was real trauma for me the night he made me move out of his room. In the country everybody slept two and three to a bed, but our family was small, so Mama had her bedroom, Daddy had his, and Carolyn had her room. My grandparents slept in the same room once in a while, but not often.

I didn't question that as a child but I've wondered about it as an adult, although it wasn't unusual in those days for farm wives and husbands to sleep with their children instead of one another. My mother slept with Carolyn after she came back from Memphis to live with us, and that's probably how I got started sleeping with Daddy. But after Mother remarried and moved out, I still slept in Daddy's bed. Then one night not long after I'd turned thirteen, I got into bed as usual, and he sat up and called to Mama, "Flora, come get this girl and put her in Carolyn's room. She's getting too big to sleep with me." Looking back, I'm sure he just felt thirteen was a little too old for a girl to be sleeping with her grandfather, but at the time I had no idea why he would do that or what I'd done wrong. I didn't ask him why. I just accepted what he said, because that's the way it was in our family, but I cried myself to sleep for nights after that. To this day I can't stand to sleep alone, and even though I now have nine bedrooms in my Nashville home for only five of us, I almost always end up with one of my daughters in bed with me.

My grandfather was the rock of my childhood, strong and steady, honest and kindhearted, and a respected member of his community. From him I formed the images I still carry of what a father and a husband should be. You could tell how much he loved Mama just by the way he would put his arm around her shoulder or reach over and pat her hand. I never heard him fuss at Mama, but she fussed at him about the mischievous things he did. For example, he taught me this song when I was little that was halfway dirty called "Sally Let Your Bangs Hang Down." When we'd have company he'd call me off to the side and say, "Nettiebelle, go in there and sing 'Sally' for them." And of course I'd do it because I loved an audience from the time I could walk. Mama would immediately drop what she was doing and come running, shaking her finger. "Chester, I *told* you not to let that child sing that dirty old song," and Daddy would laugh like a little kid.

But there was one trick he used to pull that got her more upset than any other. She raised chickens and sold the eggs we didn't need to the food peddler who came through our area once a week. She'd put five or six dozen in a basket out by the road under a big oak tree, and the peddler would pick them up and leave her money in the basket. If Daddy passed that egg basket before the peddler came, he'd make a pinhole in the end of two or three shells with his knife and suck out the raw egg. He liked raw eggs and believed in their health value—I can remember his feeding them to sick calves—but he'd leave empty shells for the peddler more as a joke to annoy Mama than because he wanted the eggs. The peddler would leave her a note saying, "Mr. Russell has been in the eggs again," and then he would deduct the money for the number of empty shells he found. When Daddy came home she'd raise the devil, accusing him of stealing egg money right out of her pocket.

She didn't care for his using snuff either, but she didn't say too much about it. No one in our family smoked cigarettes—that was almost as sinful as drinking—but Daddy loved his snuff. Once when I was about ten, my cousin Jane Hall, who lived in Red Bay, Alabama, was spending the day, and we decided to try some of Daddy's snuff. We hid in his car and tried to put it behind our lips the way I'd seen him do. It tasted awful, but we swallowed it anyway because I assumed that's what you were supposed to do since I had never seen him spit it out. About an hour later Jane was so sick she had turned greenish-white, and she was throwing up all over the place. Her mother, Hazel, said, "I'm going to have to take this child home and get a doctor for her. She's coming down with something." So I decided I'd better confess. When I told Hazel what we'd done she laughed and said getting sick was punishment enough, so for once we didn't get a whipping. Years later Daddy had to give up his snuff because he developed bleeding ulcers. But he couldn't throw it away. To this day there's a can of it on the living room mantel above the fireplace. Before his stroke he'd look up at that yellow label and say, "They never sold that stuff for as much as it was worth." He didn't touch it again after the doctor told him not to, but he never got over wanting it.

Like most kids, Carolyn and I tried to get away with things we knew our parents wouldn't want us to do. I thought she was a genius when she figured out a way to steal watermelons out of Daddy's patch without getting caught. She'd take a pair of his old shoes down to the field and put them on and walk backward into the patch until she found a ripe melon. I'd follow along behind in the same footprints, and because I was so much smaller my feet didn't leave an imprint. Then we'd both lift the melon, and she'd lead the way back in the footprints. When Daddy went down to the watermelon patch, all he saw was his own footprints coming out of the field, and I guess he figured they were left from the day before. He never did catch on.

Anything we saw or did in the country that was out of the ordinary was an event, because life on the farm was very routine. Even a little thing like gypsies coming to the house to beg food was exciting. They were very colorful in their costumes, and they were strange and mysterious, too. The women wore full skirts and big gold earrings, and the men had long hair held back in bandanna headbands. Their dress would have been right in style today. Daddy never turned them away, but one time he did get a little put out with them. It was on a cold winter night, and we were sitting around the living room fireplace. For some reason we hadn't lit the coal oil lamps, so the only light in the room was the glow from the open fire. Daddy was cooking ham on a coat-hanger skewer over the coals, and Mama had sweet potatoes wrapped up, baking down under the ashes. There was a knock on the door, and when Daddy opened it we could see several fierce-looking men with mustaches and long black curly hair standing there. In the dim firelight they really looked scary. Mama whispered, "It's gypsies," and the way she said it sent a chill through me, even though I knew there was nothing to be afraid of since they'd been coming around all my life. They asked Daddy for food, so he filled a brown bag from the kitchen and gave it to them. Then they wanted to know if he'd let them have some chickens. He took a flashlight and went out to the henhouse and came back with two live chickens. They thanked him and left. But about thirty minutes later they showed up again and asked if they could please have one more chicken. Daddy started off the porch to get it; then he came back and said to Mama, "Flora, come here. I want you to see this." He pointed to their car parked in the front yard. It was a brand-new Cadillac. He said, "Look at that. I'm giving them food when they're driving a big fancy car and all I've got is an old Ford." But he gave them the chicken anyway.

Christmas was a very special time at our house. Daddy would help me write a letter to Santa which we would then place on the mantel beside my stocking. He'd say, "Now don't ask for too much because Santa Claus doesn't like that." And he would never let me ask for a bicycle even though he knew I wanted one more than anything in the world. I never understood why he wouldn't let Carolyn or me have a bike until I was grown. Then he told me that once a man had been driving his sawmill truck when he struck and killed a little boy on a bicycle. Daddy wasn't even in the truck, but since he owned it he felt responsible so he had a bad feeling about bicycles. But I always had a wonderful Christmas. Since I was an only child, and Daddy's only grandchild until I was eighteen, I got more than some of the children in the area who came from large families. Daddy was very generous at Christmas. His personal gift was always money. He gave his children $50 each, which was a lot in those days. He'd put the money in envelopes with our names on them and pin them to the Christmas tree with a clothespin. Even though we knew what was inside, opening that envelope was one of the most exciting things about Christmas morning. Every year when I was small I begged to stay up and see Santa, so Daddy decided to arrange for me to meet him in person. He got Luther Anderson and Elmo Kent to dress up in Santa suits and come to the house. I was sitting on Daddy's lap listening to a story he was reading when they knocked on the door. When Daddy opened it and I saw two Santa Clauses standing there, it scared me so much I ran and hid under Mama's old pedal sewing machine and refused to come out until they'd gone.

Christmas had important religious significance in our home because it was Christ's birthday and the biggest event of the year in our church. Actually, we went to two churches—the Providence Baptist Church and the Oakgrove Church of God. My mother's people were Baptist, and my father's family belonged to the Church of God, so we had a lot of friends there. Both churches were about five miles away, but the Church of God used the school bus on Sundays so we could get a ride there, whereas the Baptist Church had no transportation facilities. If Daddy needed the car for some reason, and we didn't have anyone to drive us to our church, we'd ride the old homemade school bus to the Church of God. Daddy seldom went to church with us, although he lived by the Christian doctrine and believed in the Bible. He used to say he could get his religion just as well at home.

But church was more than a place of worship to the rest of us. We loved it because it was where you saw your friends and heard all the local news and gossip. I especially looked forward to going because I could sing and play piano. The old man who played piano at the Baptist Church died when I was about eight, and for several Sundays we had no music. Then the preacher asked the congregation if anyone there could come down front and play piano, and I got right up and walked down the aisle and said, "Yes, I'll play." My mother says it embarrassed her because I was so bold about it, but I knew all the old hymns by heart, and I wanted to be up there making music.

But singing and playing was more fun at the Church of God. They really got cooking over there. At the Baptist Church they were more restrained, and the hymns were the old slow, traditional church songs. The Church of God preacher, on the other hand, would let you bring guitars and play rockin' gospel more like black gospel music. When the music got rolling the congregation would stand up and clap their hands and sing out at the top of their lungs. A member of the congregation would call out "Amen" or "Praise the Lord" every time the preacher made a point. Or someone would stand up and shout that the spirit was moving him. Sister Josie Jones scared me to death one time when she stood up and began hollering in unknown tongues. I'd never seen that before, and I didn't know what on earth had come over her.

The church was the center of our social and community activities because we didn't have any entertainment. Both Mississippi and Alabama were dry states then, and there were no nightclubs or dance halls for people to frequent. Daddy was a Mason, and that organization had some family activities; and we also had school events like cakewalks and Halloween carnivals, but most of our social life revolved around the church. It was there that I first learned to sing harmony and to appear before an "audience." I get much the same feeling today when I perform on stage that I did then singing in front of the congregation or playing piano for them. It's a kind of thrill that never gets stale, and it's probably what keeps most entertainers going back out there for more. I rarely have the opportunity to go to church today because I'm usually on the road on Sunday, appearing at a concert or a fair, but my musical background is so deeply rooted in the Christian religion that I could never entirely drift away from that influence. I do a gospel medley in every one of my shows, even when I'm appearing in a sophisticated nightclub, and the audiences seems to love the music as much as I do.

I can't imagine what life would have been like in the rural South when I was a child without the church because it fulfilled so many needs, both socially and spiritually. Country people didn't have the money to spend on city-type entertainment, even if it had been available, and they certainly couldn't have stayed out all hours of the night and gotten up at dawn to do farm work. Everyone in a farming family had jobs and responsibilities, from the youngest to the old folks. I had chores to do from the time I was big enough to hold a dust rag or help make a bed. We grew everything we ate and made almost everything we wore. During the war, when leather was rationed, my mother even made me little shoes out of felt, using several layers for the soles. My grandmother never went grocery shopping in her life. The only things we ever bought from the store were sugar, coffee and flour, and Daddy would buy that when we went to Red Bay to trade. Even our cornmeal was homemade. We grew the corn and Daddy took it to the gristmill two miles away to have it ground. We kept the cornmeal in a big chest on the back porch, and I loved to climb up on it and play.

Once I saw Daddy look inside the meal chest and mumble something about the "damned old bugs" in there, so the next time I played on it, I got in trouble. Mama called out from the kitchen to ask what I was doing, and I said, "I'm out here, playing with these damned old bugs." She came out and gave me a spanking for using a bad word, and when I kept telling her I had heard Daddy say "damn" she spanked harder. "I don't care what your Daddy says," she told me "Nice ladies don't use language like that." Even now it makes me uncomfortable to be around women who swear a lot. But that day I got into double trouble. After the spanking Mama made me churn, which was her favorite punishment for both Carolyn and me any time we used slang, and it made me so mad I pumped that churn handle up and down as hard as I could and splashed milk all over the floor and walls. I got another whipping for that. I learned very young that Mama meant what she said and said what she meant.

Mama did most of the disciplining, but Daddy had his stern side too. He whipped me only three times in my life, but I remember every one of them. I got the worst one when I was about ten. It was on a Saturday and there was a county fair in Tupelo that I couldn't wait to get to. But it was harvest time so we all had to pick cotton that day. Daddy said if I picked a certain amount by noon—I think it was fifty pounds—I could quit and go on to the fair. I got up before dawn and started off the day cheating by picking before sunup. Cotton still damp from the dew weighs more, and I wanted to pick my allotted pounds as fast as possible. But when time came to quit I knew my sack didn't weigh enough, so I committed the ultimate sin of a cotton picker—I weighted my sack down with rocks. Cheating on the weight is bad enough, but rocks in a cotton sack are a real danger and one that I had been warned against for as long as I could remember.

If a rock strikes the metal pipe that sucks the cotton from the back of the truck up into the gin, it can cause sparks and set the whole place on fire. But I was determined to make it to the fair. So I drug my sack to the scales and after it was weighed I took it off to the side and very carefully took out every rock I'd put in —or so I thought. Then I climbed on the back of Daddy's old Case tractor so I could reach the wagon hooked to it, and I dumped the cotton out myself to make sure I hadn't missed any rocks. After that was done, I headed for the house to clean up. Daddy got on the tractor and started for the gin, which was no more than fifty yards away. By the time I reached our front porch he was in line waiting for his turn at the pipe, so I stopped to watch. I saw him pull the wagon under the suction pipe and then, not two minutes later, I saw smoke. I knew instantly what had happened and I thought, "Oh my God, I've set the gin on fire. I'm dead now." It was a community gin, and I could just see all the cotton picked by us and the neighboring farmers going up in smoke. I saw Daddy unhook the wagon and start for the house on the tractor. I couldn't see the men inside the gin, but I knew they'd be working frantically to put out the fire, and the only reason

Daddy would be leaving at a time like that was to get *me*.

I jumped off the porch and ran for the fields, looking back over my shoulder at him coming on that tractor. When he reached the house, he got down and started after me on foot. I was way out in the cotton fields by then, running and looking back, crying and begging him not to whip me. He didn't run after me. He didn't even speed up his walk. He just kept coming. He called to me, "The faster you run, the harder I'll whip you when I catch you," but I kept on going. Then suddenly I tripped and fell down, hitting my knee on a sharp rock. It hurt really bad and blood was running down my leg. I thought, "Oh, this is great because now he won't whip me." When he got to me I was bawling and holding my knee. I showed it to him expecting sympathy, but he just looked at it and said, "I'll take care of that after I've taken care of this." He pulled up a cotton stalk and whipped me good with it. Every time the stalk hit my legs, it stuck in my flesh because he hadn't pulled off the dry pods. But as much as it hurt I knew I deserved it.

The fire burned three or four hundred pounds of cotton before they got it put out, and Daddy had to make that up. So I had to pick the amount that had burned without pay. But he let me go to the fair that afternoon anyway. Many farmers didn't pay their families to work in the fields, but Daddy always did. I got about $2 for every hundred pounds I picked. I don't remember how much I could pick a day at that age, but I know as I grew older I got up to $4 per hundred pounds, and I could pick 170 or 180 pounds a day. The most I ever picked in one day was 204 pounds, which was really a lot for a girl.

Just as our social life revolved around the church, our home and school life revolved around the crops. I was just three weeks old when I was first taken into the cotton fields. Since my father was too sick to work by the time I was born, my mother had to pick cotton to earn money for us. She'd take me with her and lay me on a quilt on the ground. Then she'd spread another quilt on the branches of a tree above me and sprinkle that with insect powder to keep the ants off me. She'd work in the fields all day long, stopping just when she had to nurse me. But my first memory of the cotton fields is riding on Mother's pick sack when I was three or four years old. A pick sack is made of heavy cotton canvas, and it's about six feet long, according to how tall the picker is. An adult sack would be five to seven feet long. It has a strap that goes across the shoulder, padded with cotton so it won't hurt so much when the sack gets full. I would sit on top of Mother's sack, and she'd pull me along between the rows as she picked. I was sent out to pick, myself, when I was six or seven years old, and I continued to work in the fields until I left home to get married at seventeen.

The men planted the cotton in early spring, and if it came up skimpy we'd have to go back in and plant more to make a good solid row. When the cotton stalks grew to eight or ten inches high, we'd go in with a hoe and chop a space around each one so they would have room to branch out. Two or three weeks later we'd go back in with hoes and clear out the grass, because it would grow up as tall as the cotton in no time. Sometimes we'd do as many as three hoeings before harvest time. Then came the picking, which we all dreaded. On the first picking you had to be careful to get everything that was open. If you could look back down your rows and see any white spots, that meant you "goose picked" the cotton, or did not pick it all from the boll. Then you'd have to go back and clean up your rows. It was a matter of pride not to leave them messy. You walked between the rows, picking two at a time, and there would be two or three pickings each harvest, according to when the bolls ripened and opened. Picking cotton tears your hands up because the dry bolls have stickers that prick the skin and make it fester up and bleed. Your back aches from bending over all day, your hands are sore and itchy, and your knees throb from crawling on the ground to reach the lowest cotton bolls. I can remember being so exhausted after a day in the fields that I'd literally cry if company showed up at the house at night. You couldn't go to bed as long as company was there, and all I ever wanted to do after picking cotton was to go straight to bed.

School terms were arranged around planting and harvesting, so we were on a different schedule from city children. We started school in October after the harvest, but if all the crops weren't in by then, due to bad weather, they gave us the time off we needed to get everything picked before winter. School let out in May; then we had June off before we started the first picking in July. We picked in July, August, and September from dawn till dark with the Mississippi sun beating down full strength all day. If we were working anywhere near the road where people could see us, Daddy made us wear pants and long-sleeved shirts. But if we were picking way back in the fields, we could wear bathing suits and get a suntan. My skin tans easily, so by the end of every summer I was black. I still like to keep a suntan, but I'm thankful that I now get mine on the beach in front of my house in Florida or by my pool in Nashville, and not in a cotton field.

The only thing that got me through those long, hot days during harvest was daydreaming. I don't remember what I fantasized about when I was real small, but during my adolescence I daydreamed a lot about singing professionally. One of my favorite fantasies as a teenager was to imagine myself standing on a stage singing with my country music idol, George Jones. There I'd be, down on my hands and knees, fingers all cut and scratched, knees sore as boils, dusty and dirty, picking that dang cotton as fast as I could, with a vision going around in my head of George Jones asking me to sing with him in front of thousands of people. Even my best girlfriend would have laughed if I'd shared that fantasy. It was so farfetched it was ridiculous. Yet a few years later, I would not only be singing on the same stage with George Jones—I would be his wife.

Chapter 2

❦

$\mathcal{I}$ REMEMBER my first kiss as though it were yesterday. I was thirteen years old and the boy's name was A.G. Stepp. We were sitting in the balcony of the Bay Theater in Red Bay, Alabama. The theater was our Saturday afternoon hangout, the place where we met our friends and sometimes held hands with the boys. There was probably also a lot of heavy petting going on in the dark back rows of the balcony, but the girls in my crowd didn't go that far. For us, one or two stolen kisses was daring enough!

I knew A.G. wanted to kiss me. He'd been building up to it for several Saturdays, but he was as nervous about making his move as I was about being kissed. A.G. worked at the theater. He was the only usher, the ticket taker, and the concession stand operator. Between selling popcorn, taking tickets, and making sure the little kids didn't wreck the theater, A.G. was a busy young man, but he managed to sneak up and sit with me whenever he found a free minute. It was during one of these breaks that he finally got up the

nerve to kiss me. When he turned my face toward his
and touched his lips to mine, the strangest feeling went
through my body. It made me sort of dizzy, and I
liked it a lot. In fact, I liked the kiss more than I
liked A.G., because in those days my heart belonged to
Billy Cole.

I fell in love with Billy Cole in the sixth grade. He
was my first crush, and he inspired the first song I
ever wrote. I've probably written two hundred love
songs since then, but none ever came more from the
heart than that first one. It was a simple melody, and
the lyrics were made up from the letters of his name:
"B" is for this, "I" is for that, "L" for so and so, and
on through his name. All I remember is that it rhymed
and that I was too shy to sing it to him for a long
time after I wrote it. A mutual interest in music brought
me and Billy together, but it was his thick, black hair
and clear blues eyes that kept me infatuated through
the tenth grade. I met him at the Oak Grove Church
of God, where his father was the minister (the music
wasn't the only reason I liked going to that church!).
I think of Billy every time I hear the song "Son of a
Preacher Man." He was four years older than I, and
I thought he was the handsomest thing I'd ever seen in
my life. He and his brother Jamie played guitar at the
church services, and my best girlfriend Linda Loden
and I sang with them. The four of us would stand in
front of the congregation and lead the singing or do
special numbers by ourselves. So we just naturally began spending a lot of time together. At first we saw
one another mostly at church, but when Linda and I
got to the ninth grade we started dating the brothers,
and after that we became an inseparable foursome. We
went everywhere together. Yet during all the years I
had such a crush on him, I don't remember being alone
with Billy more than half a dozen times. Nevertheless,
by the time I turned fifteen we were sure we wanted
to get married. He was nineteen then, and it wasn't
uncommon for teenagers in our rural area to marry
that young. We decided to order wedding rings from a

mail order catalogue. They were $8 each. Billy gave me his money, and I used money I'd earned picking cotton to pay for mine. I had them delivered to the school because I knew if they came to the house my mother would kill me.

I was beside myself with excitement the day they called me into the school office to say I had a package. I couldn't wait to show my girl friends. I let them into the girls' bathroom one by one where we hid in one of the stalls and giggled and squealed over my wonderful secret. Of course, word got back to one of the teachers, who happened to be a good friend of my mother's. By the time I got home from school, Mother already knew the whole story, and she was fit to be tied. She said I was disgracing her by buying wedding rings and having them sent to school. She also said I might as well get the idea of marriage out of my head because it was the most ridiculous thing she'd ever heard in her life. She took the rings away from me, and I cried more about that than anything else. I hadn't even had a chance to show them to Billy.

After that incident Mother put a stop to my seeing Billy Cole for a long time, and I thought my heart would break. I'd see him in church and sit there and cry all through the sermon. I thought Mother was being mean and hateful, and I couldn't understand why she didn't see that I was *truly* in love. I recently had to stop one of my daughters from seeing a young man she'd been dating, and although it wasn't for the same reason, I was able to sympathize completely with what Mother must have gone through over me and Billy Cole. At the same time I felt heartbroken for my daughter because I *remember* the pain of first love. Mother was worried to death that I'd slip off and marry Billy Cole, and I would have in a minute if the opportunity had presented itself. I remember the last night we were together. I cried as though I would never stop. Billy had gone into the service by then, and when he came home from boot camp in his uniform he was so good-looking he took my breath away. We drove to

a little backwoods road near the church where his
father preached and parked there for hours. He talked
and I cried. He kept telling me he'd be back by the
time I was old enough to get married, but I just knew
I would never see him again. We wrote every day for
months. Then he came home on leave another time,
but Mother wouldn't let me see him. I know she was
still afraid I would run off with him.

I was appearing at the Coliseum in Memphis a couple
of years ago, and Billy's brother Jamie showed up
backstage. That was the first time I'd seen him since
high school. I asked immediately about Billy. Jamie
said he was married and living in Jackson, Mississippi,
with his wife and three daughters. I still think about
him at times and wonder how my life would have gone
if we had married. I guess you never really get over
your first love, no matter how young it hits you.

By the time I wanted to marry Billy Cole I had
moved out of my grandparents' house and was living
full time with Mother and my stepfather, Foy Lee.
Mother had married Foy when I was four. If she had
gone out looking for a husband with the intention of
finding someone who would be good to me, she couldn't
have done any better than Foy Lee. He is the kindest,
sweetest man you can imagine, and he seems to have
unlimited patience. He has been married to my mother
for over thirty years now, and I've yet to see them
fight.

After I moved in with them he was often my ally
when I had disagreements with Mother. He'd say,
"Mildred, get off the child's back. Ease up on her
some." And he always saw to it that I got to go places
the other kids went, even though he and Mother went
with me. They were really good about that. They took
me to basketball games, school parties, church socials,
and just about any place I asked to go. A lot of parents
wouldn't have bothered.

Mother and Foy never had children of their own,
and I don't really know why. When I was small I
wanted them to have a baby because I thought it would

be so much fun to have a little brother or sister. Nearly all the families we knew had a lot of children. Our nearest neighbors, the Pattersons, had twelve, and the family down the road from them had about ten. But when I asked Foy if we could get a baby, he gave me a strange answer. I was about six, and I was sitting in his lap one day, thinking about not having playmates close by, when I asked, "Please, Foy, will you and mother get me a baby brother or sister?"

He laughed and said, "Oh, I don't think we need another youngun' around here."

I said, "Why not? Everybody has sisters and brothers but me and I want one."

Then he got real solemn. He turned me around to face him and said, "If I had a child of my own, I might love it more than I do you, and you wouldn't like that, would you?" I certainly didn't want that to happen, so I never asked for a baby again. But I still wonder if that's the real reason they never had children. Foy is the only grandfather my girls have ever known and they adore him. He's their "PeePaw" and Mother is "MeeMaw," nicknames given them by my oldest daughter, Gwen, when she was still too young to pronounce grandpa and grandma.

When Mother and Foy first married they moved into a dilapidated old log house on Daddy's property, just across the cotton field from his house. It was no more than a shack and in terrible condition. They had no electricity, no plumbing, cracks in the walls, and holes in the roof. The first night it snowed they woke half buried under it. They had to shake the snow off their bed quilts to get up. They nailed tar paper and Sears Roebuck catalog pages on the walls for insulation. They lived that way for about a year. I saw them everyday, of course, but I kept on living with my grandparents until Daddy made me move out of his room. Then I moved over to Mother's and Foy's, but I wouldn't sleep in a room by myself, so they bought me an army cot and put it in their room. In some ways I was spoiled from all the attention and affection I'd had as an only child and an only grandchild. It showed when I started dragging that cot back and forth across the road from Mother's to Mama's and back again. If I'd get upset with Mother for something she'd done, I'd put my cot on my back and go sleep over at Mama's for a few days. Then if she got on me about something, I'd pack up and go back to Mother's. Daddy let me get away with that for a few months before he put his foot down. Then one day he said, "You park that cot and you stay in one place or the other." So I stayed with them for a few more weeks, then moved in with Mother and Foy permanently. But the houses were so close I still spent as much time with my grandparents as I did at home.

The only time I really lived away from them before I got married was during my tenth year when I moved to Memphis for a while with Mother and Foy. He'd gone there looking for better work because farming hadn't been good that year. Foy also raised cotton, though not on as large a scale as my grandfather, and money was tight for everybody if drought or rainstorms ruined the crops. I went along to Memphis thinking life in a big city would be really exciting. Mother took a job in the office at the University Park Cleaners, which was owned by Carney Moore. His brother, Scottie, was a part-time musician, and he and a group of friends used to practice every afternoon upstairs where they blocked hats. One of the friends was Elvis Presley. Later, when Elvis began making it, Scottie went along and stayed on the road with him for years. Mother used to come home and tell us about the noise upstairs at the cleaners with those kids playing loud music every day.

She remembers Elvis as a sweet, nice kid, polite and kind of shy. I met him when I was ten but never saw him again. We were born less than thirty miles apart in Mississippi. I idolized him as a performer. The last year he was alive, he played a concert near my home in Florida, and I happened to be off that week. I felt a real urgency to see that show and to get backstage to meet him. It was sold out, of course, and when I contacted a member of his entourage, he was so pompous about *trying* to get me in I just let it drop, thinking there would be other opportunities. But a few months later Elvis was dead, and I regretted so much that I had let a rude flunky prevent me from seeing him. From that experience, and from things I've been told by people who knew him, I believe Elvis's biggest problem was some of the group he had around him. They cut him off from the real world. That's one of the reasons you don't find many country music stars surrounded by entourages. We don't want to be too protected, too insulated. When you are, it's too easy to lose touch with reality. The minute a performer gets the idea he's better than the people he entertains, he's in trouble. He may be luckier in some ways, but he's sure no better.

As it turned out, I didn't find big city life in Memphis so exciting after all. I didn't like my school, and I missed my grandparents and my friends at home. But what really sent me flying back to Mississippi wasn't homesickness. It was word from my grandmother that my gym teacher at the old school was about to give my basketball uniform to someone else.

Mama wrote, "You ought to be here now because they're starting basketball again, and Shirley Anderson is going to get your uniform." Boy, did I get home fast after that letter came! At that age I loved basketball more than anything except singing, and it had been a long hard struggle to get Daddy to let me play. He thought the uniforms were too revealing, and at first he made me wear jeans when I played. Being the only girl on the court in long pants made me feel conspicuous, and I hated it. I brought one of the regulation uniforms home from school one day and put it on to show him, begging him to let me dress like the other girls. Finally he gave in, but with one stipulation. Mama had to sew elastic in the bottom of the shorts so there would be no danger of my underpants showing when I jumped up to make a basket. With Mama's elastic, the bloomers hugged my legs so tight they almost cut off the circulation, and my outfit still looked different from the other players, but at least I had on a uniform.

Even though I was short for my age, I was a pretty good player, and later, in high school, I made the 1958 and '59 All-State Team. What I didn't have in height I made up for in speed. I had done a lot of acrobatics as a kid so I was agile and could move fast. I'd fake out the opposition by pretending I was going to shoot, then dart between the legs of one of the tall girls when she jumped for the rebound. Before she could get into guard position again, I'd pass to a teammate under the basket and she'd plop it in. We won a lot of games that way. But in 1959 we lost the state championship by one point. It was heartbreaking.

I always loved school because, like church, it was the place I saw my friends. Living on a farm wasn't like being in a neighborhood where you could walk down the street and visit. We lived eight miles out of town in the country, and our neighbors were few and far between. I was five when I started school. They asked Mother to go ahead and let me enroll since I went to school with Carolyn most of the time anyway. During recess I'd stand on the bench by the table where the kids ate lunch and sing to everybody. The first-grade teacher, Miss Ida Lyle, thought that was cute. The next year they passed a law that kept you from starting school until you were six, so I had to repeat first grade, but I didn't mind because I loved Miss Ida. I loved my other two grammar school teachers, too. They were Miss Gertie Hyden and Mr. Leman Birch. I was in Mr. Birch's class in the sixth grade when I first confessed my ambitions to my classmates. He asked us to stand up one by one and tell what we wanted to be when we grew up. I said I wanted to be an actress or a singer. Of course, all the kids laughed. Mr. Birch took his yardstick and whacked his desk with it and told them to be quiet. "You remember this," he said. "You can be anything you want to be in life if you want it bad enough." That stuck with me, but I never again talked about going into show business in school.

My mother was also one of my grammar school teachers. She had taken college courses in Fulton, Mississippi, while I was in first and second grades, and she earned enough credits to get her teaching certificate. By the time I reached third grade, she was the regular substitute at our little three-room schoolhouse. It was called the Bounds-X school because it sat at an X-shaped crossroads. Today there's a Head Start school there. When Mother taught my class I really had to mind my p's and q's. She made a shining example of me, and I couldn't get away with a thing. It wasn't that she was trying to be mean. She just didn't want anyone getting the idea that she showed her child partiality. I was proud of her being a teacher because the kids liked her, and she always knew how to explain things if I needed help with my homework, but it was a lot easier for me in class when I had one of my regular teachers.

Bounds-X was only about 500 yards from our house, but Mother's kid sister Carolyn and I never walked to school. They had made a school bus from an old truck bed by building a wooden shed on it and putting in two rows of benches facing each other. The bus had to pass right by our house anyway, so they always stopped and let us ride the last few seconds with our friends. In the wintertime it was nice to be out of the cold even for that short a distance. Carolyn and I would nearly freeze to death getting out of those warm featherbeds to dress for school. Daddy always had a fire going in the living room by the time we got up, but the mill hands usually stopped by to have coffee with him before going to work, so we couldn't dress in there. We'd try to put on as many clothes as possible under the covers, then throw on the rest and make a beeline through the living room to the warm kitchen where Mama had breakfast waiting. The whole house smelled of fresh-baked biscuits, country ham, and strong coffee. We ate like field hands in the mornings —grits, biscuits, red-eye gravy, and eggs Mama had

gathered from her chickens. Country ham is still my
favorite meat, but it never tastes quite as good as it
did when Mama cured her own in our smokehouse.

Carolyn and I took ham and biscuits in our school
lunches, and sometimes banana sandwiches with mayon-
naise, or peanut butter and jelly. All the kids swapped
lunches' cause somebody else's always looked better.
There was no cafeteria at our little school, but there
was a country store about a hundred yards down the
hill, and they did a booming business every day when
the lunch bell rang. Kids would swarm out of the
schoolhouse, running down to the store to buy their
milk, cokes, Pepsi, or Orange Nehi.

Most of the girls at Bounds-X School wore dresses
made of flour sacks. We all thought it was terrific
when patterned sacks came out instead of the plain old
white ones. They had several pastel floral designs, and
it wasn't unusual to see the same print made up in a
variety of styles on half a dozen little girls. Most country children hated hand-me-down clothes with a passion
because the younger ones in large families seldom got
anything new except shoes. But since I was an only
child I never had secondhand clothes, and I used to
envy my friends for getting to wear their big sister's
cast-off dresses and overalls. I would beg for Carolyn's
old clothes, but the five years' difference in our ages
meant the clothes would have had to be taken apart
and completely remade. It was easier for Mother to
make me new things.

Mother was an excellent seamstress, and she took
great pride in dressing me, so I always had pretty
clothes. She would embroider and appliqué skirts and
blouses, and she even bought colored lace to sew
around the tops of my white sox to match my dresses.
I especially remember one Sunday school dress she
made for me when I was about seven. It was lilac cotton with a white organdy overskirt and a matching
Bertha collar that was wide enough to give the appearance of sleeves. She appliquéd little butterflies,
yellow daisies, and pink rosebuds on the collar and

overskirt, and I thought that was the prettiest dress in the world.

We were never rich, but we always had plenty to eat and Mother made sure I had nice clothes. We didn't miss luxuries because we had never had them, and we didn't know anyone else who did. And even though I hated it at the time, I believe the fact that we all had to work to contribute our share to the family's well-being gave me a sense of pride and accomplishment a lot of young people don't have today. Even farm children have it easier now because the big conglomerates have all but eliminated the little farmers like my Daddy, and machines do most of the hard work.

Even before I started school I had regular chores around the house. Carolyn and I had to round up the cattle every afternoon and lead them back to the barn to be fed. Then I had to bring in firewood and coal and help Mama in the kitchen. By the time I was nine I could prepare a full meal by myself. I enjoyed cooking and still do. I cook the old-fashioned way, not measuring anything, just throwing in a handful of this and a pinch of that. (After so many years of practice you know instinctively how much of what goes into the pot.) One of the reasons I liked cooking as a child was because if I helped Mama in the kitchen, it meant I had to spend less time in the fields picking cotton. She cooked for all the hands every day during harvest. I remember one time I got bored with making corn bread the same old way, so I put green food coloring in it. Foy agreed it tasted fine, but nobody would eat it because it looked so awful.

At school we often had box suppers where the girls would bring boxes of picnic goodies to be auctioned off. We competed to see who could decorate the fanciest box, with colored crepe paper and bright ribbons. The boys would bid on the boxes, and the highest bidder for each box got to sit and eat with the girl who had brought it. We also had cakewalks. Families would donate home-baked cakes which were numbered and placed on a long table in the auditorium. Corresponding numbers were placed on the floor in a circle. Contestants then paid a quarter to march around the circle, and the number they landed on when the music stopped showed which cake they had won. These events not only helped raise money for the school, they were also big social occasions for us.

I don't remember my first real date, but I do know I didn't go out with a boy alone more than a dozen times before I was married. We did everything in groups. In my case it was a matter of necessity because it was the only way Mother would let me out of the house. After I began going to junior high and high school in Tremont, Mississippi, I made a lot of new friends, and I was voted school Queen in my junior year. This was an annual event for the junior-senior prom, and Billy Brewer and I were named Mr. and Miss Tremont High. But I was never one of the most popular girls with the boys. I was not one of the prettiest girls in school, and everyone knew about my strict situation at home, which meant I couldn't do a lot of the things the other kids did. I was heavier than I am now, and I had mousy brown hair which never did what I thought it should do. I don't remember ever being told I was pretty by anyone, including members of my own family. If they commented on my looks at all, it was to remark about my dark skin which stayed tanned from the sun almost all year round.

I was less boy-crazy than some of my girl friends because my music was so important to me. In addition to playing flute in the high school band, I sang and played piano for the other students at the drop of a hat. I never had to be coaxed to get on the auditorium stage. Our principal and basketball coach, Mr. Johnson (better known behind his back as "Tater Head"), always asked me to take charge of the musical part of our chapel programs, and I loved doing it. I spent every spare moment, even my lunch hour, at the auditorium piano. Some of the kids teased me about it, which hurt because I took my music seriously, but others enjoyed it enough to gather around and sing with me at lunchtime.

Linda Loden, who had been my best friend since grammar school, loved music as much as I did, and we began singing together on local radio programs. Brother Verde Collier, her Methodist minister, gave us our first opportunity. We sang on his thirty-minute Saturday show, and he would laugh and tell Mother his listeners didn't tune in to hear his preaching as much as they did our singing. When that show ended we were invited by Carmol Taylor, a well-known country music songwriter and singer, to appear on his Saturday show on WERH in Hamilton, Alabama. It was called "Carmol Taylor and the Country Pals." My mother and Linda's mother took turns driving us over to Hamilton, and sometimes we'd stay on into the evening and sing at the Skateatorium. Mother would take us as far away as Birmingham, which was 125 miles, to enter talent contests, but we never won any. It's strange that I didn't find that discouraging, but I didn't care as much about winning as I did about singing. Just getting to appear before an audience was thrill enough for me.

Linda and I formed another group from school with Morris and Kenneth Miller and Tommy Brewer. Anytime we heard of a chance to be on radio or enter a contest, we took it. I also sang with Agnes and Geraldine Tharp, whose mother played piano for us, and later Linda and I formed a trio with Ima Jean Patterson, one of the daughters from the big Patterson family I mentioned earlier. Country music was my favorite even then, but I also liked the Platters, the Drifters, and the Coasters, and I loved all the gospel music we sang in church. Mother had the largest collection of George Jones albums in the area, and I played them over and over on my little Mickey Mouse record player. George was her favorite singer and he became mine, too. Years later when I first met him, he was surprised that I knew the lyrics to just about every song he'd ever recorded. It was because I grew up singing along with his records.

But as I grew older, music wasn't enough to keep my mind off the boys *all* the time. I was just beginning to balk at Mother's restrictions on my social life when a tragedy struck our family that made my problems seem so petty I put them out of my mind for months.

Carolyn had married and moved to Zion, Illinois. She'd been gone almost a year, and I missed her terribly because we had become even closer after I was a teenager. I could talk to her about things I wouldn't discuss with Mother or Mama. In some ways she was better than a sister because she never picked on me the way older siblings sometimes do. If anything, I picked on her. She'd be out sweeping the front yard, and I'd run by and pinch her just for meanness. Once I kept it up until she chased me into the washhouse loft, and I almost stepped on a snake trying to get away from her. Instead of saying it served me right, she consoled me because the snake had scared me half to death. Another time I hid under the bed by the front window so I could listen to what she and her boyfriend were saying while they sat in the porch swing. Mama caught me that time and whipped me good, but Carolyn said, "Oh, Mama, she's just a kid."

When I got upset with someone, I'd fume and carry on and say, "Carolyn, I hate him, I *hate* him!" And she'd sit me down calmly and tell me it was wrong to feel that way.

"Now, you don't mean that," she'd say. "If he died tomorrow, think how horrible you'd feel for talking so ugly about him."

I was high-strung and impatient, but Carolyn had the patience of a saint and the temperament to match. I know that growing up with me underfoot must have been irritating at times, but if she ever resented me it certainly didn't show. I thought she was the sweetest, prettiest thing in the world. Naturally I was excited when she wrote she was coming home to celebrate her twenty-first birthday in June. She was to drive down from Illinois with her husband Gerald Jetton and his aunt and sister.

While they were on their way, a big thunderstorm hit at home, so Daddy made Mother, Foy, Mama, and me sleep in the storm cellar that night. For some reason he stayed up in the house alone, and in the middle of the night we heard him pounding on the storm cellar door yelling, "Get up, get up, Carolyn's had a wreck, Carolyn's been in a wreck." I had never seen Daddy so upset, so I knew it must be something really serious. It was raining torrents, but we put on our clothes and jumped in the car anyway and headed toward Fairfield, Illinois, where they'd had the accident. All we knew was that Carolyn was in the hospital with a broken leg, but I think we sensed it was a lot worse than that because during the long drive up there everyone was unusually quiet.

One incident happened on the way that shows what kind of man my Daddy was and how he spoiled me. We were passing through Paducah, Kentucky, the next morning, and Foy was driving. I caught sight of a purple felt dress in a store window that I thought was just about the prettiest thing I'd ever seen. Daddy was sitting beside me, and I grabbed his arm and said, "Oh, look at that *beautiful* dress. Oh, I wish I could have it!" And Daddy said, "No, Nettie, we can't stop. We have to hurry on to Fairfield to see about Carolyn. She's been hurt and she needs us." I said, "Okay," and slumped back down in the seat. We drove on for a few blocks and I looked at him and said, "But it *sure* was a pretty dress." Daddy said, "Turn around, Foy. We're going back to buy Nettiebelle that dress."

When we arrived at the hospital we were told the horrible truth about Carolyn's accident. Their car had collided head-on with another automobile carrying seven people who were on their way to church. All seven had been killed instantly. Gerald, who was driving, had been deeply cut across his chest. His sister, who had been asleep in the back seat, had only been bruised. His aunt, who was sitting beside her, was thrown under the front seat, pinned down and badly smashed up. But Carolyn had taken the full impact of the crash in the front passenger seat. Her face had struck the windshield like a sledgehammer, shattering the glass into a million pieces and wedging her half in and half out of the car so tightly she had to be cut out with a blowtorch. Her shoulder was dislocated, her pelvis was crushed, she had a brain concussion, and her face had been cut to shreds. When they finally freed her from the car, they pronounced her dead and laid her under a blanket on the roadside with the seven other bodies. But while they were waiting for the ambulance Gerald saw her finger move, so he picked her up in a daze and carried her around in his arms until the ambulance got there. He was bleeding badly and in need of attention himself, but he wouldn't put her down, even when he tripped and almost fell over one of the dead bodies from the other car. When they got her to the hospital, they sewed up her face as best they could, but she was barely alive. Mother was the first to go into the room to see her. She took one look and fainted dead away.

Carolyn was bandaged from head to toe like a mummy. There were two holes for her eyes and a slit for her mouth and one little place for her nostrils, and that's all you could see. Her legs and arms were in casts, and she couldn't move or speak. We all thought she was going to die; we couldn't accept what had happened. It just didn't seem possible. She was still a newlywed, so young and beautiful and happy. One minute she was celebrating her twenty-first birthday with everything to look forward to, and the next she was broken to pieces like a china doll.

We found motel rooms close to the hospital and took turns sitting with her. Doctors were amazed at the way she clung to life. Every passing day brought us renewed hope that she was going to pull through. By this time it was July and miserably hot. There was no air conditioning in the hospital, and Carolyn not only had to endure unimaginable pain, but also horrible discomfort from being covered with bandages in the suffocating heat. They had put her in traction so her pelvis would heal correctly, and she pleaded and begged us to take the weights off her legs for just a little while. I felt so sorry for her I'd have to leave the room so she wouldn't see me cry.

After a few weeks Mother and Foy decided to drive up to Zion to pack Carolyn's things, because it was obvious by then that she'd have to come home with us when she was released so someone could take care of her through her long recuperation. Mama and Daddy went too, leaving me there alone with Carolyn to keep her company and help the nurses in any way I could. The doctors had removed most of the bandages from her face and stressed the fact that under no circumstances was I to give her a mirror. They were afraid she would go into shock if she saw herself. She had been such a beautiful girl with good features and naturally curly hair that fell down past her shoulders. Now her head was shaved, she had no lips, the side of her nose was gone, one eyelid was missing, and there was a split from the tops of both eyes all the way to her hairline. She was swollen, black and blue, and had scabs all over her face. She looked worse than any Frankenstein monster I'd ever seen in the movies, and it was all I could do not to burst into tears every time I looked at her.

One day soon after the family left, I was sitting there with her when she asked very quietly, "Wynette, go get me a mirror."

I said, "Well, I don't have one with me and nobody else is here because they're not back from Zion yet."

She said, "Go find one." I put her off by pretending to go ask the nurses for one, but when I came back empty-handed she gave me a determined look and without raising her voice ordered, *"Get me a mirror!"*

I went out and told the nurses what she'd said and they panicked. They called the doctor immediately, and when he came he had a mirror in his hand. I didn't want to be in the room when he handed it to her so I waited outside. I heard this pitiful, anguished cry, then screams so loud they seemed to fill the whole hospital. The nurses all stopped what they were doing, and most of them had tears in their eyes. They knew the patient from the car cash had taken her first look in a mirror.

Hearing her suffer that way and knowing there wasn't a thing I could do or say to comfort her tore me apart. I cried for days. Carolyn was so hysterical they had to knock her out. She was kept heavily sedated for almost a week. I'd sit there watching her moan in her sleep and think how unfair it was. I knew that if it had happened to me I would be filled with bitterness and resentment toward the whole world. I loved her so much, and I didn't see how it would be possible for her to face the life ahead of her. The disfigurement alone would have been disaster enough, but she had also been told that she would be risking her life if she ever had children. She and Gerald had so looked forward to having a family, and now due to her crushed pelvis and other internal injuries that dream was gone too. I thought if it were me, I'd probably pray for the courage to kill myself. But I can't count the times in the past twenty years when I've looked back and thankèd God Carolyn was made of stronger stuff. She soon became an inspiration to us all.

When they released Carolyn from the hospital two months after the accident, she had already started to regain her sense of humor. Daddy hired an ambulance to take her back home with us, and we followed along behind it in the family car. She was still in traction, but she could touch the back window of the ambulance with her toes. She'd use her big toe to write us messages in the dust on the window, like HAMBURGER. Of course, there was no way she could eat a hamburger or anything else solid, with half her teeth gone and the rest of them still loose, but that was her way of making a joke. So Daddy would stop and get her a milkshake.

I spent a lot of time with her at home that summer, and I was constantly amazed by her attitude. Gerald was inducted into the Army that first week we brought her home. When he got ready to leave for boot camp, she asked him to bring her their wedding picture. He looked at her like, Please don't make me do that, but she insisted, so he brought it.

She had tears in her eyes and she said, "I'll never look like the girl you married again. It wouldn't be right for a wife with my face to hold you to the vows you took with a bride who looked like this, so there's the door and no one will blame you for not coming back."

Gerald fell to his knees beside her bed and cried, "Don't ever talk like that. I didn't marry a face. I married you, and my love for you hasn't changed one bit. I love you, and I'll always be with you." They'll celebrate their twenty-third anniversary this year, and Gerald is still a devoted husband.

It must have been doubly hard for Carolyn at first, having to face so much plastic surgery with him gone too, but she never complained. Instead of the family having to cheer her up, more often than not she was the one who made us laugh. And she made Gerald laugh, too. One of the most difficult operations was to build her a new lip. They had to take skin from underneath her toes because that's one of the few places on the human body devoid of hair. The next time Gerald came home on leave, he kissed her on the mouth and Carolyn said, "Well, how does it feel to be kissing the bottom of my feet?" It broke him up!

Somehow she learned to handle it when people stared or made remarks, but she was always concerned that she might be an embarrassment to one of us. The first time I drove her to the doctor for a checkup, she asked me to wait in the car, explaining that she would be only a minute. But I knew exactly what she was doing. She didn't want me to feel uncomfortable sitting in the waiting room with her, because she knew the other patients would stare. I said, "No, I'm going in with you," and she just smiled and said, "Okay."

Carolyn's accident gave me a new appreciation of life. Good health and a sound body were things I had simply taken for granted, until I saw firsthand how quickly they can be wiped away. It also made me more impatient to get on with my own life, and Mother's restrictions became more irritating than ever. By the time I was a senior in high school, our relationship had become very strained. There were occasions when we still had fun together, but not often. We argued almost constantly, usually over my not being allowed to do things my friends and classmates were doing. Mother always seemed to expect and suspect the worst. If I came in as little as fifteen minutes late, she met me at the door embarrassing me in front of my date and insinuating by her attitude that we'd been doing something wrong.

I think the thing I resented most during that time was her lack of faith and trust in me. My girl friends' mothers trusted them, and it hurt me that mine didn't, especially when I felt I had done nothing to deserve her attitude. When one of my classmates got pregnant, Mother acted like it was a contagious disease that might spread throughout the senior class. I was forbidden to see the girl again, and I thought that was mean. It seemed to me the girl needed friendship then more than ever. She was disgraced, forced to drop out of school, labeled immoral, and left with the responsibility of raising an illegitimate child while the boy she'd been dating went on about his life as though nothing had happened. If anything, it boosted his reputation with the other boys. I used to see him in school, flirting with girls, and I'd think, How can he do that when he knows what she's going through. It was so unfair.

Nothing makes me angrier, even today, than to hear a girl called names for doing the same thing a boy will brag about. I'm raising my daughters to know they're just as good as any man and have just as much right to a full life. But I'm also trying to teach them that they'll be much more loved and cherished if they have a meaningful relationship with one person than if they experiment with many. I'm so grateful my daughters are growing up in a time when it is acceptable for a girl to leave home after high school, if she wants to, and go out on her own. In my day you had no choice. You stayed home until you got married.

Looking back I know that my mother's restrictions were simply her way of trying to protect me from getting hurt or getting into trouble. I was her only child, and she loved me and wanted the best for me. She was doing what she thought was right, and I'm sure the fact that we didn't get along hurt her as much as it did me. But the importance of communication between parent and child wasn't stressed then the way it is now. Those were the days when parents laid down the law and children obeyed—and that was that!

My mother and I never had a discussion of any kind about sex. In fact, we still don't talk about things like that even though we are close now and have a good relationship. What little I knew about sex I learned at school, so it's not surprising that a good deal of my information was wrong. It would be dishonest to imply that I didn't have sexual urgings before I married, but I would no more have done anything about it than rob a bank. Between my own conscience and my mother's stern hand and with the knowledge that if I ever got into trouble it would break my grandfather's heart, I would have run like a scared rabbit if a boy had tried to get out of line with me. But I did want the freedom to go out on dates without feeling I was being spied upon. Mother and Foy would show up at the most surprising places—parked two cars away at the drive-in movie, for instance! But Linda's mother would come into her room at night when I stayed over and sit on the bed and ask us all about our dates and tease us about whether or not we'd been kissed. I longed for a relationship like that with my own mother. Linda got married toward the end of my junior year, and after that I really missed spending the night at her house.

I was beginning to get a little more popular with the boys by then, but I still didn't date around. After I was voted "Miss Tremont High" at the junior-senior prom, I went out with "Mr. Tremont," Billy Brewer, a few times, but mostly I liked older boys who were already out of school. Generally Mother didn't approve of that, but I did date one "older man" she liked. His name was John Wilson and he had been a classmate of Carolyn's, which meant he was five or six years older than I. During the time we dated he was substituting for my math teacher who had taken a leave of absence due to illness. It was strange being his student during the day and his girlfriend at night. But it helped my math grades.

Mother liked and trusted John and encouraged me to see him instead of some of the other boys I knew. He took me to basketball games, church socials, and movies, but I wasn't allowed to go to dances. With the exception of the junior prom I can remember going to only one dance in my life. My cousin Jane and I were invited to a VFW dance in Red Bay and Aunt Hazel let us go. But I didn't know how to dance so it wasn't much fun for me, except when I got up on the band-stand and sang a few songs. To this day I've never learned to dance. Musicians and singers are probably the worst dancers in the world because we're up there entertaining while everybody else is down on the floor dancing. We never have a chance to learn.

Even though Mother favored John she was still just as strict about the hours I kept and the places I went. When we'd go to basketball games she and Foy would be there too, making sure we all left at the same time so we could follow them home. We had to arrive within minutes after they did or I'd be in real trouble. I not only resented this; I was embarrassed by it. John was a grown man, and I was afraid Mother's rules would make him think of me as a kid. Of course, I thought of myself as grown up. I figured if I was expected to do an adult's share of work in the cotton field, I ought to be treated like one at home. I was headstrong and immature, and I was sure no one in the world had ever gone through the struggle I was going through at home. There must have been many times then when Mother wanted to wring my neck!

Linda visited me often enough to make me envious of her new life. To hear her tell it, marriage was nothing but fun! She was living away from home with a man she loved, and she didn't have to answer to anyone. Marriage meant "escape," and the idea became more attractive to me all the time. Several of my friends had married by then, and I began daydreaming about meeting someone, falling in love, getting married, and, of course, living happily ever after.

When Euple Byrd came into my life I thought my dream had come true. I met him through his brother, D.C., whom I had dated casually off and on for months. We had known the family for years. They lived about twelve miles from us, and some of the kids had gone to school with Carolyn and some with me. But D.C. and Euple were even older than Carolyn. They had both been in the service, and Euple especially seemed like a real man of the world and good-looking too, with his medium build, sandy red hair, and pretty blue eyes. I was attracted to him in a special way, and after we began dating I wasn't interested in seeing anyone else.

Mother didn't approve of Euple at all. She thought he was too old for me, and since he had been in the Army she was certain he was wild and a drinker. There had never been any alcohol in our house, except the jug of home brew my grandfather kept in the storm cellar. That was used only for medicinal purposes and then only as a last resort. No one in my family drank. I don't think they even had friends who did. It was against their religion and their principles. Euple did drink beer, but only moderately, and he never tried to persuade me to join him. When mother saw that I was more interested in him than I'd been in anyone since Billy Cole, she started trying to get me to date John

Wilson again. The fact that she was pushing John made me like Euple all the more.

One night, about ten months after we started dating, Euple leaned close to me in church and whispered in my ear, "I want you to marry me. Will you?" His proposal didn't come as a shock, because he'd been leading up to it for some time, but I hadn't expected it so soon. I felt more relieved than thrilled. Here was my way out if I wanted it. I was more physically attracted to Euple than I had been to anyone since Billy Cole, and I was infatuated enough to believe this was the real thing. The thought of marrying Euple, having our own little apartment, both working, taking trips on weekends, not having to answer to my mother—and never having to pick cotton again—was certainly more appealing than the life I had known. Still, something held me back, and I told him I'd have to think about it. Graduation was only a few months away, and I didn't want to miss that. Mississippi had a law that if you got married while in high school, you were automatically expelled.

About a week later Euple brought me home thirty minutes late from a date. I don't remember why now —we probably just weren't watching the time—but it was the chance Mother had been waiting for to put a stop to my seeing him. She met me at the door, fuming. "You're never going out with him again because he doesn't respect you enough to get you home on time," she said. I argued furiously, but she wouldn't listen. "That's it. I'm not going to discuss it anymore and you aren't going to see him anymore," she said flatly.

"Well, I *will* see him," I yelled back. "If I can't see him any other way, I'll marry him!"

She said, "That's the stupidest thing I've ever heard in my life. If you're that dumb, go ahead and marry him."

I said, "Okay, I will. Anything would be better than what I'm going through living here."

With that, she picked up a belt and hit me with the buckle end hard enough to draw blood. Then she gave me the worst whipping of my life. I was seventeen years old and it hurt my dignity as much as it did my backside. The next day I called Euple from school and said, "Okay, I'll marry you."

When I came home that afternoon, I told Mother I was going to get married, with or without her permission. We got into another loud argument, and she said, "You can't get married unless I sign the papers and I won't do that." So I said I would get Foy to sign them for me, and she said, "If you do that you can just leave my house right now. If you're determined to get married, I don't want you sleeping here another night."

I threw a few things into an old, beat-up suitcase and waved the school bus down as it was going back to Tremont. I got off at my friend Peggy's house and asked if I could spend the night with her. When her mother found out what I planned to do, she sat me down and talked to me for hours, pleading with me not to run off and get married.

"You're going about this all the wrong way," she said. "And you're getting married for all the wrong reasons. Marriage is hard enough if you do it for the right reasons. Please go back home and think it over. You've got to really love someone deeply to spend the rest of your life with him."

I remember saying, "I *will* love him." I think that was the first time I admitted to myself that I wasn't totally in love. "I like him so much, and I love being with him, and I know I can live with him. Besides, I could never go back home after mother kicked me out." That streak of stubborn pride has gotten me into deep trouble more than once in my life!

Foy did sign the marriage papers, even though mother was against it. He knew if he didn't I'd elope and lie about my age. I was only a few months away from eighteen anyway.

The next day Euple and I drove to Fulton, Mississippi, where we took blood tests and found a preacher who would marry us. We were married that morning at the preacher's house with his wife as our only witness. Euple had on a dark suit and white shirt, and I had on a little navy blue school jumper. I was very nervous during the ceremony, but I wasn't worried about what I was doing. I really didn't feel I had any choice, and I was sure it would all work out. I didn't resent missing the traditional white wedding. We wouldn't have had the money for one if I'd wanted it, and most of my friends had gotten married just the way I was doing it. The ceremony was so brief I almost missed the preacher's cue to say "I do." Afterward we drove back to Tremont, to the high school, and parked there so I could see some of my friends when they came out. When I told them what we'd done, the girls all crowded around me, hugging and kissing me and congratulating Euple. Some of them said they were going to get together and give me a shower. As I remember, that was the most exciting part of the day.

Later we drove to Euple's house and had supper with his family. We had no money and no place else to go, so they said we could sleep in his sister's room. I was very embarrassed. He had a large family, and I knew every one of them would go to bed that night thinking about what was going on in our room. He had two younger sisters and one younger brother who was my age and in my class at school. There was some snickering and whispering going on between the little sisters, and that made me uncomfortable. I remember we went out on the front porch and sat and watched the traffic for a long time because we didn't know quite what to do.

Then, finally, somehow we got to the bedroom. They lived in a big old unpainted house with bare wood floors which felt cold to my feet, even though it was April. I undressed and crawled under the covers as quickly as I could. I could hear his mother and father still up and walking around. It was definitely not the kind of romantic atmosphere a girl dreams of for her wedding night. There was no soft music, no candlelight, no champagne, and no satin sheets. There was a four-poster bed, but it was very old and the springs squeaked something awful. Euple was gentle and patient with me, but I couldn't get my mind off those bed-springs. I was sure every move we made could be heard all over the house.

I lay awake long after my husband's steady breathing told me he was asleep, trying to think about the happy life we were going to have together, instead of what had just happened. I had a let-down feeling, and I wasn't sure why, so I didn't want to dwell on it. There were a lot of good things to think about. For months I'd been dreaming about getting away from home. Now I'd done it. I was free at last!

Chapter 3

❧❧❧

WITHIN six months I was back home living with Mother and Foy again. And my so-called freedom was short-lived. I had returned to school the day after the wedding as though nothing had happened, hoping my secret wouldn't get out so that I could graduate with my class. But the principal came to Euple's parents' house one afternoon about a week later and told me not to come back. He wanted to know why I hadn't told them the truth and saved my family embarrassment, because my grandfather was on the school board. I hated to miss graduation, but I hated the thought of embarrassing Daddy even more. I guess in the back of my mind I thought that because he was on the board and held in high regard in the community, they might make an exception and let me graduate. The ceremony was less than a month away. But ole "Tater Head" wouldn't budge, so I put aside my disappointment and told myself it wasn't important anyway. After all, I was now a married woman!

Euple didn't have a job, and he couldn't find one in

Tremont, which is a very small town. After we'd lived with his parents for a couple of months, his brother found him work with a construction company in Tupelo, twenty-three miles away. We moved there and rented our first apartment. We had three small rooms over a garage, and although it was run down and we didn't have a dime to fix it up, I thought it was wonderful because we finally had a place of our own. I got a job at the Genesco shoe factory in Fulton, twelve miles down the road. But Euple was soon laid off and we had to move back to Tremont. He worked for a while in Red Bay but lost that job too.

But this time I knew I was pregnant, and I was getting worried about my husband not having a steady job. Mother and I hadn't spoken for several months after my marriage, but when I learned I was going to have a baby, I just had to share the good news, and she was very happy for me. We never talked about the hard feelings between us when I decided to run off and marry Euple; I guess we both wanted to forget the past. She invited us to come and live with them until Euple could find a good job, so I brought my husband home with me and we moved back into my old room.

I was thrilled about being pregnant because I wanted a large family, but I was depressed about having to live at home again. I wanted to feel independent, to be able to show Mother that Euple and I could take care of ourselves. But we were just as dependent on her and Foy as I had been before I married. This embarrassed me, so I worked hard to be useful. Mother had always preferred working outside to doing housework, so I cleaned, cooked, and did laundry while she helped Foy in the fields. At night we'd all sit around and play Rook, which had been Daddy's favorite pastime for as long as I could remember.

By the time I found out I was pregnant, Carolyn was about to give birth to her first child. She was still having plastic surgery on her face, but her body had mended as well as could be expected. Her pelvis was not strong enough for child-bearing, and we were worried about it. But she was determined to have a baby. I was two months pregnant when they took her to the hospital. Dr. Robert Pegram, who was also my doctor, stood by her through a hard twenty-hour labor before her healthy baby girl Kathy was born. I had been Mama and Daddy's only grandchild for eighteen years, so they were delighted about the new baby, and Carolyn and Gerald were the happiest parents imaginable.

Euple was looking forward to becoming a father too, but he was not overly concerned about the fact that he didn't have a steady job or the money to support a family. All his people had a gypsy attitude about life —moving around from job to job, never worrying much about where the next month's rent was coming from, or even the next meal. I hadn't been raised that way. When Daddy was Euple's age he already owned a sawmill and was saving every dime to buy land. Security for his family was more important to him than anything, and Foy felt the same way about taking care of Mother. Euple's nonchalant attitude about work made me a little uneasy, but I was too excited about the prospect of having a baby to let it get me down. Euple would lay beside me in bed at night and rest his hand on my stomach, hoping to feel the baby kick. I told him he could pick out the name if it was a boy, but if it was a girl I wanted to call her Gwendolyn, the name Mama had wanted Mother to give me. I added Lee for Foy, because he'd always been so good to me.

Gwendolyn Lee Byrd arrived in fine shape at 11:20 A.M. on April 15, 1961. It was an easy delivery, and she was an easy baby from the beginning. I had decided not to breast-feed her because I wanted to go to beauty school as soon as she was old enough to stay with someone. By then we had moved into an old log house built in the 1800s that sat back in the woods on Daddy's property, and there I became pregnant again.

When I first learned I was going to have another baby so soon, I was disappointed. Gwen was only five-and-a-half months old, and she took up most of my time. Also, I still hoped to go to beauty school so at least one of us would have a trade that would bring steady work. But then I thought, Well, I wanted a big family anyway, so maybe it's better to have the first two close together so they can be company for each other.

The old cabin we lived in was really nothing more than a shack. We had no indoor plumbing, not even a water pump in the kitchen. I had to bring water from the spring about 100 yards from the house for drinking, cooking, bathing, and washing clothes. I boiled diapers outside in a wash pot over an open fire. I cooked in the fireplace because the old electric stove never worked right, and the electricity was out half the time anyway. The cabin had been abandoned for years and it was a mess. I scrubbed the warped plank floors with a brush and Lysol every day so they'd be clean enough for Gwen to play on. Cold winds whipped through the cracks in the log walls faster than the two fireplaces could warm the rooms, so I insulated the walls by nailing up flattened cardboard boxes. It wasn't the best-looking "wallpaper" you can imagine, but it kept us from freezing to death. The front porch swayed, the tin roof leaked, and the outhouse looked like it wouldn't hold up in a stiff breeze, but at least we were on our own instead of living with my family or Euple's.

I was tired all the time during my second pregnancy. Keeping house under pioneer conditions is hard work, and it's no wonder settlers' wives were old at thirty. I was beginning to feel like an old woman at nineteen! In addition to the chores around the house, I had to watch Gwen every second after she started crawling because I had no playpen to put her in. I came up with some ingenious ways to get my work done. To keep her safely in one place while I went to the spring for water, I'd put her on the floor with a toy, then set one leg of the heavy iron bed on the edge of her dress. When I was sure she couldn't move around, I'd grab the buckets and run to the spring and back as fast as I could.

Sometimes it's hard for me to realize I lived like that just fourteen short years ago. I would have been overjoyed then just to own an old secondhand car. Now I have a Corvette and a Thunderbird, a pickup truck and a van, a bus and an airplane. And am I any happier? You bet I am! It kills me to hear people who are well off talk about the "good old days" when they didn't have a dime. I wonder how many of them would really go back to that. It's true that money can't buy happiness. But it can buy conveniences, and it sure can take the edge off misery!

I was at home alone with Gwen when I went into labor the second time. Euple then had a job setting out trees for the government and he was gone that day. So I put my suitcase under one arm, Gwen under the other, and walked a half mile down the road to Mother's house. By the time we got to the hospital, my labor was stopping then starting again. Dr. Pegram, who had also delivered Gwen, examined me and said the baby was a breech, and the cord was wrapped around her neck. He kept trying to turn her but he couldn't. I had been having hard contractions for a day and a half when Aunt Ruby came by the labor room to see me. She was my grandmother's sister, an "old maid" who was a registered nurse but still believed more in home remedies than in modern medicine. She had worked at the Tupelo Community Hospital for years, and all the doctors there respected her opinion. I was in agony by this time, but she said, "Don't worry, honey. We'll fix you right up." She made a mixture of orange juice, castor oil, and baking soda and made me drink it. Then she got me up, held onto me, and made me walk the floor.

Dr. Pegram came in and said, "Ruby, what are you doing?"

She answered, "I'm helpin' this here baby get out."

So he said, "Well, go ahead. You've probably delivered as many as I have."

Sure enough, within an hour I was ready to give birth. Even though they gave me a shot the pain was incredible. I wasn't prepared for it to hurt so much because I hadn't gone through anything like that to have Gwen. I remember Dr. Pegram telling me I had another pretty little girl, then I passed out. We named her Jacquelyn Faye, for Jacqueline Kennedy (although I spelled it differently) and for my mother, Mildred Faye.

From her delivery on August 2, 1962 through her first year, Jackie was as difficult as Gwen had been easy. She cried a lot at night and wouldn't go to sleep unless the light was on. She slept in a bassinet by my bed, and I had to keep my hand on her all night because if I moved it she would wake up and start crying again. No formula agreed with her until we tried soybean mulch. It was the only thing she could keep down. If I'd been tired before she was born, I was exhausted afterward. I hadn't completely recovered from a kidney infection I'd gotten while I was carrying her, and taking care of two babies and a house all day without a solid night's sleep was getting me down. I felt sluggish and exhausted all the time. I was also beginning to resent the fact that my life was all work and no play. I was tied down with the kids day and night, and we had no money for anything other than necessities. We couldn't even afford a movie once in a while. Euple was drawing unemployment half the time, and we literally had to count pennies. We couldn't even afford to buy a radio.

I had dreamed of married life in a vine-covered cottage with starched white curtains blowing in the breeze, but I was living in a shack with cracked window panes and no curtains at all. I had pictured myself standing in the doorway in a cute dress and frilly apron greeting my husband when he came home from work. But my husband didn't even have a steady job, and I was too tired at night to put on a cute dress even if I'd owned one. I wanted to take little trips on weekends with the children, but there was no money to go anywhere. We were expected to spend every Sunday at Euple's parents' house, where the men stayed out in the yard fooling around on old cars, and the women sat in the kitchen and talked and cooked. I hated it. I had tried bringing my father's old guitar over to Euple's on Sundays, thinking I could at least amuse myself pickin' and singin' but I soon stopped that; his family wasn't interested in listening. There was no place I could go to be alone, and he kept kidding me about my "hillbilly" music.

By the time Jackie was born I had put music out of my mind altogether. I resigned myself to the fact that I had a family to raise, and I knew I was going to have to go to work to help Euple support us. Music wouldn't bring in any money, but hair-dressing would, so my goal was beauty school. But I couldn't even get out to do that. My life was dull, drab, and exhausting. The only thing that kept me going was the kids. I enjoyed being a mother, even under these circumstances, and my only fun was playing with my children. Mother helped me out as much as she could, keeping Gwen some of the time so I could rest, but she soon went back to teaching school, and I had it all to myself again.

Finally, Euple got a job in Red Bay selling farm equipment, so we moved back there into a little white frame house that looked like a palace compared to the old log cabin. We had two bedrooms, linoleum on the floor, and *indoor plumbing!* I made curtains and fixed it up as cute as I could on our tight budget. By this time Jackie was a year old, and I was itching to get to beauty school. It cost $25 a month, more than we could afford on Euple's salary, so Mother agreed to pay my tuition. The school was forty miles away in Tupelo. Euple let me use his old car and he got a ride to work. I left home by 6 A.M. in order to drop Gwen and Jackie off at nursery school and get to beauty school by 8. Then I'd pick up the girls at night, drive home, fix dinner, and do laundry and housework. After three months I had just settled into the routine of my new schedule when Euple quit his job again. This time we were off to Memphis. He convinced me life would be better there because it would be easier for him to find a good job in a big city. We moved into a small apartment in a run-down neighborhood, and he went to work for an upholstery factory while I stayed home with the kids.

One afternoon I was out walking on Front Street with Gwen and Jackie when I heard country music coming from a bar. I wouldn't have dared go inside. I'd never been in a bar in my life, but the music sounded so good I just had to stop by the door to listen. Soon a beautiful redheaded woman came out and invited me to come in with the children. She said it would be all right since the bar wasn't open yet. Her name was Mary and she owned the place. The piano player I had heard from the street was her fiance Carl. It was just a small beer joint, but it was clean and Mary was very nice. Before we left she offered me a job as a barmaid. I told her I'd have to ask my husband about it. That night Euple said it sounded okay to him. We could use the money, and since he had a day job he could watch the children at night while I worked.

Years later I recorded the song "Your Good Girl's Gonna Go Bad" that starts off "I've never seen the inside of a barroom." I really identify with that line because I truly never had seen the inside of a barroom when I went to work in one. It was like throwing a lamb to the wolves. I was married and the mother of two children, but I was still a country girl who had never been anywhere.

Mary's place was a riverfront bar in big-city Memphis. It was like a den of iniquity compared to the places I'd seen back home. Boy, did my eyes open fast!

Most of the customers were nice men, but there were always some who thought it was real funny to pinch you on the fanny while you served their table. The first time it happened to me I was so shocked I almost dropped my drink tray. Mary didn't let anybody get too far out of line—there were no brawls or anything like that—but there were a lot of smart remarks, dirty jokes, and men who just couldn't go home until they'd made a pass at you. It didn't take me long to learn how to get around them without being hateful, but I still felt guilty about working in a place where Mama or Daddy wouldn't have gone for the world.

What kept me coming back night after night was the music. Mary and Carl were really sweet, and little by little Carl began asking me to sing for the customers. Then some of the regulars started giving me extra tips to sing their requests. I remember one man offering me $20 to sing his favorite song, but I figured for that much money he expected a lot more than a song, so I turned him down. Carl played fantastic piano in the Memphis rock/blues style of Jerry Lee Lewis or Charlie Rich, and I loved listening to him.

One night after I'd sung two or three songs he said, "You know, Wynette, you've got a good voice, but you're strictly country. You belong in Nashville."

I had never thought of going to Nashville before, and I didn't think of it again for a long time after that, but Carl had planted a seed. It just needed to germinate a while before it was ready to sprout.

My hours at the bar were 3 P.M. until midnight, which made it possible for me to be with the children most of the day. When I left home in the afternoon, a neighbor lady in our apartment building watched them until Euple got home at 6 P.M. I'd fix dinner before leaving, so all he had to do was warm it up and serve it. He was patient with the girls and never complained about having to watch them at night. But I could feel us drifting further and further apart. I didn't want to admit it, but marriage had not brought me the happiness I had thought it would.

One afternoon while I was cooking supper before going to work, I noticed that Jackie didn't look right. I wondered if she was coming down with a virus and made a mental note to ask Mary that night if she could recommend a doctor since I didn't have one in Memphis. But by the time I got ready to leave for work Jackie was limp and clammy, so I looked up a doctor in the yellow pages and called a cab to take us there. After examining her, the doctor said Jackie was in a diabetic coma. Apparently she had been born with diabetes, but we had never known it. He put her on medication and a special diet and said she would probably grow out of it by the time she started school. But after I found out about her condition I didn't want to be away from her at night, and since Euple was tired of his job at the upholstery factory, we decided to move back to Tremont. We found a house owned by a woman named Pat Brown. She used it as a beauty shop during the daytime and she said we could rent it and live there, if I would help her with her customers on weekends. It was a good opportunity for me because the beauty school where I had re-enrolled agreed to count the hours I worked with Pat toward my graduation.

Euple got a traveling job with a construction company which meant he was gone two or three weeks at a time. I didn't mind his being away so much because we argued almost constantly when he was there. By this time I knew my marriage was not going to get any better. I wanted out, but even thinking about that made me feel terribly guilty. Divorce was unheard of in my family, and I knew Mother would just die if she found out I wanted one. I told myself how lucky I was to have two beautiful daughters and I should be thankful for that instead of being so unhappy with my husband. I worried about God punishing me if I didn't show more gratitude. I was afraid He would take one of my children. I even felt guilty about the fact that I didn't enjoy our sex life. I was sure there was something wrong with me. I wondered why other girls thought it was so great. I found it very disappointing. I thought I was doing what I was supposed to do, but I couldn't be sure since no one had ever told me any details about lovemaking. I knew for certain that it wasn't anything like movies and novels lead you to believe, and I felt cheated; kissing and hugging when I was dating had actually been more exciting. Of course I never discussed any of this with Euple or anyone else. I would have been ashamed and embarrassed to talk about anything so intimate, and I didn't want Euple to know our sex life left me frustrated and discontented, because I thought it was probably my fault, and he would think I was frigid. That was a word used a lot in magazines then, and although I wasn't sure what it meant, it sounded cold, ungiving, and abnormal. So I kept quiet and reminded myself that it was a wife's duty to have sex with her husband when he wanted it.

But sex was one of the few things we didn't argue about. I was tired of moving around. We had been married four years, and we'd lived in half a dozen different places. I could see Euple was never going to settle into a steady job because he didn't want to. He worked hard when he worked, but every job soon bored him, and he thought nothing of quitting to look for something better. I knew we would never have anything at the rate we were going, and I was fed up with not being able to afford even the ordinary pleasures, like a movie now and then. I would have given anything to own a television set, but with Euple changing jobs so often we couldn't even get credit to buy one on time. About the only entertainment I had in the evenings, after I'd fed the girls and gotten them to bed, was reading movie magazines. Pat Brown kept them around the house for her beauty salon customers. I would pore over the pages, believing every word. I had no way of knowing the stories weren't always true. Like most people I thought that what was in print had to be the truth. And I certainly didn't dream my own name would one day be appearing in some of those same books. It was fun reading about other people's romances, marriages, divorces, and personal traumas, but I hated it when they started writing about mine. It is still a shock when I see my name or picture alongside movie and television stars. I feel so *exposed,* and it isn't because I have anything to hide. I am not secretive by nature, but I do need privacy. I think we all do. I understand now why stars like Elizabeth Taylor never read anything about themselves in those magazines. If it's false it makes you mad as blazes; and if it's true it's usually something that is nobody else's business. But I guess that's what makes people want to read it.

I had one customer at the beauty school who loved movie magazines more than anything. She'd raise the devil when she came in if we didn't have any new books she hadn't read yet. She was a rich old lady, but she was too stingy to go to a regular salon. She came to the school because the shampoos and sets were free. Customers were expected to tip since the students had no other income, and I could always depend on her for the same amount—25 cents! When she died, her family called the school and asked if I would come to the funeral parlor to fix her hair. They offered me $50, which was more than I made in a whole week, so I couldn't turn them down. But I was petrified at the thought of working on a dead body, and the fact that I'd known her made it even worse.

I persuaded a classmate named Jane, who was an absolute nut, to go with me. We took rollers, a wave set and portable hair dryer, and drove to the funeral parlor. They had her laid out on a slab that supported her from the neck down. Her head, which was shaved in the back, was resting on a metal pole that came up out of the floor. They had left only the hair around her face. A sheet was pulled up to her neck and she looked very pasty.

I stood there for the longest time trying to get up the nerve to touch her, and Jane kept saying, "Come on, Wynette. You know she doesn't like to be kept waiting." The attendant who was sitting over in the corner kept looking at Jane like she was crazy, especially when she started talking to the dead woman, asking how she was and how she wanted her hair done.

When I lifted her head, her skin felt cold and powdery, more like a rubber doll than a human being, and it gave me the creeps. I dampened the front of her hair and set it, then wheeled the dryer into position.

Jane had brought movie magazines to read while we waited for her hair to dry. She looked at them and said, "Oh, we forgot to bring her the new ones. She's read these." Then she told me to go check the dryer.

I said, "Why? She can't be dry yet."

Jane said, "Yes, but you know how she hates it if it gets too hot." I could have killed her.

Next she told me she saw the sheet move! I combed the old lady's hair as fast as I could, and we didn't leave there a minute too soon. Before we were a block away Jane had to stop the car so I could throw up. The odor of the embalming fluid made me sick, and for days afterward I still thought I could smell it on my hands.

By the time I finished beauty school we had moved back to Tupelo, and Euple had changed jobs again. I hadn't had time to take the state exam to get my beauty operator's license, so I went to work as a waitress. My marriage had hit rock bottom. My kidney problem had flared up again and Dr. Pegram was worried about it. He told me I was not to have intercourse until it was cured. He also took me off birth control pills while he was treating me. I don't know whether Euple didn't believe the doctor had said I was not to have sex or whether he didn't care, but he wouldn't listen. He became a lot more interested in our love life after I told him there wouldn't be any for a while, and he was so persistent that it was easier to give in than argue about it.

The infection continued until one of my kidneys was barely functioning at all. Dr. Pegram said I was on my feet too much as a waitress, so I went to work as a receptionist for a chiropractor, a dear man named Dr. Smith. Euple and I were still arguing all the time, and he seemed to think the bed was the place to solve all our problems. But for me it only made matters worse. In addition to being physically uncomfortable I was also emotionally turned off. I no longer even had the desire to fake enjoyment.

The tension kept building until we had a huge blow-up. I told Euple, "I can't stand it anymore. Please just get out and leave me alone, at least until I get well again." So he left. But every few days he came back, and he would not leave until I went to bed with him. Afterward I'd lay there hating myself and him too, knowing all I'd done was buy a couple of more days peace before he'd be back again. The strain was beginning to show. I felt on the verge of tears all the time. This had been the pattern for weeks when I went back to Dr. Pegram for another checkup. I knew I wasn't any better, but I hadn't guessed he would make a new discovery.

"You're pregnant," he said, and the words hit me like a jolt. This couldn't be true! It was the last thing I wanted to hear at a time when my marriage was falling apart. It was pretty obvious to Dr. Pegram that I hadn't followed his instructions about not having sex.

He told me that being pregnant complicated the kidney infection and vice versa. "Pregnant women have died from this same problem," he said, "and if you don't make your husband leave you alone until we get this thing cleared up, you could be in serious trouble."

I tried to explain about my marriage and why I'd gone against his orders. Then I begged him not to tell Euple I was pregnant. "I want a divorce," I confessed, "and if he finds out we're going to have another baby, he'll never give me one." Dr. Pegram agreed to keep my secret and told me to take a week off work so I could go to bed and get some rest.

That night I told Euple he had to get out for good. I tried to explain why I couldn't take it anymore, but we got into a heated argument and he refused to leave. It was a sticky summer night so I took the kids and drove around for an hour or so. When I returned he was gone, but I knew he hadn't moved out because I had his car and all his things were still there. My nerves were so on edge that when I went into the attic to turn on the fan, I saw something that scared me half to death. It looked like a man lying down up there. I could see the bottom of his shoes. I hurried down the attic stairs and put the girls in the car again. We drove around another hour. When I got home Euple was there. I asked him to go into the attic and see what was there. It turned out to be just a pair of old mildewed work shoes that had fallen over and were lying sideways. I felt like a fool.

I wanted Euple to go so I could get some sleep, but he refused. He said if anyone was going to leave, it would have to be me. We got into the worst argument ever over that and I just went to pieces. I was screaming hysterically. He slapped me, shook me, did everything he could think of to snap me out of it, but I kept on screaming. All the anger and frustration that had been pent up for nearly five years exploded, and it was like a dam had burst. I couldn't control myself. I knew what I was doing, but I couldn't stop. I guess I collapsed, finally, but by that time Euple had called a doctor who told him to bring me to the hospital.

When we got there Euple said he couldn't understand why I had been carrying on so. He told the doctor he thought I was going crazy. I heard all their conversation, and when the doctor talked to me I understood everything he said, but I couldn't answer him; I had withdrawn into myself and I couldn't come out. The doctor suggested I stay in the hospital a few days for rest and observation. He also wanted to treat my kidney problem, which he said was dangerously close to uremic poisoning. I let him lead me away like an obedient child. Between the infection in my body and the emotional state that had kept me in turmoil for months, I was totally helpless. I had no defenses left. I couldn't fight back. Every time the doctor came into my room, I burst into tears. I wanted desperately to talk to him, to pour out my heart, but I couldn't. Tears came but no words. I was lost in deep depression. I would cry myself into exhaustion, feeling completely drained and certain I didn't have a tear left. Then the doctor would walk in and I'd begin crying all over again.

After consulting with another physician the doctor decided to try to bring me out of my depression through electric shock therapy, which at the time was a popular form of treatment for nervous disorders. I understood what they were going to do, but I was too sick to protest. I felt tired all the way to my soul, and there were days when I didn't care what they did to me.

I was given twelve shock treatments all together, and they were just as horrible as I had imagined they would be. But they helped me. I came out of my depression, and when it was all over I was able to go home and tell Euple calmly that he had to leave because I was getting a divorce. He seemed to understand for the first time that I really meant it and he didn't argue. He just packed everything and left.

Euple had taken the car with him, so when I went back to work Dr. Smith offered to loan me $200 to buy an old Chevy. I was to pay him back $20 a week out of my salary, which was $65 a week. That didn't leave much for the girls and me to live on, so we moved to a small efficiency apartment that was much cheaper. Meanwhile, I had seen an attorney and filed for divorce. Mother was dead set against my doing this. She wouldn't even discuss it with me except to say that I was disgracing the whole family. She didn't know how unhappy I'd been or for how long. I couldn't talk to her about my marital problems because I felt she'd say "I told you so." Her attitude was "You made your bed, now lie in it."

The second night I was in my new apartment I decided to take the girls and visit my friend Ruby, who lived in a trailer park nearby. She was one of the few people I could talk to about my situation with Euple. I stayed at her place for several hours, and when I returned to my apartment I knew immediately that something was wrong. The front door was unlocked, although I was sure I had locked it before I left.

When I switched on the light inside the door I exclaimed, "Oh, my God!" The place had been stripped. *Everything* had been taken—the dishes, the towels, the bedclothes, the flatware and pots and pans, my clothes and the children's clothes—even the bathroom medicine cabinet and the refrigerator had been emptied! The girls began to whimper. They were scared and confused. I searched the rooms, but there was no evidence anywhere to indicate who had been there. I didn't believe it was a thief. I didn't have anything worth stealing, but what had been there was all I owned in the world. I fell to the floor and bawled like a baby. Gwen and Jackie tried to comfort me and the three of us sat there hugging one another until we were all cried out. I put them to bed on the bare mattress and covered them with their little coats. We had no clothes left except what we had on our backs.

They had already fallen asleep, and I was sitting on the floor again, still crying, wondering what to do, when I heard a knock at the door. I opened it to find a policeman standing there. For a minute I thought he'd somehow heard about the robbery and had come to investigate. Instead, he said, "Are you Mrs. Euple Byrd?" I answered yes, and he handed me a paper and said, "I have a warrant for your arrest."

I couldn't believe it! "What have I done?" I asked. He said he would explain on the way to the station. I asked him if I could follow him in my car since I had two little girls inside and would have to wake them up and take them with me. He said we'd have to ride with him in the patrol car and that someone from the juvenile department would meet us at the station to take the children.

I was horrified! "The juvenile department? Why do they have to go to the juvenile department? Why can't they stay with me?"

"It's the rules," he answered.

The children couldn't understand why they were being awakened in the middle of the night and taken away in a police car, and they were terrified. I was too. I had no idea what I could possibly have done. I was sure they had mistaken me for someone else.

I didn't learn anything until we arrived at the police station and they had taken the girls from me. They left me alone in a room. I didn't know where Gwen and Jackie were, if they were crying for me, scared to death, or what. I was beside myself with worry. No one would give me any information at all.

After what seemed like hours, a man came into the room and introduced himself as a doctor. "I'm here to examine you because your husband thinks you are mentally and emotionally incapable of taking care of your children," he said. He explained that he was one of three doctors who would question me that night to determine if the charge was true.

I was stunned. I knew Euple didn't want a divorce, but I had no idea he would go this far! He had taken out a warrant on me, knowing that the threat of losing my children would make me agree to almost anything. I was so distraught and frightened I couldn't concentrate on the doctor's questions. To be told you're being "tested" for sanity and whether or not you get to keep your children depends on whether or not you "pass" is terrifying. I was a nervous wreck for fear I would answer a question wrong or say something that would make them think I really was crazy.

The "examination" seemed to go on forever, and when it was finally over I felt numb. The policeman who'd picked me up came in to apologize for what he'd had to do. Then the second doctor appeared. Again, the same routine. Questions and more questions, some of them the same as the first doctor had asked. When he finished it was well past midnight, and the third doctor was brought in.

When I saw him, I all but fell into his arms. I'd never been so relieved to see anyone in my life. Dr. Pegram, my own personal physician! He hadn't known I was the "crazy woman" he had been brought in to examine, and they hadn't known he was my doctor because he'd been chosen at random. He said, "My God, what are *you* doing here?"

I burst into tears, trying to explain, but the policeman in charge interrupted and told him what had happened.

"This woman is no more crazy than I am," Dr. Pegram said. "I've been treating her for months for several things, including a severe kidney infection, and there's nothing wrong with her mentally at all." (He never mentioned pregnancy as one of the reasons I'd been seeing him.) "The pressure she's been under in the past year would be enough to drive anyone crazy. And now she's being tormented by her husband, who won't leave her alone long enough for her to get physically well. She's unhappy and she wants a divorce. If that's crazy, then half the married people in this state are crazy!"

The policeman asked if it were true that I had been given electric shock treatments. Dr. Pegram said, "If it is true, it took place under another doctor's care, not mine. And if she needed them it was because she was driven to the point where she desperately needed help. I won't even examine her, much less sign any paper. Now, I want to talk to the other doctors who've seen her tonight."

The first two doctors agreed that I was not mentally unstable. One said the only thing he concluded was that I was scared half to death. The other one said I had answered all his questions intelligently and coherently, but that I was in a state of extreme nervous agitation from worrying about my children's safety and comfort. They released me on the spot and the police drove me home.

But the juvenile authorities wouldn't release Gwen and Jackie until the next morning because it was so late. I had to go home without them to that empty, looted apartment. Just the sight of that bare mattress brought tears again. It had been the worst night of my life. I was exhausted, but I couldn't sleep. My mind was spinning a mile a minute trying to figure out how I could get away from Euple. I knew he wasn't going to leave me alone, and I couldn't imagine how he would try to harass me next. I knew he had arranged my apartment being cleaned out, and if he could go so far as to have me arrested he was capable of anything. But I felt so beaten I didn't even have the energy to hate him for what he'd put the girls and me through that night.

Two weeks later I drove to the nursery school as usual after work to get my girls. The lady in charge told me they had already been picked up. I asked by whom. She said she assumed it was someone I'd sent. She described a woman and a man—my mother and Euple!

I went to a pay phone and called Mother to ask if she had Jackie and Gwen. She said she didn't.

I said, "My God. The woman at the nursery school described someone who looked like you as the person who picked them up." Mother repeated she didn't have them.

I called Euple's family and they said they didn't know where he was, and they hadn't seen my children. I called everybody I could think of, and no one knew where they were. By this time I was a wreck. I felt certain Euple had the kids, but I didn't know where he was or where he could have taken them. For all I knew, he had left the state. I didn't go to the police because my recent experience with them was too painful in my memory. I didn't want them involved at all if I could help it.

For the next six days I tried everything I knew to track down my husband, but I couldn't find a clue to where he'd gone. It never occurred to me to call Mother's house again, and she was too far out in the country for me to drop by after work. But one afternoon I couldn't stand it any longer, so I took off early from work and drove thirty-five miles to her place to see if she had any idea about where I could find Euple. When I pulled into her driveway I was shocked to see my kids playing in her front yard! And Euple's car parked in her garage! I was furious. So it *had* been my mother at the nursery school! She had conspired with Euple to take the children! I knew my mother and Euple had one thing in common. Neither one wanted me to get a divorce, but I couldn't believe they would do something like this.

I was so incensed I grabbed the girls, put them in my car, and backed out of her driveway as fast as I could. Euple heard my engine and ran out the front door of her house, jumping into his car and backing out after me. I tossed my purse to the girls in the back seat and told them they could play with anything in it if they would just stay down on the floorboard. I was driving like a reckless fool, trying to outmaneuver Euple because I knew my old car couldn't outrun his newer model. Half the time I was straddling the white line so he couldn't pass me and block my way.

All of a sudden I saw a school bus stopped ahead of me unloading children. I was almost on top of it, and there was no way I could stop, so I ran off the road onto the shoulder, passing the bus on the wrong side to avoid hitting anyone. Euple stopped behind the bus which gave me a little time to get ahead of him, but he soon caught up again. It was the wildest thirty-five mile drive I've ever had. He forced me off the road three different times, but somehow I managed to get back on and dodge him again. He stayed right on my rear bumper all the way into downtown Tupelo, where I came to a screeching halt in front of the courthouse. I grabbed the girls and ran up the steps. Once he saw where I was going, he tore out of there burning rubber, and I had a peace bond sworn out on him so he couldn't come near us again without risking arrest.

I was still fuming, but the anger did me a world of good. For months I had felt like a victim. I had been mentally beaten and physically dragged out. I had been torn between guilt and resentment, and it had left me confused and too tired to make decisions. But that burst of anger sent the adrenalin flowing again, and all of a sudden my thinking was clear. I knew exactly what I had to do. I would take the girls and move to Birmingham where my father's family lived. I had visited them almost every summer while I was growing up, and I loved all his relatives. My grandparents Margaret and William Pugh lived with my father's sister, Aunt Earleen, her husband Jack Robbins, and their son Donnie. I called them, and when I told them my predicament they said, "Of course you can come. We'll help you all we can."

I gave Dr. Smith two weeks notice the next day and prayed that Euple would leave me alone until I could get out of town. I didn't call Mother at all. I was still too mad and too hurt to talk to her, and I didn't want any more arguments with anyone. (I later learned that the kids had not been at her house that first day when I called, but she had been with Euple when he picked them up from nursery school. He had persuaded her that he was doing it for my own good as well as the children's. He told her he loved me and wanted to stay married to me, but that I had just flipped out for some reason and needed help. She had known about the shock treatments, and he convinced her that doctors wouldn't have subjected me to them unless they thought I was "off my rocker." He wanted her to sign papers with him to have me committed, but he wanted the children safely out of the way first. She was worried about me, and she went along with him because she didn't want me to get a divorce either.)

I was three-and-a-half-months pregnant when I arrived in Birmingham with Gwen and Jackie. We moved into my aunt and uncle's little two-bedroom frame house, which was already crowded with five people living there. I started looking for a job. I had passed my state board and received my Mississippi beautician's license a few months before, so I didn't anticipate having any problems finding work. But I was wrong. First they told me that my Mississippi license was no good in Alabama. Then I found out they wouldn't even accept my hours of training from another state. If I wanted to be a hairdresser in Alabama I would have to start *all over* again and go to school for 1500 hours instead of the 1000 required in Mississippi. I also heard they wouldn't accept pregnant girls as students. The only good thing I learned was that the tuition was free under a state occupational training program.

If it hadn't been for the kindness shown me by my relatives I would have had to go back to work as a waitress or a receptionist. But Aunt Earleen and Uncle Jack gave us free room and board, and watched the children while I was in school. Uncle Harrod found me an attorney so that I could refile for my divorce in Alabama, and I enrolled at the American Beauty College.

The woman who ran the school was named—believe it or not—Dolly Pardon. (Later, when I first heard Dolly Parton's name on the radio, I thought it was spelled the same, and I wondered if she was any relation to the lady who had been so nice to me back in Alabama.) When Miss Pardon found out I was pregnant she told me I'd have to quit school or the state could close her down for breaking the rule. I explained my situation and persuaded her to let me stay on if I could hide my pregnancy from the state inspectors who came around periodically. Those were the days when beauty operators favored big full smocks for uniforms, and since I had gained only a couple of pounds it really wasn't difficult to hide my slightly protruding tummy.

One of the students at the school was a divorcee named Dolores ("Dodie") Chapman with two small children, Bubba and Dana. Dodie and I became good friends, and I stayed with her often on weekends so we could do things with the children, like take them swimming to a nearby public pool. My old Chevy had given out by then, so Dodie would drive all the way across town to pick me up at my grandmother's and take me to work every day. She was really kind and I appreciated all she did, even though it made me feel bad to know I could never repay her.

Meanwhile, Euple had called to tell me he knew I was pregnant. He said he wanted us to get together again. He drove from Mississippi to see me at my grandmother's house, but I told him there was no chance for us, and I didn't want to start it up all over again. By that time I was five months pregnant, and I had begun having complications carrying Tina. I was on my feet fourteen to sixteen hours a day at the shop, I wasn't eating properly, and my health wasn't good. Euple kept calling, and he finally caught me at a weak moment when I was telling myself I'd never make it alone. So I agreed to try again. He came to my grandmother's and moved his clothes in. But the next morning I woke up to find him gone. I asked my grandfather if he'd seen him leave, and he said, "Yes, I guess he's gone back to Mississippi, 'cause he took everything with him that he brought."

Then I saw a note on the coffee table. It said, "Now, file over again." I didn't know what it meant, so I called my attorney. He said that since Euple and I had spent the night together my petition for divorce was automatically canceled and I'd have to refile. When the attorney contacted Euple about the new filing, Euple said he would never grant me a divorce because he didn't believe the child I was carrying was his. That didn't make sense to me. You'd think that would be all the more reason he would want a divorce, but I guess it was just his way of making more trouble. The attorney said if I wanted him to continue with the case I'd have to submit to tests to determine whether Euple was the father of the baby. I went into the hospital, and they put a needle into my stomach and drew blood from the baby to see if it matched Euple's blood type. It did, so the attorney refiled my divorce petition.

About a month later I was in the shop giving a permanent to a registered nurse, when all of a sudden I felt a rush of water down my legs. I knew instantly what had happened. Since the customer was a nurse I told her I was pregnant and that I thought my water had just broken. She advised me to get to the hospital as soon as possible because I wasn't quite six months pregnant. The other operators were running around bringing me towels, and the water continued to pour. I was so embarrassed I wanted to crawl in a hole somewhere.

It was pouring rain but Dodie got me into her car

with towels all around and under me, and we took off. On the way I explained that Euple had dropped his medical insurance on me, but that Uncle Harrod had left a check with Aunt Earleen for me to use when the time came to go to the hospital. "We'll have to pick it up," I said, "because they'll never let me in the hospital with no money and no insurance."

When we got to Aunt Earleen's, only my grandparents and Donnie were there. Donnie was sitting on the floor wrapping newspapers for his paper route. Papa Pugh was sitting by the window looking out at the rain. I told Mama Pugh I needed my check, and she said, "Oh, Lord, Earleen and Jack went fishing down on the river, and since this rain's come up, I don't know where to find them." She started making phone calls to try to track them down.

Water was still running down my legs and I was beginning to have pains, but Mama Pugh was more nervous than I. She couldn't locate Jack and Earleen anywhere, so she walked the floor wringing her hands. All of a sudden she turned to Papa Pugh, put her hands on her hips, and said, "There's come a storm; it's raining cats and dogs out there, thundering and lightning. Donnie's motorbike is broken, and he ain't got no way to ride with his papers; Earleen and Jack is gone to the river, and they've got Wynette's money, and she's having a baby. *My God,* William, won't you say *something!*" Dodie and I had to laugh, but Papa, who never did talk much, just looked at her and turned back to the window again.

We decided we'd better go on to the hospital without the money because my pains were about fifteen minutes apart. Just as I expected the admittance office refused to take me without money or insurance, but Dodie wasn't having it. She went behind the partition and took a wheelchair and put me in it. She said, "I'm not going to let my friend have this baby in the lobby," and she wheeled me through the swinging doors down to the labor room. The nurse there put me in one of the beds and called a doctor to examine me. He said he was going to stop labor because judging from my size and the fact that I was only six months pregnant, the baby wouldn't weigh more than three pounds and would have no chance of survival. He gave me some pills, but every time they wore off hard labor started again. This went on all night long.

By the next morning I was bleeding. Aunt Earleen had come down by then to bring my check, and the doctor told her he thought I was in false labor and wanted her to take me home. She said, "That's ridiculous. She's had two children. She wouldn't be hemorrhaging if she were in false labor." He ordered more pills to stop labor, but this time I spit them out. I knew the baby was coming no matter what he did, and sure enough, a little while later Tina was delivered by a nurse in the labor room. She placed the baby up on my stomach, then wheeled me quickly into the delivery room where the doctor cut the cord. They were so anxious to get her into the incubator they didn't even clean her up or weigh her. They estimated her weight at two pounds three ounces and her length as eleven inches. She was so tiny she looked more like a doll than a baby.

A few days later Dolly Pardon came to the hospital with the best present she could have given me. She handed me an envelope, and I opened it to find my graduation certificate from the beauty school! I had completed only about half the required hours, but she said that since I had already been through the entire course in Mississippi, she was going to go ahead and let me graduate so I could get a decent job to support my children. She was really a jewel.

I knew I wouldn't be able to bring Tina home for quite a while, because they had told me they wouldn't release her until she weighed five pounds. I went ahead and got a job at the Midfield Beauty Salon. Every day after work I'd go by to see my baby. She was the talk of the hospital and everybody's pet. The nurses had put a sign on the incubator when she was born that said "Tiny," and that had become her nickname.

Finally at twelve weeks old she weighed four pounds and fourteen ounces, so they said I could take her home.

Uncle Harrod went with me to pick her up. He pointed to the sign on her incubator and said, "Wynette, we're not going to call this child Tiny. It sounds like a dog's name. Let's change it to Tina."

I said, "Okay, but I'd also like to name her Michelle."

He said, "No, I don't want no old French name. I want to call her Denise."

Since he was the one paying the hospital bill to get her out, I thought he ought to have the privilege of naming her. So I laughed and said, "That's all right with me. But don't you know Denise is a French name, too?"

"I don't care," he answered. "At least it's a pretty one."

Jackie and Gwen were thrilled finally to see their baby sister. They didn't understand how anything so small could grow to their size. She wasn't as big as a bag of sugar. My uncle could hold her in the palm of his hand, and her little legs barely hung past his wrist.

A few days later Euple called from Alabama and said he wanted to see the baby. When he arrived, he told me he knew he'd done wrong to come and stay with me, then leave again. He really acted sweet for the first time in a couple of years, and he asked me to forgive him for all he'd put me through. He wanted us to try one more time to make a go of it. I thought, Well, I can't be much worse off than I am now, and it would be nice for the girls to have their Daddy around, so I agreed. We moved into Elyton Village, a government housing project, where we rented an apartment for $23 a month.

It was less than a month later when Tina came down with spinal meningitis. The day I took her to the hospital I kept calling the apartment to ask Princie if Euple was home from work yet. I wanted him with me during those long hours when I was pacing the waiting room floor not knowing what was wrong with Tina. But he never showed up. He didn't come home for several days, and by then I was already in isolation with Tina.

During the seventeen days I stayed with her he was away from our apartment more than he was in it. He said he was looking around for jobs in other towns. Mother had come over to keep Jackie and Gwen by then, and even she had lost all patience with him. She finally realized what my life had been like with Euple. He wasn't even there the day we brought Tina home from the hospital, but he came back shortly after and stayed for four months. We didn't fight during that time. We just didn't communicate at all. I was more concerned about Tina's recuperation than I was about him. I no longer cared enough to argue. One day he went to work as usual and never returned. We hadn't had words of any kind the night before. He just never came back.

I saw Euple only twice after that. The day I was leaving Birmingham he drove past as I was packing up the car. He stopped, came over, stuck his head in the car window, and leaned on the steering wheel. "So, you're going to Nashville to be a hillbilly singer, huh?" he asked sarcastically. I said that I was going to try. He laughed and said, "Dream on, baby. Dream on!"

Ten years later, almost to the day, I was signing autographs on the stage after a concert in Birmingham when Euple came down the aisle. He waited in line, then handed me a Tammy Wynette publicity picture and asked me to sign it.

I said, "You got your autograph a long time ago."

He said, "Well, now I want another one."

I couldn't resist. I turned the picture over and wrote on the back, "Dream on, baby. Love, Tammy."

Chapter 4

DURING the five-and-a-half years I spent with Euple I gave up my fantasies about singing. I no longer even played for my own pleasure. I didn't have a piano, and half the strings on my old guitar were broken. But living in Birmingham around my father's family rekindled my longing to sing, and I started thinking about it more and more. They were the type of people who just automatically sat around and picked and sang anytime they got together. Music brought them as much pleasure as it did me, and I felt good when they said, "Sing for us Wynette," or, "Let Wynette sing the next song." They had been telling me from childhood that I had inherited my father's talent, and hearing them say it again made me a little ashamed that I wasn't doing anything with it. My mother's side of the family took my voice for granted, but they never took it seriously. Euple and his family were even less encouraging. But in Birmingham I was surrounded by people who told me I was as good as the singers they heard on the radio. I soaked up their enthusiasm like a sponge.

Uncle Carl and Uncle Harrod, two of my father's brothers, owned a small radio station in Alabama and another one in Waynesboro, Georgia, so they were up on all the current popular songs. When they were young men they had both played in a group with my father, but after his death Uncle Carl never played a guitar again. Uncle Harrod couldn't pick after he lost his arm in a railroad accident, but Uncle Harvey Truelove, my father's brother-in-law, who had also been in the group, still loved to play. His wife, Aunt Athalene, was a good singer, so the three of us would get together and entertain the family, with me on piano, Uncle Harvey on guitar, and everybody joining in to sing.

Uncle Harvey was (and still is) the chief engineer on WBRC-TV, Birmingham's channel six. There was a show on the station called "Country Boy Eddie" that came on from 6 to 7 A.M., five days a week. I watched it while I was getting dressed in the mornings to go to work, and I noticed they didn't have a girl singer. I asked Uncle Harvey to find out if they'd let me try out for the show, and when he came home with the news that I could have an audition I was thrilled to death. I got the job easily enough, but keeping up with it was hard. The pay was only about $35 a week, so I had to keep my beauty shop job too. That meant starting my day at 4 A.M., Monday through Friday. I'd get up, dress, and drive across town to the studio in time to rehearse my two songs before air time. When the show was over I'd drive back across town to Midfield Beauty Salon, where I worked until 7 P.M. Then I'd go home, feed the kids, and play with them a little while before bedtime. After they were asleep I'd take care of household chores, then fall into bed myself, exhausted but happy.

My father's oldest sister, Aunt Princie, and his mother, Mama Pugh, took turns watching the girls for me so I didn't have to worry about what kind of care they were getting during my long work day. I didn't really mind the hours because I was getting to sing again, and I was free from the strain and tension I had lived under for so long with Euple. With two jobs and three children demanding my attention I had no time for a social life, even if I'd wanted one, but I honestly can't remember a day during that period when I missed male companionship. I didn't hate men by any means, but I was going through a stage many women go through after divorce when they need a breathing space. I wasn't anywhere near ready to get involved in another relationship, and the idea of casual dating didn't appeal to me. I had a lot more fun fooling around with my kids than I would have had going out with some man I didn't care about.

Tina was doing better and I was extremely grateful for that. I still had no way of knowing if she'd be mentally retarded because she was too young to tell, but I didn't let it worry me because I was so thankful she was alive. I couldn't help but feel partially responsible for the horror she'd gone through, because all of us—Euple, Gwen, Jackie and myself—had been carriers of the germ that had given her meningitis. It's a pneumococcus germ which is carried in the throat. A healthy child or an adult may develop only a sore throat from it or throw it off completely, but Tina had been too small and weak to fight it off, so it developed into meningitis. When the doctors found out she had a highly contagious disease they wanted to know where it came from, so they did throat cultures on all of us and discovered we were the carriers, even though we hadn't been sick.

Tina was still the tiniest thing you could imagine. At five months old she was carried around on a pillow, and she slept in a shoe box by the bed because I didn't have a bassinet and she would have slipped right through the bars of a crib. Her little body was sore all over and she cried a lot. Usually the older girls were very understanding about Tina's crying, but I remember one night when Jackie lost her patience. She was just three, at that really cute age before she could talk plain. Tina had been exceptionally fussy all day.

Jackie toddled into the kitchen where I was cooking supper and said, "Mama, all that baby done all day is jus' cy, cy, cy."

I said, "Well what do you want me to do about it?"

And she said, "Kill it, Mama; *kill* it."

I couldn't help laughing. She was so cute, a red-headed, freckle-faced, chubby little thing, stompin' her foot as mad as she could be. I hugged her and explained that we ought to be grateful Tina had the strength to cry, even though it did get nerve-racking at times.

Gwen and Jackie grew up helping me take care of Tina, and in many ways it made them more responsible than most kids their age. I'm sure there were times when they resented the responsibility, too, because it wouldn't be normal if they hadn't, but they never complained about it to me.

After I'd been doing the "Country Boy Eddie" show for a few months, I met Fred Lehner, a disc jockey at WYAM. He was writing songs and I started working on some of them with him. He invited me to go to Nashville to the Disc Jockey Convention with him and Tony Lee, another deejay. He explained that the convention was sponsored every year in October by the Grand Ole Opry, and he said we could meet more important people in the music business during the convention than any other time of the year. He wanted to try to get some of his songs recorded, and I wanted a full time singing job—and he thought we might meet someone who could help us. Disc jockeys who fly into Nashville that week from all over the country are entertained by the record labels and music publishing firms, and all the big artists stay in town to perform live for the men they hope will play their records on the air throughout the year. The more I heard about "Deejay Convention" the more I wanted to go. I knew the Country Music Association also held their annual awards banquet that week, and I thought it would be really exciting to be in Nashville when so much was happening in the music business. Mother agreed to come over from Mississippi to watch the girls and I got all set to go. I didn't have many clothes, which was a good thing because I would never have been able to decide what to take. I was so excited I just packed everything. Going to something as important as Deejay Convention was a real adventure for me, and I couldn't have been more thrilled if I'd been getting ready for a world cruise.

When we arrived in Nashville on Friday night we headed straight for the Ryman Auditorium, legendary home of the Grand Ole Opry. The weather had already turned cold, and the smell of fall was in the air. There was a carnival atmosphere in the streets around the area known as Printers Alley, and we were immediately caught up in the spirit of it. People were walking back and forth, milling around in front of the Ryman and Tootsie's Orchid Lounge next door. Tootsie's was the most famous hangout in Nashville for pickers, songwriters, and singers, and if you were lucky you could see Opry stars sitting at the bar or in a booth having a drink and swapping tall tales about their life on the road.

In 1974, when the Opry moved to its beautiful new headquarters at Opryland USA on the outskirts of Nashvville, many tears were shed over the memories left behind at the old Ryman, but some of those tears were for Tootsie's too. Stopping by to see Tootsie Bess, the generous, spunky woman who ran the bar, was a routine part of going to work for many of the people connected with the Opry. Tootsie was as famous as the stars who patronized her place, and she knew everybody worth knowing in the business. She died of cancer in 1978, but she isn't forgotten. She had a soft touch for struggling musicians or songwriters who needed a little money to tide them over, and they all loved her.

But the first thing that caught my eye that night outside the Ryman wasn't Tootsie's place; it was a country music band playing on the back of a flatbed truck parked in front of the auditorium. The truck belonged to WENO radio, and a big sign said anyone who wanted to could step up and sing with the band. That was all the encouragement I needed. I had been thrilled at the idea of going to a live performance at the Opry, of getting to see and hear the big stars in person, but just watching them wasn't enough. I wanted to be right up there on stage with them, to be one of the chosen few who receive the applause instead of one of the many who give it.

When I saw a man standing by the truck I walked over and asked if the sign really meant what it said. He said "Sure, you can get up there with the boys. What do you want to sing?" I said I'd sing anything his band could play.

He kinda grinned and asked, "Are you sure you can sing?" I told him to just give me a chance!

I didn't find out until much later that I was talking to Cal Young, the owner of WENO. Today he's a neighbor next door to my house in Nashville.

With his help I jumped onto the back of the truck and asked the band if they knew "Your Cheating Heart." They looked at one another as if to say "Is she kidding?" Asking a group of country pickers if they know that old Hank Williams classic is like asking the United States Army Band if they can play "Stars and Stripes Forever." Those guys must have thought, Boy, what a hick.

I'll never forget how good it felt standing up there in front of the Ryman, singing above the street noise. I don't know where I got the nerve to do it, but at the time I didn't even think about being scared or whether I was making a fool of myself. The two couples who'd brought me from Birmingham were about the only ones actually standing there listening to me. People were wandering back and forth, and one or two would stop for a second, but I wasn't getting near as much attention as pleasure from being up there. I remember a chill passed all the way through my body when I realized I was actually standing on a stage in

Nashville. The fact that my "stage" was a flatbed truck didn't matter. I thought about what the piano player in the bar where I'd worked in Memphis had said—that I belonged in Nashville—and I knew he was right.

I went home from the 1965 Disc Jockey Convention more fired up than I'd ever been about making singing my life's work. I was determined not to give up until I'd done everything I could do to earn my living as a country music singer. I didn't even think in terms of becoming a star, or even getting rich. All I wanted was to get paid enough to take care of myself and the kids. In fact, if I hadn't had three children to support, I would have been willing to sing for free.

I wasn't back home in Alabama a week before I was ready to come to Nashville again. I was eager to start making the rounds of record producers and music publishers in the hope that somewhere I'd meet someone who would say, "Hey, you're just what we've been looking for!" I told Mother my plans, and although she didn't share my enthusiasm she agreed to come over again from Mississippi in a couple of weeks to watch the girls. I counted the hours, pinched pennies, and did without lunch so I'd have the money to stay in a motel when I got there. I had no contacts in Nashville and absolutely no idea of how you went about getting into the business, but I figured the way to learn was to get there and find out.

I had Sunday and Monday off at the beauty salon, so I asked for an extra day and took off for Nashville in my old beat-up Volkswagen. When I arrived I checked into the Anchor Motel because that's where we'd stayed during the Deejay Convention, and it was the only place I knew. I made friends with Don Chapel, the night clerk; he was the first person I met and I confided my hopes to him. Don told me that he was trying to get into the music business too, both as a songwriter and singer, and he offered to introduce me to his sisters Martha Carson, a well-known singer in Nashville, and Jean Chapel, a great writer, who had already had several of her songs published.

Early Monday morning I headed for Music Row, a section of town around Sixteenth and Seventeenth Avenues where most of the music-related businesses are located. I had no appointments set up because I didn't know anyone to set up an appointment with, but I thought if I went to the record labels first maybe I could at least get in to see someone who would take the time to give me advice. I was too ignorant to know you don't just walk in off the street and get to see the important people in the business. A few years later I would never have made it past the receptionists, but the attitude along Music Row was looser and more relaxed in 1965, and my ignorance worked for me instead of against me. Since I didn't know you couldn't do it, I went ahead and did it.

My first stop was Hickory Records. I told the secretary my name was Wynette Byrd and I had come up from Alabama to talk to somebody about singing. She must have taken pity on me because she said, "Well, let me go and find out if one of our producers will see you." When she returned she led me into an office that had more hi-fi equipment in it than I had ever seen anywhere outside a department store.

I don't remember the man's name there, but I do remember the first thing he asked me was, "Do you have a tape?" I didn't know I was supposed to have a tape.

I said, "No, but I have a guitar out in my car and I could sing for you." He told me to go ahead and get it. He must have been laughing up his sleeve. Here was this little bleached blonde from Birmingham, too dumb even to know she was supposed to have her voice recorded on tape, and he's sending me out to get my beat-up $25 guitar. He listened while I sang a couple of songs, but when I finished he didn't comment on my singing at all.

He said, "Don Gibson is our biggest recording star. Do you know who he is?" I said yes, that I was a big fan of his and thought he had a fabulous voice.

He said, "Well, we're looking for a female Don

Gibson, so why don't you take some of his records home and try to learn to sing and phrase like he does."

His secretary brought me the albums, and I went rushing back to Alabama to tell my mother I was going to become a "female Don Gibson." She just shrugged her shoulders and didn't say anything. In the next few months she heard me say a lot of silly things like that, and I'm sure she never believed one of them. That week I played Don Gibson records till they were coming out my ears. I'd listen to a line, then try to copy it, but I didn't sound any more like him at the end of the week than I had at the beginning. This didn't discourage me, however. Even in my ignorance something inside told me that when I sounded like myself I sounded better than when I was trying to copy someone else.

A couple of weeks later I was off to Nashville again. This time I went to KAPP Records and was somehow able to get in to see Paul Cohen. He turned out to be one of the most straightforward, honest men I met during those months I traveled back and forth from Alabama, trying to get my foot in the door in Nashville.

I sang for him and he said, "I think you've got a great voice. Your sound is really different. I could record you tomorrow, but we don't have a big budget here like they do at the larger labels, so it might be two or three years before our company would get around to releasing your record. That would only hold you back because you couldn't record for anyone else as long as you were under contract to us, and until you've got a record out you won't get anywhere. My advice to you is to try the big labels like RCA or CBS."

What Cohen said made sense, so the next day I went to RCA. I did get in, but that's about all I got. A man who is no longer with the company saw me and said they already had all the female singers they could sign for that year. He didn't even listen to me sing.

In those days "girl singers," as they were called, were still in the process of proving themselves as money-makers to the industry. About ten years before, Kitty Wells had recorded, "It wasn't God Who Made Honky Tonk Angels," which was the first hit for any woman in country music. After that Patsy Cline became a big seller, and by 1965 Loretta Lynn was starting to make the top of the charts, but male vocalists still accounted for the great majority of sales. Because of this the producers would always sign a man before a woman; the labels were convinced that women, who buy most of the records anyway, would spend money to hear a male singer quicker than they would to hear another woman. In the past ten years that theory has been proven wrong. It doesn't matter now whether it's a man or a woman singing if it's a good song. But back then most producers thought of women singers only in terms of finding a "female version" of some male star. Things have improved tremendously and women in country music have definitely come into their own, but I doubt very much that even today you'd hear a producer say he was looking for a "male version" of Tammy Wynette or Loretta Lynn. When I met United Artists' producer Kelso Hurston, who was a big man in Nashville then, he told me he had just signed "the female George Jones." He played me her single and she was great. It was Billie Jo Spears. But she was no female George Jones. She was herself.

In January of 1966 I packed the children, our few belongings, and my old guitar into the back of my '59 Chevy and headed for Nashville. After three-and-a-half months of driving back and forth to see producers, I decided it was time to make the move and give it my all. Too many people I met had indicated that I would have a better chance to get my foot in the door if I lived in Music City rather than 200 miles away in another state. After all my trips to Nashville, I had no more assurance of getting a record contract or even a singing job than I'd had back in October when I'd sung in front of the Ryman, but my determination to go all the way with my music was stronger than ever.

There were two reasons for this—the road and

Porter Wagoner. I had gotten just enough taste of the road to make me hungry for more, and Porter had goaded me into a quick decision without even knowing it. He's helped a lot of people in country music get their start, but I'll bet I'm the only one he's ever helped by not helping. He had come to Birmingham to do a concert just after his longtime duet partner Norma Jean left him. In those days the girl singer opened the show for the male star, and Porter had no one with him to do this. By that time I had made friends with the people at radio station WYDE, and they recommended me for the job. I jumped at the offer. Porter was one of the biggest stars in country music and a chance to work with him was a golden opportunity. I had visions of him hiring me to replace Norma Jean after one song. She had retired from the road after seven years with Porter, and everyone knew he'd have to get another girl sooner or later. As it turned out I didn't even meet Porter until the show was over. I didn't know whether he heard me singing or not because he was still in his dressing room while I was opening the show. Afterward he came over and thanked me and shook my hand, and that was that. What a letdown!

I felt totally dejected. I left the building and started across the parking lot toward my car when suddenly Speck Rhodes, a comedian who worked with Porter's show, came running after me. He said Porter had sent him to ask if I wanted to go on the road with them for the next ten days. They had bookings in Alabama and Georgia, and my pay would be $50 a night! It sounded like a fortune. Speck made it clear, however, that I would not be allowed to ride on the bus with Porter and the band. I would have to furnish my own transportation.

I didn't care. I was thrilled beyond words, I just *knew* my big break had come at last. After ten days of working with me, surely Porter would want to hire me permanently. And if anyone in the business could get you a recording contract, he could. It didn't bother me a bit that I had to drive my own car. I was so excited I would have been willing to run along behind the bus for a chance to tour with him.

My Aunt Earleen agreed to go with me, and we left the following morning. I had the best time during the next ten days I'd ever had in my life. There were other acts traveling with the show too—Wilma Burgess and Jim and Jesse with their Bluegrass group—and it was like entering into a very special little clique. I guess it's like a college girl feels when she's asked to join her favorite sorority.

Performers either hate the road, or it gets into their blood like a fever; if that happens they're usually hooked for life. I took to it immediately, like a fish to water, and I knew after the first night that I never wanted to give it up. It's like being in love. You experience the highest of highs and the lowest of lows, but even at the worst of times it still has a hold on you. And just when you think the thrills won't get bigger or better, they do.

I've spent more than ten years on the road now —usually averaging about eighteen days a month—and I'm still hooked. When we've been home for a week or so and a new tour is about to begin, the excitement starts to build around my house even before my bus arrives. My boys fly in from their various home states (only one member of my band lives in Nashville; the rest are spread out around the country), and I usually have a big pot of beans or something I know they like simmering on the stove, waiting for them. They help themselves to supper, and we sit around the kitchen table catching up on one another's news till my driver brings our bus over from his house. Then the boys start loading up, and there's an organized scramble to get everybody's stuff together and on the bus. There's usually at least eight of us going out, and friends often come over to see us off. My girls are always there, and the chatter and noise is so loud you can't hear what anybody's saying, but it doesn't matter. It's all been said before anyway.

There's that same feeling of adventure in the air every time we pull out, even though we've done it a thousand times. Most of us will be sound asleep in our bunks before we get as far north as Louisville. By now the routine of driving, sleeping, working, checking in and out of motels week after week, month after month, ought to have become as dull as dishwater, but somehow it's always as new as the first time. There's a feeling about it that you can't quite put your finger on, almost like the scared but happy thrill you get as a kid when you cut school.

That's exactly how I felt that first time out with Porter—like I was playing hooky from real life, but at the same time doing something really important. And I wasn't even on a bus. When the ten days were over and I had to go back to work at the beauty salon, it was the biggest comedown of my life. I had always enjoyed doing hair before that, but after being on the road, I hated it so much by comparison that it took every bit of self discipline I could muster to drag myself out of bed in the morning and go to work. I thought I'd scream if I saw one more hair roller or smelled one more bottle of permanent wave solution. I had been so sure Porter would at least offer to help me get a recording contract. But he never said a word. His band members had complimented me after shows with standard pats on the back like "good job" or "nice show," but none of them ever said, "You're good enough to be recording." I was thoroughly disheartened. My depression lasted for about a week before it turned into anger, and I became more determined than ever. I thought, Well, to heck with all of them. If no one will help me I'll move to Nashville and get my own recording contract.

Looking back, I wonder how on earth I had the guts to leave the security of a job and family who loved me. In Alabama I was at least sure I could support my children, and there were relatives nearby ready to help if I needed them. But in Nashville I had nothing —no job, no money, no family, no friends. What I did have was three children, all under five, who were totally dependent on me as their sole provider.

I doubt if I could make such a risky move today, but back then youth gave me the courage, and ambition gave me the push. When I was twenty-three it never occurred to me to worry about the possibility of failing. I worried only about how long it would take me to get where I wanted to go. What bothered me the most was a nagging guilt that I wasn't being fair to my children by not providing for them as well as I could have as a hairdresser. But I fought those doubts by telling myself the sacrifice was worth it because in the long run they'd be much better off. If things worked out, I could eventually give them more security than I ever could by working in a beauty shop.

I knew my mother didn't agree with this line of thinking, so we never discussed it. Our family just didn't take unnecessary risks. You worked hard, made an honest living, and took care of your own. Only fools chased rainbows. After every trip to Nashville I would come back telling her I had met someone or learned something that was sure to lead to a record contract. I kept saying, "It's just a matter of time." If nothing encouraging had happened I'd make something up to save face. I knew she thought I was wasting my time, but at least she had been willing to help me out by coming over from Mississippi when she could to watch the kids. My only real encouragement came from my father's family. Their attitude was, "If you get turned down at one place, go to another." I wanted to live up to their expectations and I wanted to prove to Mother that I wasn't just chasing a silly dream.

Most of my experiences in Nashville had been good, and I had learned a lot, even though I hadn't gotten anywhere. Only one man tried to take advantage of me, and I like to think I've paid him back because if I'd been recording for him all these years, he'd be a lot richer than he is now. He led me to believe he was interested in signing me to his label, then closed his office door, unzipped his pants and said, "You take care of me, honey, and I'll take care of you." I shot out of that room so fast his secretary must have thought he'd set fire to me. In a way, he had; I was so burned up I was sizzling. I wanted to strike back, but instead I did what a lot of women do when a man insults them. I ran to my car and sat there in the parking lot, bawling like a baby.

Mother's silent disapproval of my trips to Nashville was nothing compared to her grim opposition when I actually picked up and moved. She was worried about me and the children in a strange city where I had no job, and when I discovered how hard it was to find a place to live I secretly thought she might have been right. Nobody wanted to rent me a room. I couldn't afford an apartment, and boarding houses didn't take children. But that wasn't the worst of it. When people renting rooms asked my occupation and I answered "singer," the reaction was like I'd said "thief" or "prostitute." They would practically slam the door in my face! They thought of pickers and singers as hillbilly trash who wouldn't take care of property or pay the rent on time. One woman told me flat out she didn't want any "hillbillys" living around her place, and to this day I get mad when I hear that word used by anyone outside our business.

I had saved a little money to support myself and the girls until I got some kind of singing job, but living in a motel and eating meals out was draining that away fast. I finally had to tell a lie in order to find us a place to live. I found the name of a beauty salon in the yellow pages and told a landlady I worked there. She rented us one room in a motor court for $12 a week, agreeing to put in a crib for Tina. But she warned me I'd have to move out if the children made any noise and disturbed the other tenants. I knew she meant it so I was afraid to leave them with a baby sitter. I didn't have the money to hire one anyway, so I took them with me to appointments and auditions and left them in the car with Gwen and Jackie watching Tina. Leaving a four-and-a-half- and a five-and-a-half-year-old to watch over a thirteen-month-old baby would scare me to death now, but it didn't then. I had complete confidence in Gwen and Jackie and they never let me down. Of course I didn't leave them alone for more than a few minutes at a time, even if I had to run out to the car and check on them in the middle of a meeting, but I don't wonder that Mother worried about how we were getting along. If I knew today that Gwen was off in a strange city with my grandchildren under similar circumstances, I'd be fit to be tied.

I took the girls with me the first time I met Billy Sherrill. I had been sent to his office by Kelso Hurston, who had no idea he was doing me the biggest favor of my life. Kelso had told me he wasn't interested in signing another female artist because he had Billie Jo Spears. I said, "Well, do you know how I can get in touch with Pappy Daily who produces George Jones?"

"You might as well forget that," he said. "Pappy and George both live in Texas. But there is someone else here in Nashville you should go see. His name is Billy Sherrill and he produced David Houston's hit single 'Almost Persuaded' for Epic Records. He just might be ready to sign a girl singer."

The next day I piled the kids into the car and drove down to Music Row, looking for Billy Sherrill's office. When I found the building I went inside but no one was around. The outer office, where you'd normally expect to find a secretary or a receptionist, was empty. Since I didn't see anyone, I didn't know what to do, so I stood around for a few minutes before getting up the nerve to knock on the door to his private office. I heard a voice say, "Yeah?" I didn't know if that meant to open the door or what, so I knocked again. This time the voice was louder and sounded a little impatient. "Come on in." I hesitated a minute, then thought, What have I got to lose?

When I stepped inside the door, I saw a small-framed man with light brown hair, leaning back in a big leather chair with his feet propped up on his desk. He looked to be in his late twenties, not much older than me. He had on ordinary clothes—an open-collared shirt, casual pants and loafers—and he didn't appear very prosperous. He just sat there looking at me in a disinterested way, waiting for me to say something. He made me feel uncomfortable; he seemed so cool and detached.

In my nervousness I blurted out, "My name is Wynette Byrd and I've recently moved here from Birmingham."

He said, "Well, I'm from Alabama myself, but you probably never heard of the place. It's a little town called Haleyville."

I said, "Yes, I have! That's the town where my father was born, and my grandparents still have a little house down there."

He almost smiled then and I thought, Well, at least the ice has been broken a little bit. He asked, "What can I do for you?"

I stammered, "I want a recording contract."

His expression didn't change at all. He said, "Do you have any tapes?"

I said, "No, but I'll sing for you if you'll loan me a guitar."

He reached over behind him and handed me his, then leaned back in his chair again. I sang a couple of songs I had written with Fred Lehner in Birmingham. Then I did a Skeeter Davis song and a George Jones song. His expression still didn't change, and he made no comment whatsoever about my singing. He didn't say anything at all for a minute or two, then spoke in a very matter of fact tone: "I don't have time to look for material for you, but if you can come up with a good song, I'll record you."

Just like that! At first I didn't believe I'd heard right. It couldn't be this easy, this casual, after a year of knocking on doors and facing one rejection after another. He didn't say *when* he would record me and he didn't mention a thing about a contract, but I couldn't have been happier if I had just signed one for a million dollars. Even if this man didn't seem the

least bit enthusiastic, someone had at least offered me
a chance to record. Billy has never admitted it, but
I think the only reason he made the offer was because
he felt sorry for me. He once described his first impression of me to a reporter as "a pale, skinny little blond
girl who looked like she was at her rope's end." And
I guess he was right about that.

The next morning I was out bright and early making
the rounds of publishing offices, looking for a song, but
I didn't come up with anything I thought was good
enough. That night I took the kids to a Burger Chef for
dinner, and I was sitting there making a list of places
to go the next day when a man walked up and asked,
"Didn't I see you coming out of Billy Sherrill's office
yesterday?" I told him he had and he introduced himself as Scotty Turner. He had written a big song a few
years before called "Shutters and Boards." He had also
worked for both Dot Records and Liberty Records
on the Coast. He said he had just finished a new song
called "She Didn't Color Daddy" and he thought it
could be a big hit. I said I wanted to hear it and he
drove me and the girls to an office nearby where he
could borrow a turntable to play the song. I loved it!
It was very touching, about a little girl and her coloring
book. She colored the trees green, the sun yellow, and
so on. But she didn't color Daddy because he was
gone.

The next day I couldn't wait to get the dub to Billy;
I thought I'd found my hit for sure.

When I played it for him he was just as cool and
unconcerned as he'd been that first day. "It's a good
song," he said, "and it probably could be a hit. You
hang onto the dub and let me have a phone number
where I can reach you." I couldn't even afford a
decent meal, much less a phone, but I didn't want
Billy to know that, so I gave him my landlady's number and prayed she would agree to take a call for me.
Then I went home to wait.

The days drug by. I dreaded leaving my room for
fear I'd miss the call, so I played with the girls and

worried and fretted. By the end of the week I couldn't stand it any longer so I called him back. He said to come on down to his office. He had something he wanted me to hear. I grabbed up the girls and rushed out immediately.

When I got there he said, "I still like the song you found and we'll probably record it, but I think I've found one that's even better. It was recorded by Bobby Austin on a very small label with poor distribution. I think if we released it on Epic, it could be a hit." He played me Austin's single of "Apartment #9" and I knew instantly that it was my song. You can get a feeling like that about a song the same way you can about a person—that it was just meant to be. Billy set a recording date for the following week. Then he asked what name I wanted to use as a singer. It had never occurred to me to change my name, but he said, "I didn't think you'd want to use Byrd since you're getting a divorce, and Pugh doesn't fit you."

I said, "Well what does fit me?" He thought for a minute, then said, "With that blond ponytail you look like a Tammy to me."

I said, "Well, can I at least keep Wynette?"

He said "Sure. How about Tammy Wynette?"

I left his office saying the name over and over under my breath. It sounded strange, but it sounded right too. "Tammy Wynette." I said it out loud. It didn't sound like me, but it sounded like someone I wanted to be. I sensed it was more than just a new name. I felt I was also about to start a new life.

Chapter 5

*T*HE first time I met George Jones he was in bed with another woman.

Don Chapel told me one night he was taking some songs by to George and asked me if I'd like to come along. I jumped at the chance! I hadn't met Billy Sherrill yet and I thought, Boy, if anybody can help me get a start in this business, it's George Jones. He was the king! We drove to the Biltmore Motel, where George always stayed when he was in town from Texas, and Don knocked on the door of room 127. The anticipation was killing me. I was worried about how I looked, what I was going to say—everything. Someone finally opened the door and there was George, propped up in the middle of a king-sized bed, watching television. He had on silk pajamas, and a girl dressed in a lounging robe was sitting close beside him in the bed. Four or five other people were in the room, some sitting in chairs, others on the bed, and they were all laughing and talking and drinking. I immediately felt like an intruder, and uncomfortable, and I wished I could think of something clever to say. But I just stood there and stared.

We weren't invited to sit down or to join the party. Don handed George the songs, then introduced me and said I was a singer. George nodded, barely acknowledging my presence. When Don told him I was trying to get a recording contract and would like to have the name of someone at his label, Musicore, George told him whom to call in Nashville, but he was obviously indifferent to me. We left right away and that was that. I was really disappointed. I told myself I had been silly to expect a big star like George Jones to take an interest in an unknown to begin with, but that didn't keep me from being depressed for days afterward.

A few months later, when Billy gave me the opportunity to record, all the disappointments and rejections I had faced in Nashville—from producers to stars like Jones and Porter Wagoner—made me doubly determined to prove myself. My ego said, Now I've got the chance to show them all, but another side of me was satisfied just knowing I was at last going to be paid to *sing!*

About a week after Billy christened me Tammy Wynette, I went into CBS Studios to record for the first time. I was scared to death! I felt my whole future was riding on the results of the session. I still had no contract, and although Billy hadn't come right out and said so, I thought that if my first session didn't come off good, I wouldn't get a second chance. I had never even made a tape or a dub (a demonstration record), so I had no idea what went on inside a recording studio. The musicians sensed my nervousness and went out of their way to make me feel comfortable. Pete Drake, who still plays steel guitar on most of my sessions, was there, along with Jerry Kennedy, who played lead guitar. Jerry is now a producer for Mercury Records and has recorded some of the biggest hits in country music with artists like the Statler Brothers, Johnny Rodriguez, and Tom T. Hall. But he was still a studio musician then, and I found out months later that he made a phone call after the session that day which proved important to me. He telephoned Al Gallico, the biggest independent music publisher in the business, at his New York office. "I just sat in on a Billy Sherrill session with the goddamndest little singer I ever heard in my whole goddamn life," he said. "She's going to be the biggest goddamn female star in this town."

Al asked, "Well, who is she?" and Jerry answered, "Tammy Wynette."

Gallico said, "I never even heard of her," and Jerry said, "Then you'd better call Sherrill and find out what he's up to because it won't be long before everybody in the goddamn business will be hearing about her." That conversation led to my meeting Al on his next trip to Nashville, and he became my publisher as well as a helpful advisor during my early career.

But that day after my first session, I had no way of knowing whether Jerry or anyone else was enthused over what we'd done. The musicians left without commenting one way or the other. Billy asked me to stay behind so we could overdub. I had no idea what that meant but I said, "Sure, I'd love to," just as though I'd done it a hundred times. He must have seen through me because he waited until we were alone to explain that he was going to play back the tracks we had just recorded so I could sing harmony over my own voice. I had wanted to do that ever since I had learned to harmonize as a child singing in church, but I had never known it was called "overdubbing."

I left the studio happy but a little perplexed. Billy hadn't said a word about whether he liked what we had on tape. If he thought it was good, wouldn't he have said so? Maybe he thought it was so awful he was embarrassed to say anything. I worried about it all that night. I hadn't yet learned that Billy's way is to be noncommittal. He wouldn't show enthusiasm if Gabriel came into the studio to record a trumpet album. Some of his artists think he's superstitious, afraid that it will jinx a record if he acts too sure of it, too confident that he's got a hit. But I think it's just Billy's personality. You seldom know what he's really thinking. The first six months I was around him I thought he was the strangest man I'd ever met. He did peculiar things. For example, if there were five or six people in his office, he would suddenly get up and walk out without saying a word to anyone. Eventually I learned that people in groups make him nervous. He's a loner, and he puts a lot of people off by being blunt and outspoken or by being so cool and indifferent you don't even know if he's paying attention. But he also has a very dry sense of humor and often comes out with lines as funny as any comedian. Musically he's a genius. His track record in country music is unparalleled, not only as a producer, but also as a writer. Nearly 85 percent of all the songs he's written have become number one singles, and I don't know of any other writer who can top that figure. As a producer he's not only discovered and made stars of unknown artists like myself and Tanya Tucker, but he's also made smash hit records with older artists, like Charlie Rich who had been recording for twenty years with no luck until Billy produced "Behind Closed Doors." I don't know how many number one singles Billy's had since his first, "Almost Persuaded," but the count must be way up in the hundreds. He's produced twenty-six top five singles for me alone, and eighteen of those went to number one. When you consider all the other big-selling artists he's recorded—George Jones, Marty Robbins, Johnny Duncan, Johnny Paycheck, Kris Kristofferson, Barbara Mandrell, Jody Miller, Bobby Vinton and many more—you can imagine the success he's had.

Billy has often been criticized for recording so many of his own songs with his artists. A writer came up to me once and said, "I'll never send you any more material to Sherrill's office because the only songs he ever cuts are his own."

I said, "Well, any time you can write one better than his, I'll record it."

And that's exactly how I feel about my association with Billy. I have so much confidence in his taste and judgment that I'd record "Yankee Doodle" if he asked me to. He encouraged me to develop as a songwriter from the beginning, though I had no confidence at all in that area. Even if I thought of a line while Billy was working on a song for me, I didn't have the nerve to tell him for fear he'd say, "Why, that's the dumbest line I ever heard." But he kept after me to contribute until I offered meek little suggestions now and then. Years passed before I gained enough confidence to sit down with him and actually co-write a song. Now, writing is one of my greatest pleasures, and nothing thrills me more than to have another artist record one of my songs.

My first single, "Apartment #9," was released just in time for the October 1966 Disc Jockey Convention. Imagine my excitement at being invited to the parties as an artist when just the year before I'd been there as a fan, happy for the chance to sing on the back of a flatbed truck. I didn't have the money to buy a new dress for the Epic party, so Don Chapel's sister Jean offered to make me one. I had been seeing more and more of them, as they were the only two friends I had in Nashville. Jean worked on the dress for days and I was so proud of it. It was blue knit with a matching chiffon top and big, blousy sleeves. Don took me to the party, and I remember standing off in the corner of the huge hotel suite where it was held, looking all around at the important people, listening to my record playing in the background, and thinking it was like being on the sidelines watching my own dream come true.

Billy and Al Gallico did everything possible to make me feel at ease. I've always been nervous at large get-togethers where I don't know the people. I'm not good at small talk, and I never know what to do with my hands so I smoke too much. Billy and Al kept bringing people over one by one to meet me while Don mingled around the room. When I was introduced to Len Levy, who was then president of Epic, he shook my hand and said, "I believe you'll go all the way, girl. I really do." I don't know how many new artists heard the same thing from him, but I know he made me feel very special, and I was determined to live up to the faith everyone seemed to have in me.

The praise and attention I received that week really boosted my ego, but I was learning fast that you can't live on compliments. I was desperate for work. My money had run out, and I knew there would be no royalties coming in from my record for several months. It was ironic that Euple chose that time to sue me for a cash settlement, even though we'd already had our divorce hearing.

"Apartment #9" was getting played on the radio back in Mississippi and Alabama, so Euple naturally thought I was making a lot of money. He hired an attorney to try to get some of it. When the lawyer contacted me I went running to Billy and explained that my soon-to-be ex-husband had now decided I should pay *him* money. I couldn't afford to hire an attorney to battle it out in court, and I was afraid a legal hassle could hold up the money that would eventually be coming to me from the label. Billy turned the whole matter over to CBS attorneys who made it clear to Euple's lawyer that not only wasn't I making any money as yet, but that I was in debt to the company several thousand dollars for the cost of my recording session. (It is standard practice in the business for the label to charge recording costs to the artist. That money is then paid back before the artist begins receiving royalty checks.) The CBS attorneys suggested that Euple ought to help me pay off my debt before he started asking for money, which must have shaken him up, because the suit was dropped and he never asked for money again.

I made the rounds of the booking agencies trying to get someone to sign me. In my ignorance I thought that everyone would want to book me once I had a record out, but I found out that wasn't the case. The

Moeller Talent Agency was the first to turn me down. Larry Moeller said, "We don't have good luck with girl singers. They don't like to work clubs where people are drinking, and they've usually got a husband or children who need them at home. It's just not worth the trouble to book women." His attitude really burned me up. I didn't think it was fair that all female singers should be labeled "troublesome" without a chance to prove otherwise, and I told him so. I knew that if ten of his male singers got drunk and missed dates he still wouldn't stop booking men.

After I'd been turned down by several other agencies, I went to see Hubert Long, who booked George Jones. By that time I was really desperate. The weather was turning cold, and the children needed shoes and warm clothes. Jackie was wearing a pair of scuffed-up white go-go boots with frayed tassels and loose soles that flip-flopped every time she walked. We were living on biscuits and gravy for breakfast and fried cornbread patties and milk for supper. About once a week I splurged and bought the kids a hamburger at Burger Chef. I wrote Mother and asked her to send me $25 to tide me over until some money started coming in, but she didn't answer the letter. I guess by then she was tired of hearing how things were going to be better tomorrow. Finally I swallowed my pride and called Uncle Harrod in Birmingham. I hadn't forgotten how good he had been to me when Tina was in the hospital. When he answered the phone I burst into tears. I was ashamed to have to ask for more favors, but he was as sweet as he could be. He wired me $100 the next day, and I knew I had to make it last until I got my first singing job.

When I walked into Hubert Long's office I told him the plain truth—that I had a record out which was getting air play, but I couldn't get anyone to book me. I said, "I have three children who need clothes and food. I've *got* to find work. Please won't you help me?"

Hubert is gone now, rest his soul, but I'll never forget how kind he was to me. Years later he told me I was so pitiful his conscience wouldn't have let him turn me down even if he'd wanted to. He signed me to a contract on the spot and told me he would get me work just as soon as he could. By that time I had moved into the trailer court where Jean Chapel lived, and I had my own phone. When it rang a few days later I could hardly believe Hubert's good news. "How would you like to work a place in Atlanta called The Playroom?" he asked. "The pay is $500 for one week."

Five hundred dollars! I would have played the South Pole for that. I couldn't imagine making $500 for one week's work!

Hubert explained I would have to pay the staff band out of my salary as well as my own expenses while I was there, but it still sounded like a fortune to me. He asked if I had transportation to get there, and I told him my old '59 Chevy would make it if I had to push it all the way. I had planned to take the girls along with me, but Mother came up from Mississippi to visit and asked if she could have them with her for a couple of months. I agreed, knowing it would make more sense for them to be with relatives back home than to be hanging around motels with me. I knew I could visit them often because Mother lived only about three hours from Nashville.

When I arrived in Atlanta I discovered the band-leader at The Playroom was Kirk Hansard, who was married to Lois Johnson, a singer I had met in Nashville. Kirk was just starting out, so he remembered how it felt to be on your first booking and was very helpful. We rehearsed for two days, putting together a show made up of everyone else's hits because I didn't have any of my own. By that time "Apartment #9" had made it to the top forty on the trade charts, which is good for a first record, but you can't sing a medley of one. So we worked out arrangements of songs that were my favorites then, like Jeannie Seely's "Don't Touch Me," which had been the number one record at home when I left Alabama. We had to come up with a lot of material because I had to do five shows a night, forty-five minutes a show—they were going to make sure I earned that $500. I needed two completely different programs. I sang Patsy Cline songs, David Houston songs, George Jones songs, and a lot of others.

On opening night I was stiff with fright, but not because I had to stand up in front of an audience. I was afraid I would forget the words to one of the songs, or hit a wrong note, or do something to make a fool of myself. Joe Casey was CBS's promotion man in Atlanta then (he's now Director of National Promotion for the Columbia label), and he brought me three dozen red roses on opening night. I had never received roses before in my life, and it made me feel very special. He put them on a ringside table, and all the time I was singing I could look down at the flowers and see him looking back at me with a big smile of encouragement. A whole table of Atlanta CBS people showed up that first night, but Joe was the only one who returned every night and sat through all five shows. By the end of the week, he knew the program as well as I did. I don't know whether he felt sorry for me because it was my first job and I was anxious about it, or whether he liked my singing that much, but seeing him there every night sure made me feel confident. During the day he took me around to radio stations and introduced me to disc jockeys. I learned a lot from Joe about the promotion end of the business and how important it is for an artist to keep in touch with the people who play the records on the air.

At the end of the week I owed the band $250, half of my earnings. I also had to pay my motel, food, and gas bills. When I got back to Nashville my rent was due. After paying everything I had exactly $82 left out of $500. I couldn't believe it. I had hoped to make that money last for weeks in case I didn't get another booking right away, but the Atlanta date was my first introduction to road expenses. When fans hear about an artist making thousands of dollars a night they think it's an enormous amount of money, but they don't consider our business expenses. My overhead now runs between

$35,000 and $40,000 a month, and that has to be paid whether I work or not. It costs me at least $250,000 a year just to keep my band on the road, and that doesn't include my stage costumes or the initial investment in the bus.

That first date was also my introduction to the unique way country music performers receive and handle their money. When my week was up at the club I expected to receive a check; instead I was paid in cash. I had never seen so many bills in my life, and I was nervous about having that much money in my purse. When I mentioned it to Joe Casey he laughed. "You'd better get used to it," he told me. "It won't be long before you'll be receiving thousands in cash for a night's work. It's standard practice in country music. In the old days too many performers got burned too many times with bad checks, so they stopped accepting any payment that's written on paper. The old-timers won't even take a cashier's check."

He went on to explain another reason they deal in cash. On a tour of one-nighters there's no time to wait for the banks to open the next morning, so the money received from ticket sales is divided up as soon as the auditorium empties. The promoter and the road manager (or whoever collects the performer's money) sit there and count it out like kids dividing paper money —one for you, one for me, etc. After he leaves the promoter's office the road manager doesn't want to take a chance on getting robbed before he gets back to the bus, so it's not unusual for him to stuff his share in a brown paper bag because that's much less conspicuous than a canvas bank bag. Each bus has a safe where the money is kept until the return to Nashville, where the money is deposited. I'll never forget the time I found myself in the Denver airport with $28,000 in cash—I was carrying it in a Safeway market bag! My bus was still out on the road, and I had decided to bring the cash we had already collected back to Nashville to deposit it. I knew that by the end of the tour we'd have over $50,000 in our bus safe and the thought made me nervous. But I discovered that walking around an airport with a bag crammed full of small bills made me even more nervous, so I never tried that again!

I began to get regular bookings after Atlanta, and within five or six months I was averaging about $500 a night. But nearly a year passed before I started making any money off my records. You don't get rich on one hit—or even two. An artist has to have several top five records before he starts making any real money. I was lucky. My second single, "Your Good Girl's Gonna Go Bad," made it to number one on the country charts.

Then my first duet, "My Elusive Dreams," which I recorded with David Houston, also went all the way to number one. I was flabbergasted when my third and fourth singles, "I Don't Wanna Play House" and "Take Me to Your World," also made it to the top, and I followed the charts like a Bible every time we released a new record.

First you pray to get a number one record, and then you pray that your follow-up won't bomb out and prove it was all a fluke. The more number ones you get, the more you want to stay up there, knowing full well you can't be in the top position every time. So an artist is never satisfied and never relaxed enough to rest on past performances. In the record business you're only as good as your last hit or as important as your next one. But in country music we do have an edge over the rock and pop stars; if you stop recording hits your label will eventually drop you, but the country music fans don't. If you've recorded just one song that they remember and love, you can go on getting bookings the rest of your life. Ernie Ashworth has been singing "Talk Back Trembling Lips" for twenty years on the road, and the fans still come to see him and still love him. I never knew if my current hit record would be my last—and I still don't—but since those first two or three singles that launched my career, I've had the security of knowing I could always make a living in country music. It was—and is—the greatest feeling in the world for me.

When the girls came back from Mississippi I took them with me to most of my out-of-town bookings. We'd pile in the car and take off looking like a band of gypsies, with me driving and the three of them hanging over the back seat. They stayed backstage while I worked, with Tina crawling around on a blanket (she didn't walk until she was two-and-a-half) while Gwen and Jackie watched her. They were as good as gold and never once disrupted a show. Sometimes I'd drive all night to get to the next show while they slept in the back seat. When we could we stayed over in a motel and drove on the next day. They traveled with me almost all the time that first year because I didn't have anyone else to keep them.

My first trip out of the South was to Toronto, where I was booked at the Edison Hotel. It was an experience I'll never forget. I played with Mel Tillis and Marion Worth. While I was there I received a call from CBS in New York saying there was a prepaid ticket waiting for me to fly down for the day for meetings regarding my contract and other business. Billy Sherrill was flying up from Nashville also to be there. I had driven to Toronto, so I left my car there and flew to New York.

We landed in the middle of a rainstorm with hurricane winds. As we hit the runway a huge gust of wind caught a wing and flipped the plane over. The crash caused an engine to catch fire and pandemonium broke loose. Passengers were screaming, and the stewardesses were trying to keep everyone calm and line us up to slide down an evacuation chute. Fire engines roared onto the runway with sirens blaring and red lights flashing, and it all happened so fast I didn't have time to think about how scared I was until I slid down the chute into the pouring rain. Billy was there to meet me, and I fell into his arms, drenched to the skin and looking like a drowned rat.

He teased me until I was able to laugh about the crash, which was a good thing because I had to return on a plane to Toronto that afternoon. When customs asked for my papers I explained they were in my car at the hotel because I had driven across the border and had flown down to New York just for the day. They asked me to step aside as though they didn't believe my story. I told the immigration officer I had to hurry or I'd be late for my show at the Edison. He looked at me—disheveled from the crash landing and the rainstorm—as if to say, "Sure lady, you're an entertainer and I'm the Prime Minister." He allowed me one phone call, but the manager of the hotel was not there and they didn't know where to reach him.

I was more nervous about being late for my show than I had been about the plane crash, and by the time they finally released me I was an hour and a half late getting to the hotel. The manager was pacing the floor, smoking a cigar as big as he was.

When he saw me he started to yell. "What the hell happened to you?"

I put my hand up to stop him. "Don't," I said, and he knew I meant it. "Just don't say a word." I was surprised I had the nerve to stand up to him, but I had been through enough for one day and wasn't going to let him put me through any more.

I had begun to realize I was working in a man's world, and most of them looked down on women in the business. The same men who treated wives and girl friends with respect and consideration treated girl singers like a piece of merchandise. As a woman I could never have gotten away with some of the tricks male singers pulled, like missing bookings, or getting drunk and wrecking hotel rooms, or having one night stands on the road. Everybody joked about what the "boys" did, but if a woman stepped out of line her reputation was ruined, and she could kiss her career goodbye. We had to be professional, dignified, prompt, and always ladylike. But we also had to be tough enough to stand up for ourselves. Otherwise they ran all over us. Every career woman knows the fine line you walk to succeed, and there are times when you can't help but resent it. On the other hand, making it to the top in a man's business world is so rewarding it's well worth the effort.

Professionally I was learning to stand alone, but personally I still needed a partner. It had been lonely for me in Nashville and without the friendship of Don Chapel and his family, I don't know what I would have done. We were more or less thrown together because they were the only people I knew outside of a few business associates. I had met Don on my very first trip to Nashville when the group of us came over from Birmingham to the deejay convention. He had been friendly and interested in my career from the beginning. I loved his sister Jean and her daughter Lana, and I spent most of my social time with them. Jean was always encouraging Don and me to go out together, especially after I moved out to the trailer court where she lived. She'd say, "Ya'll go on to the movies and I'll watch the girls for you." Don was divorced and had three children just like I did, and on weekends we'd sometimes take them all out together. Jean fascinated me because she knew so much more about the music business than I did. Don picked guitar a little bit and was trying to get some of his songs recorded, but Jean already had a number of hers on record, and she was always willing to answer my questions or give me advice.

My divorce from Euple had been final a few months when Don asked me to marry him. I knew I wasn't madly in love, but I honestly thought it was more important that we were friends. We had so much in common—both divorced with three children, both trying to make it in the music business—that I thought we could be happy together. I even talked myself into believing romantic love would come after we were married. I had thought I loved Euple but that hadn't worked, so I figured this time at least I would marry someone who shared my ambition. I had been on the road alone for nearly a year, and I knew how lonely that life can be without someone to share it. Don wanted to travel with me, to pick and sing with my show, and the idea appealed to me. I didn't like single life even though my marriage to Euple had not been a happy one.

Jean was delighted when she heard Don and I were going to get married, and it made me feel good to know his family liked me. As soon as I had a few days off we drove across the Georgia line and were married by the first justice of the peace we found. Then we drove back to Nashville, and Don moved into the trailer with me and the girls.

I was getting enough bookings by then to bring in several thousand dollars a week, so it didn't take me long to save enough for a down payment on a house. I found one I liked at Imperial Point out on Old Hickory Lake. It cost $50,000, and it was a mansion compared to the places I'd lived with Euple. I was as proud of owning my own home as I was of the fact that I'd been able to earn the money to pay for it. Shortly after we moved in Don's three children came to live with us. Their mother thought they would have better advantages with us than they would with her. Donna was sixteen, Michael twelve, and Gary just four. My Gwen was almost six, Jackie nearly five, and Tina two. We had children of all ages spilling out of every room, but they got along surprisingly well. We never had problems with any of them except Michael.

At first I thought Michael was just having trouble adjusting to a new household, but I learned he'd been as much of a troublemaker at home as he was with us. If he did something wrong he blamed it on one of the other children. He constantly bullied his little brother, who was a very sweet boy, and he tried in every way possible to cause bickering among my girls. He was very jealous of the other children, and any time he wasn't the center of attention he'd take it out on one of them by doing something petty or mean. Donna tried reasoning with him over and over again, hoping she could make him see that he was causing problems for the whole family, but he would either yell and scream at her or pay no attention at all. Don realized his son had problems but he didn't want to admit it, which is natural.

Donna was a big help to me during that period. We hit it off right from the start and I loved her like my own. She's married now and lives in Iowa, and I see her every time I play Des Moines. She has two darling children and seems very happy, but when I was married to her father her dream was to have a career as a singer. She had a super voice, and I put her on my show as soon as she came to live with us. On weekends she went with us on the road and sang backup for me. But in the end she wanted a family most of all.

I didn't have my own band then. Don picked and we had another guitar player who traveled with us. Don also sang, though not very well. He was more interested in writing than performing, but he was anxious to get a recording contract because he said we could get bigger bookings if we both had records out. He wanted me to go to Billy Sherrill about it, but I was reluctant to because I honestly didn't think Don was good enough to get a contract, and I didn't want to put Billy in the embarrassing position of having to turn him down. So I kept putting Don off, hoping he'd start making it as a writer and forget about recording.

After I'd been working on the road for about six months, Hubert Long began booking me on a few shows with George Jones. I still hadn't actually stood beside him on a stage or sung with him, but at least we were sometimes on the same bill. George always closed the shows, so as soon as I finished my part I'd run backstage and change, then go out front to watch him work. It was an education. He could hold an audience in the palm of his hand from the first note, and he made it look so easy you would have thought he was singing in his own living room. I studied him like a textbook, and I wondered if the day would ever come when I would have that kind of confidence on a stage. I hadn't learned yet that George gets just as scared as any of us. But he knows how to hide it so well you'd never guess when he's shaking in his boots.

I have Tillman Franks, who was then managing David Houston, to thank for my first duet with George. "My Elusive Dreams," the duet Billy had cut with me and David, had reached number one, so Hubert booked us on a tour together with George. Normally I opened the show, with David following and George closing the show. But one night in Winnipeg, Canada, the promoters asked me if David could go on first because he and Tillman had some place to go later and wanted to leave early. It didn't make any difference to me, so David went on in my spot.

While David was singing, Tillman came over and said, "You'll have to go out and sing your duet with David during this part of the show."

I said, "No, I can't do a number on his show before I've even been introduced or done any part of my own. It wouldn't look right. Instead, why doesn't he go ahead and finish, then I'll go out and do just one song before I bring him on for our duet? That way you can still leave early, but I can at least start my show before we sing together."

Tillman wouldn't hear of it. "David Houston is not going to be a part of anybody else's show!" he snapped and stormed out of the dressing room.

A couple of minutes later one of the promoters came hurrying in and said, "David is about ready to call you out for the duet. You go do it now." I tried again to explain why I couldn't do it. I pointed out that we'd always sung the duet after we'd both done separate segments in the show, and that it added to the overall effect to build up to it that way. He wouldn't listen but kept insisting that I go out and sing with David, then come off, and then go out again for my own show after David left the stage. I refused and he went to tell Tillman. By this time David was finishing his act. Since I didn't have my own band, his musicians were paid extra to play for me. However, someone had told them to leave the stage with David if I didn't come out and perform the duet with him, so they did.

Tillman sent the promoter to say he wanted to see me in David's dressing room.

I was so mad you could hear my heels clomping on the cement floor all the way down the long hallway. Several members of the press who had come to cover the show were sitting in David's dressing room with him and Tillman, and I realized the scene was being staged for their benefit. Tillman started on me immediately about refusing to go out before I'd done any of my own show. Then he said, "David Houston made you what you are by recording with you, so if you can't sing the duet when he wants you to, then you don't use his band."

I reminded him that I'd had a couple of hits on my own, and he smiled in a nasty way and said, "Well, everybody knows how girl singers make it in this business anyway." I was already hopping mad but his remark made me furious. I blew up. I told him if he was insinuating I'd gotten where I was by sleeping with somebody he was badly mistaken. I also told him that if his client was the last singer on earth, I'd never record with him again. Then I turned and left, walking so fast the fringe on my mini-dress was swinging in time to the clacking of my heels.

When I passed the back of the stage I saw that George's band, the Jones Boys, were already playing for intermission. I went to the side of the stage and motioned frantically until I got the attention of Charlie Justice, the fiddle player. Charlie was nicknamed "Grumpy" because he had such a dry sense of humor you usually didn't know whether he was teasing or serious. I was motioning for them to stay out there and play for me, putting my hands under my chin in a prayer gesture. He shook his head and silently mouthed, "No way," so I got down on one knee as though I was begging. He kept shaking his head, then he turned his back on me and I didn't know what to do. I was about to walk away when I heard him announce, "Here she is, ladies and gentlemen, Miss Tammy Wynette." He had been teasing me all along and I'd been too upset to see it.

I had never sung with George's band before and I was very nervous. They didn't know my material, and there was certainly no time to rehearse. But they faked it beautifully and somehow we got through it. I fell in love with all six of them that night, and it's a good thing it happened in that way, because many of them are still with me today.

Although I didn't know it, while I was on stage someone got word to George about what had happened between me and Tillman. After my show I pulled up a chair backstage, as I always did, to watch George work. He was about halfway through his show when I heard him say, "You know I've recorded duets with a lot of girls—Melba Montgomery, Margie Singleton, and others—but there's a girl here tonight that I'd rather sing with than anybody else in the world. She's got a big hit duet out now with David Houston, but to-night I'd like to sing it with her. Let's see if we can get her out here—Miss Tammy Wynette."

The crowd started applauding, and before I knew it I was out there on stage standing beside my idol, George Jones. We had never sung together before, and I was scared to death. I knew George shouldn't be doing David's duet with me, and I knew David's manager would hear about it; I was shaking so hard the fringe on my gold dress was in constant motion. I stood there with my hands behind my back, fidgeting, stammering, too scared to speak a word, and all the time George was clowning around saying funny things, trying to make me relax. It seemed like he carried on for about ten minutes before he finally started singing "I followed you to Texas, I followed you to Utah." The crowd went wild. They were screaming and applauding like mad. Some of them even began to stand up, and it was the most exciting moment that had ever happened to me as a performer.

George didn't know all the words to "My Elusive Dreams," so I had to whisper his lyrics while I sang my own. We kept getting tickled and breaking up, but the audience loved it. After that we did about fifteen minutes of his duets because I knew the words to every song George Jones had ever recorded. It flashed through my mind that my fantasy had actually come true, but a part of me still couldn't believe it. My daydreams in the cotton field hadn't been anywhere near as fantastic as the real thing, and I was on cloud nine.

After the show I thanked George for what he'd done. He said, "Look, I heard what happened, and no one is going to put you down if I can help it. If anything like that happens again on this tour, you just let me know. I'll sing duets with you anytime."

Hearing that from the great George Jones was all the encouragement I needed to stand up to Tillman once and for all. He heard about my duet with George, and the next night he made a point of insisting again that we reverse the show order so I would have to go onstage with David before I'd performed as a single. Again I refused, and this time the promoter told me that if I didn't do my duet with David when Tillman told me to, I wouldn't work at all. He added that I wouldn't be doing any more songs with Jones on his show either.

I pulled out my contract and asked him to show me where it read that I had to sing with David or couldn't sing with George. The contract didn't mention anything about my doing duets one way or the other, so I knew I had him legally. "Unless I do the duet with David the way we've always done it, after we've both been out and done our shows, then I won't do it at all. And if you try to keep me from working, I'll go back to Nashville and sue you for breach of contract," I told him calmly.

Tillman came up then and said, "We won't have you going out there again singing with George Jones and making us look like fools."

I said, "Then you'd better work it out to keep the show in the right sequence."

He refused to give in which suited me fine, because

for the rest of the tour I sang my duet with George and loved every minute of it.

In those years there weren't more than a half-dozen women headlining their own shows in country music, and every time one of us stood up for our rights she made a point for us all. We had our own "liberation movement" going, but I don't think any of us was aware of it. I know I wasn't. All I wanted was the right to work in my chosen field and be treated with as much respect as the men who did the same job. Those few of us who were out there performing in the sixties had to work extra hard to prove to bookers and promoters, as well as to the male entertainers, that we could handle the business and hardships of the road as well as they could. We also had to prove we could bring in audiences. As a result of our success a female singer starting out in country music today can easily find a booker. Things have improved 100 percent, and I'm proud that I played a part in making that happen.

The incident with David Houston's manager wasn't the only time George Jones "rescued" me during that first year on the road. My own group had grown to four, with Don, Donna, and a guitar player, and we were still traveling by car. Don kept talking about wanting to buy a bus. Custom-designed buses, which are commonplace among country music stars today, were just getting really popular then, and we all wanted one. It's a much more comfortable way to travel because the bus serves as a home on wheels as well as a dressing room during performances. Many of the places we play on the fair circuits don't have facilities for artists to change clothes or rest between shows. I also wanted a bus so we could take all the kids along when they weren't in school. And I was tired of doing one-nighters by car, which is an exhausting way to travel. But I didn't see how we could possibly afford to buy a bus. I knew the bus alone would cost about $50.000, and customizing the inside with bunks, tables, a bathroom, stereo equipment, refrigerator, television, and all the rest would run another $40,000. (Today stars pay as much as $200,000 for their customized buses, but things were cheaper in 1967.) I had used all my cash to make the down payment on the house, and since the size of my family had doubled, my bills had too. In addition I now had road expenses for four, and since the children could no longer travel with me, I had hired a couple to live in so I could be certain they were well taken care of at home. I told Don there just wasn't enough money to buy a bus, and I resigned myself to traveling by car for a long time to come.

Just a few weeks later we were working a date in Texas with George, and he mentioned that he was buying a new bus. I asked him what he was going to do with the one he had and he said, "Oh, that old thing isn't worth much. It's not fixed up nice inside, and the heat doesn't work right. You freeze to death. I'll try to get what I can out of it."

Thinking he meant to sell it for $15,000 or $20,000, I asked, "Well, how much would that be?"

He laughed and said, "For you, it would be $2,000."

I said, "George, that bus is worth a lot more than $2,000 no matter what condition it's in."

He just kept on smiling and said, "For you, it's $2,000."

I decided I'd better grab it quick before he changed his mind, so I wrote out a check then and there.

When we got back to Nashville we put together a six-piece band for the road, but we didn't hire a bus driver. We decided to save money by taking turns driving ourselves. It was very cold that first trip out, and we soon realized George hadn't been exaggerating when he said you could freeze to death on that bus. Drafts of cold air came in from everywhere. It was worse than being outside. We bought masking tape and crawled all over the inside of the bus, trying to seal up the cracks. We stuck the tape around windows, under the seats, behind the bunks, and along the sides of the floor. It really looked tacky, but it helped some. We bought two little butane heaters to heat the bus when it was parked, but we never did get it really warm. In fact trying to keep from freezing almost cost me my life.

On our third or fourth trip out, we stopped at a truck stop in New Brounsfel, Texas, to fuel up. Everybody got off to go eat except me. I was asleep in the back room where we had a couch that opened into a bed. I woke up when I realized the engines had stopped; then I heard a voice yell, "Get everybody away from the bus. She's gonna blow."

I jumped out of that bed and hit the floor before I realized what I was doing. In a split second I was down the aisle and out the front door, nightgown and all. Just as I hit the cement I heard a loud explosion, and half the back end of the bus blew off. One of the butane tanks had blown up. Someone had opened an outside door to a back compartment where we kept our instruments and had seen the flames just in time to shout a warning.

It was a long time before I got a good night's sleep on that bus again. But I loved it anyway. It was an old Flex, and I had more fun driving it than I do now riding along in the back of a luxurious Silver Eagle. Daddy had taught me to drive when I was just nine years old and could hardly reach the pedals. He took Carolyn out in his pickup truck one day with the intention of teaching only her. But I tagged along and begged until he taught me too. By the time I was twelve I could handle any piece of equipment on the farm including the tractor, so driving a big bus was easy by comparison. I put in just as many hours behind the wheel of our bus as anybody else, and I handled it just as well, too. Sometimes I'd sit up alone for eight or nine hours driving while everyone else was asleep.

Sometimes, Donna liked to sit up with me. We had more laughs over my driving! Every time a trucker would pass he'd look our way, then do a double take when he saw two girls sitting up there by themselves in the front of that big bus. We'd be coming down the side of a steep, winding mountain road, and Donna would pretend she was praying, "Oh God, please let her keep this thing on the road." If I drove in behind an auditorium where we were working, the fans would fall out when they saw who was behind the wheel. George Jones's band teased me about it all the time. Like George, several of them were from Texas, and they couldn't get over a *woman* driving her own bus. Once in a while now, if I'm bored, I'll go up front and ask my driver to let me have the wheel. Those same guys start getting very nervous when they see me get into the driver's seat. Even after all these years they still don't trust me.

In some ways road life became easier for us with a bus, but it proved to be a point of friction between me and Don. He wouldn't let me put my name on the outside of the bus unless his was on it too, and although I didn't think that was fair since it was my show, I went along with him because he was my husband. The lettering read "The Don Chapel and Tammy Wynette Show" and it irritated me every time I saw it. He wasn't a good enough musician or singer to get a sideman's job on his own, much less headline a show, and he knew that as well as I did. I felt I was being used and I resented it.

I kept getting complaints from promoters about Don singing too many solos on the show and doing too many duets with Donna. They said they were paying for me, not my family, and if I didn't do more of the show alone, they were going to take their complaints to Shorty Lavender, my booker at the Hubert Long Agency. I was afraid to tell Don about their criticisms because I knew he'd argue with them and cause me trouble with the agency. I had been on the road only about six months and didn't want to do anything to jeopardize my relationship with my booking agency, or my reputation with promoters. I wanted them to call back Shorty and say what a good show I had, not to complain about it. Don was pushing harder than ever for me to talk to Billy about a recording contract for him and Donna, so I finally did that. Billy knew the pressure I was under at home, so he agreed to record them. Nothing ever came of Don's two singles, and Donna's was never released.

Meanwhile I had bought a larger home on Old Hickory Lake about three blocks from Johnny Cash's house. With six kids, Don and me, and the live-in couple, Geraldine and Norman Rogers, we had ten people under one roof and needed more space. I kept the house on Imperial Point and leased it out. I had gotten the mortgage down to $8000 by putting extra money into it every time I had a good week, so I wanted to keep it as an investment.

We were no sooner settled into the new house than Michael's problems grew worse, and we had to put him under a psychiatrist's care. He seemed to delight in doing anything that would disrupt the family. He constantly lied to Don about me, and to both of us about the other children. He would deliberately break something, then say, "Look what Gwen did." Or, "Look what Gary broke while you were gone." He was setting a terrible example for the younger children, and I was at my wits' end as to what to do about it. One day when I scolded him for sassing me, he told his father I'd made him spend all morning ironing shirts. He brought them out on hangers and said, "See what she made me do while you were gone." I stood there dumbfounded that he could tell such a bald-faced lie right in front of me. I had ironed every one of those shirts myself. It was true that I had asked him to iron them; Geraldine and Norman were off that week, so we were all going to pitch in and do the work ourselves. Donna did her laundry and part of Gary's, and I did mine, Don's, and my girls'. I didn't think it was unreasonable for Michael to help out by ironing his shirts. But he refused to do anything around the house, then shut himself in his room until his father came home. Don knew Michael was lying about who had ironed the shirts because Donna backed me up, but he stood up for him anyway and said I shouldn't have tried to make his son do "woman's work."

Arguments with Don became more frequent at home and on the road. We did have fun when we worked with George Jones because there was never a dull moment with him around. I was still in awe of him, Donna worshiped him, and even Don liked being with him because George was recording some of his songs. I knew George had a drinking problem—it was common knowledge in the business—but we had seen only his best side, and I had convinced myself that the only reason he drank was because he was unhappy. I didn't know about his demons. I thought to myself that any man who had spent most of his life on the road had a good reason to drink, and although he had never discussed his private life with any of us, I had heard from others that he didn't have a happy marriage.

George knew things weren't going well in my marriage either, because it was obvious to anyone who spent any time around me and Don, but he never mentioned it. We never spoke about personal things, just the business. Then one day be stopped by our house to go over some songs with Don, but instead, kept singing my single that had just come out, "D–I–V–O–R–C–E." After he'd sung the first line, "My divorce became final today," several times, he said, "Did you hear what I said?"

I didn't even know he was getting a divorce, so I didn't catch his meaning at all. I said, "Yes, I like the way you sing my song."

"No, *listen* to me," he said, and he sang the line again, "My divorce became final today."

I said, "You mean *you* got a divorce?"

"Yes," he said, "and it *was* final today." He laughed and suggested we toast his divorce. We knew he'd been married about seventeen years and that he had two sons and an older daughter, but we didn't ask any questions and he didn't say any more.

After George left that night, Don blew up. It was the first time he had ever said anything suggesting he thought George had a special feeling for me. I was shocked, and I told him he was being ridiculous. In my heart I was hoping Don was right, but I didn't believe it for a minute. I worshiped George, but I had him so high up on a pedestal I couldn't imagine us being together any way except on a stage. He had certainly never said anything to indicate he was interested in me—other than as a singer. We had never even been alone, although I admit there had been times when I wished I were with him instead of with Don.

My husband had done something that had turned me off so completely I didn't see how I could ever forgive him or feel the same about him again. We hadn't been married long when he popped into the bathroom one day and snapped a picture of me just as I was stepping out of the shower. I laughed and told him to cut it out. He said, "Oh, don't be such a prude. I like to take pictures of you, and no one will ever see this but me." After that he began getting the camera out whenever he could catch me without clothes on, and I found it very annoying. One day I was doing exercises on the bedroom floor. I had taken off my robe so I could move around more freely. Don walked in and saw me and immediately grabbed the camera. I really got mad that time and told him I was sick and tired of his little game and asked him not to do it again. He said I was being silly, so after that I locked the door when I wanted privacy.

A few months later we were working the Edison Hotel in Toronto, the same place I'd been late the time I had trouble returning through immigration. Customers had been dancing during the show, and they gathered around the stage to listen while I dedicated a number to someone. Suddenly a man stepped to the front of the crowd and just stood there watching me. I noticed him because of the way he was staring, not like a fan usually does, but with this smug look on his face. He was bald except for a gray fringe around his ears and neck, and he had on green pants and a green-and-white striped shirt opened at the collar. I could

see an envelope sticking out of his shirt, and I thought
that was an odd place to carry a note.

After the song was over, several people handed me
requests written on paper; then he reached forward
and handed me the envelope he'd taken from his shirt.
He said, "Read this while you're on your break." I
laid it on the top of the amplifier with the other requests, and when I'd finished my last song, I grabbed
them all and left the stage. The manager had provided
a table for us ringside, so I sat down while Don went
to get a Coke for me and a drink for himself. While I
was waiting for him to come back, I started reading
over the requests for the next show. I came to the envelope, opened it, and pulled out a picture.

When I saw it I felt like someone had hit me in the
stomach hard enough to knock the wind out of me. I
couldn't speak, and my heart was pounding in my
chest. I was looking at a picture of myself stepping out
of the bathtub, reaching for a towel. I was totally nude.
I wanted to die of shame, and I ran into the ladies
room and cried my heart out. I couldn't understand
how the picture had gotten out of Don's hands into the
hands of a stranger.

By the time I composed myself enough to leave the
restroom, the next set was about to begin, and I had
to go right onstage. The man who had handed me the
picture stayed in front of the bandstand, dancing with
a young girl throughout the whole show, and I was so
embarrassed I couldn't concentrate on performing. He
kept looking at me and grinning, and I wanted to jump
down off the stage and slap his face.

After the show I went straight to the bus and Don
followed, not knowing why I was so upset. When I
confronted him with the picture, he was very nonchalant about the whole thing. He said, "Oh, that's
just a little hobby of mine. I get names out of ads in
porno magazines, and we swap pictures. What difference does it make? Your name's not on the picture.
No one could ever prove it was you."

I was furious with him, and hurt and humiliated at

the same time. What kind of man would show other men nude pictures of his wife? It was a sickening, low-down thing to do. I tore the picture to shreds and told him what I thought of him. He finally apologized and promised he would destroy the pictures and negatives he had at home. But I knew that wouldn't change the disgust I felt. I had lost all respect for Don, and our marriage was never the same after that.

Shortly after George told us he had gotten a divorce, we did a show together, and he asked me where I was working the following night. I told him I was doing a benefit in Red Bay, Alabama, where I'd spent so much of my childhood. I explained they were trying to raise money to put air conditioning in the new school. All George said was, "I never heard of Red Bay, Alabama," and he left. After the show Don and I drove on to Mother's house in Mississippi, which was just across the state line from Red Bay. The next night, when we pulled up in front of the Red Bay auditorium, a brand new burgundy Eldorado Cadillac drove up beside us. I thought, Who on earth owns a car like that in this town? Then George stepped out of the Cadillac and said "So this is Red Bay, Alabama?"

I was flabbergasted. George was a huge star, a giant in country music. A town as small as Red Bay couldn't possibly have afforded his show. "What on earth are you doing here?" I asked.

"I came to do a benefit," he said. "Didn't you say they needed air conditioning?"

It was the nicest thing imaginable, and I was thrilled and so was my mother. She was beside herself with excitement over meeting the great George Jones. He had been her idol since his first record came out in 1953, and it pleased me no end to be able to introduce Mother to George. It was the first time she'd shown any sign of being impressed by my career. Relatives and friends had told me she bragged behind my back, but she never complimented me to my face. When "Apartment #9" came out I couldn't even get her to listen to it. She was too busy playing with the kids, and when

I asked her what she thought of my record she said, "Oh, I don't know, all that country music sounds alike to me," so I never asked her to listen to a song again. But George Jones impressed her, and she was beaming all night, introducing him to everybody in Red Bay. Don, however, did not share her enthusiasm over George's showing up; he was sulking all night.

We agreed that we wouldn't announce George was there until Don and Donna had done their part of the show, and I had done most of mine. Then I told the audience I had a surprise for them, and when they heard George's name they went wild. He worked for over an hour and put on the kind of show only George Jones can do when he's in top form. They loved him so much they would have built another new school that night if he'd asked them to.

The following year, after George and I were married, we played another benefit for Red Bay, and Mother and I had a good laugh over it. I said, "Mother, last year when I was here I was married to Don, and I introduced George as my special surprise guest. Now this year I'm back again as his wife, and all those country people are sure to think something was going on between us all the time."

But it wasn't. In fact, the day George blurted out that he loved me I was shocked to death. He had never so much as touched me, except to shake my hand or pat me on the back, nor had he ever said anything personal to me. And we had never been alone. It wasn't exactly what you'd call a romantic setting, either.

Don and I were in the middle of one of the worst arguments we'd ever had when George showed up at the house. The night before we had come in off the road to find Gwen, Jackie, and Gary down with some kind of food poisoning. Norman and Geraldine had taken them to a ball game that afternoon, and they'd all eaten hot dogs, so we figured they must have gotten sick from the meat. That night they all had cramps and were vomiting. I could tell they were becoming dehydrated, and when I called the doctor he advised me to bring them to the hospital. Don said for me to go ahead, and he would unload the bus and join me there later. Norman played semi-professional baseball, and I knew Geraldine wanted to go with him to an out-of-town game, so I told her there was no need for her to stay at home; Tina was visiting my mother, and Michael and Donna had gone to see their mother. I figured Don could help me out with the sick ones if I needed him.

When we got to the hospital they pumped the children's stomachs, then put them all in one large room with three beds. They were being fed intravenously and were whining and fussing; they were still sick to their stomachs. I was running between beds trying to take care of all three of them.

By 10 o'clock that night Don still hadn't shown up at the hospital, and I was tired and irritated. I got no answer at home, so I called George's manager Bill Starnes to see if he could find Don for me. I checked back with him about an hour later, and he said he hadn't been able to find my husband anywhere, but that he was coming over to help me out. When he arrived George was with him. I hadn't even known George was in town. The kids were crying and begging me to take the needles out of their little arms, and they still couldn't keep water down, so George and Bill helped me wait on them and try to quiet them down. They stayed with me until all three were asleep, which was about 2 in the morning. I dozed a little after they left until the children woke up again at 6 A.M. The doctor saw them at 10 and released all three.

There still had been no word from Don, even though one of the sick children was his own son. Since he hadn't even called the hospital, I was surprised to find him at home when we got there. He said he had fallen asleep after he unloaded the bus and hadn't woke up until just before we arrived.

I said, "Don, I know that's a lie because Bill Starnes came over here looking for you last night, and no one was at home."

He said "Where the hell did you see Bill Starnes?"

So I explained what had happened. When he heard George Jones had been at the hospital he hit the ceiling. He said he was sick and tired of George hanging around all the time because he knew he had eyes for me. I told him he was crazy, and it went back and forth like that all afternoon, with him following me around the house drinking. All our bills were spread out on the dining room table, along with the cash from our last date and the checkbook. I was trying to take care of our monthly books, with Don still ranting and raving.

Then the doorbell rang. I answered it and there stood George. I thought, Uh oh, this is really bad timing, but I didn't know what to say except to invite him in. He'd been drinking too, but that wasn't unusual and I didn't think anything about it. I had never seen George's temper on display, so I had no idea what to expect. Don offered George a drink, then while he was mixing it, he started making hateful remarks to me. We argued again about his not coming to the hospital the night before. He was standing at the refrigerator door, putting ice in George's glass when I said, "What you did last night was inexcusable."

Don whirled around and said, "Well, you bitch. You're not fit to sleep with anyway."

The words were no sooner out of his mouth than George went berserk. He grabbed the end of my huge dining room table and flipped it over like a matchbox. Money, bills, drinks, and papers went flying everywhere. Don and I just stood there gaping. George is a small-framed man (five-foot-seven-and-a-half, about 150 pounds) and you don't expect such power from a man his size. All of a sudden he was like a tornado, wrecking my house. He picked up a heavy dining room chair and threw it into a window, shattering the plate glass into a million pieces. He looked straight at Don and said, "You don't talk to her like that." His voice was so menacing it sent a chill through me.

Don stammered, "Wha-what's it to you? She's my wife!"

George shot back, "That may be so, but I *love* her." I was so shocked at his words that my knees gave way, and I collapsed into a chair in the corner. George walked over and stood behind me, resting his hand on my shoulder. "And you love me, too . . . don't you?" he asked gently.

"Yes, yes I *do,*" I answered quickly, and at that moment I realized it was true. I *was* in love with George Jones, and I had been for a long time.

"Okay." George squeezed my shoulder. "Let's go."

I stood up in a daze and followed him into the children's room where we gathered up Tina, Jackie, and Gwen, and we walked right past Don out the front door. We left my husband standing in stunned silence in the middle of a room that looked like a hurricane had blown through it. George's Eldorado was parked in front of the house. We got in and drove away. I turned around once to look back at the house I'd been so proud to own and at my brand new limousine sitting in the driveway. Tears welled up in my eyes and I thought, Oh, Lord. What have I done? We left with nothing but the clothes on our backs, after I had worked so hard to buy us the first nice things we'd ever had and to furnish the house the way I wanted it. Now I was leaving everything behind.

George knew what I was thinking. He reached over and patted me on the arm. "Don't worry, honey," he said. "There's nothing in that house I can't buy you again. Let him have it all. It's not worth going back for. From now on you'll have everything you want, and you won't have to pay for it yourself, either. I promise you that."

As his big car sped through the night I wondered if this was really happening to me. The legendary George Jones, my idol, in love with *me,* Wynette Pugh from Tupelo, Mississippi? It was far too wonderful to be true.

Chapter 6

I DIDN'T know where George was taking me and I didn't care. I would have gone anywhere with him. My heart was so full of love for this man I'd worshiped since childhood that I felt as though it would burst in my chest. He had rescued me from a husband I didn't love, just like the knight on the white charger saved the captive princess in fairy tales that I'd read as a little girl. The fact that his "white charger" was a burgundy Cadillac and that he wore cowboy boots instead of shining armor didn't make the impact any less romantic. I wanted to bask in the safety of his arms forever, and I would have done anything he asked.

But George didn't ask for anything; instead he was concerned about my well-being and what was best for me. He could have taken me home with him that night. I would have gone willingly. I'm sure he knew that, but he never brought it up. He took me to the Hilton hotel near the airport where he checked me and the girls into adjoining rooms. When we got to the door he held me for a moment and told me not to worry. Then he kissed me on the forehead and left. I tucked the girls into bed, then lay down in my room and tried to watch television. But I couldn't concentrate. Thoughts kept racing through my mind about all that had happened that day, and I smoked one cigarette after another. I knew Tennessee was one of the few states that still had an "alienation of affection" law where you can sue someone for taking away your husband or wife, and I wondered if Don would try to use that to get back at George. I worried about the scandal it would cause in Nashville when word got out that Tammy Wynette had left her husband for George Jones. I didn't want my family to think there had been anything between me and George before that day because there hadn't, and I knew it would hurt them to have people talking about me.

I had just dozed off about 4 A.M. when the phone rang. It was George. He was laughing. "Well, I guess we fooled old Don. He just left here with the police. They showed up with a search warrant and went all through the place looking for you and the kids. I thought he'd come and I was right. He was so sure I'd bring you here! He should've known I've got better sense than that." He told me to get some sleep because he was coming to pick me up early the next morning. But sleep was out of the question after that news, so I paced the floor until the girls woke up. We had just finished breakfast when George arrived. He told me he had made arrangements for his secretary Shirley Phillips to stay with Gwen, Jackie, and Tina so we could fly to Mexico to get me a quick divorce. He had made reservations for us to leave the next day. Meanwhile he was taking us home with him where we'd all be more comfortable.

That night, after the house was quiet and the children were asleep, George said there was a movie he wanted to watch on television. He asked me if I'd like to watch it with him in his bedroom. Like every girl who has ever fantasized about making love to her movie or singing idol, I had often wondered what it would be like with George Jones, but now that I was about to find out I was too nervous to look forward to it. I was more anxious than I'd been on my wedding night with Euple. Even though I'd had two husbands and three children, I still didn't know much about sex, and I was afraid I wouldn't be a skillful enough lover to satisfy a man who had been around as much as George. I wanted so much to please him, to show him how much I loved him, but I could never have admitted my feelings of inadequacy. I still had hang-ups from the way I was raised, where talking about sex was taboo, so instead of telling George how I felt, I lay there the whole time he was watching "Requiem for a Heavyweight" worrying about what was going to happen when the movie was over.

I thought the room we were in was the most beautiful bedroom I'd ever seen. It was all done in Spanish decor with a huge four-poster bed, red carpeting, black velvet drapes, red velvet valances, paintings of bullfighters, and massive hand-carved furniture. It was coordinated and complete down to the last detail, and I was very impressed, knowing that George had done it all himself. The only thing out of place in the room was a bottle of whiskey he had brought in and placed on the night table beside the bed. I remember feeling a twinge of disappointment that he was drinking on our first night together, but the setting was so perfect otherwise that I pushed it out of my mind.

George had become so completely engrossed in the movie that I began to think he'd forgotten I was there. He suffered through every trauma with Anthony Quinn, getting so carried away that when it was over he was lying there with tears rolling down his face, murmuring, "They can't do that to him, they *can't*." No woman can resist a man who cries over a book or a movie, and I was so moved by his show of emotion that I forgot all about my own anxieties. It proved to be a beautiful night. He was as gentle and tender and loving as I'd hoped he would be, and I fell asleep in his arms certain that I was the luckiest woman in the world.

The next day we flew to Mexico City in a flurry of excitement, eager to make me a "free" woman so we could share our love with the world. Before we left for the airport, George led me outside his house where a brand new white Continental Mark IV was parked. "This is yours," he said, handing me the keys. "Now you don't have to worry about going back to that house to get your car." He also took a four-carat diamond ring off his finger and put it on mine. "Wear this," he said, "until I can get you one of your own." I was overwhelmed by George's generosity. No one loves presents more than I do, and no man had ever given me expensive gifts. All the way to Mexico City I kept holding my hand up to admire the diamond. After we arrived we found it was easier getting a divorce there than it is to get married in the United States. I felt giddy and lightheaded the whole time I was in Mexico City. George said it was the altitude, but I was sure it was love.

We arrived back in Nashville the next day to discover we'd made the front page of the Banner. The headlines read: "Tammy Wynette Leaves Husband for George Jones." The article insinuated I'd abandoned Don and run off from a perfectly good marriage to be with a "superstar." It was the first time I'd ever seen my personal life smeared all over the newspapers, and I hated the feeling that I couldn't defend myself. I knew people would believe what they read without hearing my side of the story. I've gotten used to that feeling now, and I don't let it bother me anymore, but it's been only in the last couple of years that I've stopped taking it so personally. I suffered a lot of pain over things I read about myself before I realized it doesn't do any good to get upset over something you can't control. People are going to believe what they want to believe. So the best defense is to tell the truth if you're asked, but don't read the papers.

After reading the article I went immediately to see

my attorney, Jack Norman, Jr., and told him about my Mexican divorce. He just shook his head and looked worried. "A Mexican divorce doesn't mean a damn thing in this state," he said. "Tennessee doesn't recognize Mexican divorces. You're no better off now than you were before you left. You'll have to file for divorce here, and I feel certain Don will crossfile."

Jack was right. Don filed a countersuit against me the very next day, charging me with desertion and adultery, naming George as the corespondent. He also filed a separate alienation of affection suit against George, suing him for $100,000 in damages. While my attorney was preparing the case, George's manager Bill Starnes happened to go to Alabama on business. He ran into a lawyer friend there and told him about the mess we were in back in Nashville. The attorney advised him to look up the date my divorce from Euple was final. "Alabama has a law that states you must get permission from the judge to remarry within a year after your divorce," he explained. "If she married Don within a year from the time her divorce from Euple was final without permission from the judge who granted it, there might be a legal loophole for her." Bill checked it out right away and discovered I had married Don less than two months after my divorce from Euple was final. Since I didn't know about the law stating I needed the judge's permission, I didn't get it, so we were able to obtain an annulment of my marriage to Don on the grounds that it hadn't been legal in the first place.

The annulment came through just two days before I was to give a deposition for Don's case against me. His attorneys didn't know about the annulment, and my attorney wanted to keep it that way until he found out exactly what Don was going to ask for in the property settlement.

Don's attorneys began asking me questions like: "Is it true you drove here today in a new Mark IV given to you by George Jones?" "Have you been wearing a diamond ring he gave you?" "What is your current address?" "Are you living in the house with George Jones?"

I evaded the questions as best I could until my attorney stood up and said, "That's enough! You have no right to ask her these personal questions because her marriage to Don Chapel has been annulled." You could have heard a pin drop. Don's attorneys were stunned and obviously disappointed that they had lost their bargaining power.

Still, I was determined to be more than fair in the settlement with Don, so I gave him the bus, the new limousine, the first house I'd bought at Imperial Point and all my furniture. I felt that was a generous agreement since we had lived together only nine months, and I had paid for everything we owned. His attorneys kept trying to push the alienation of affection suit, but since George and I had never been together before the day I left Don, he didn't have valid grounds. He finally settled out of court for $2000. Later he lost the house at Imperial Point even though there was only $8000 owed on it. He could have rented it out for more than the monthly payments, but he let it go back to the bank instead. And he abandoned the limousine somewhere in Nebraska.

After the legal hassles with Don had been settled, George and I kept talking about getting married, but our work commitments kept us apart more than we were together. We had both been booked about six months ahead and had to fulfill those separate dates before Shorty Lavender could begin booking us together. If he had a night off, George would fly out to see me wherever I was working, and if I had a night off, I'd do the same for him, but there never seemed to be enough time to plan a wedding. I lived for the times we were together and dreaded the days when we weren't. Our phone bills during that period were outrageous.

George's birthday was in September, a month after I'd moved in with him. We both had dates that night —his was in Oklahoma and mine in Milwaukee—and he complained bitterly about the fact that we couldn't be together to celebrate his first birthday with me. I loved the fact that he was sentimental about things like that, and I kept trying to make him feel better by saying we'd make up for it the next year. On the morning of his birthday we talked on the telephone and he told me he had two shows that night, one at 7 and one at 9. That evening, just before I left for the Nickobob Club where I was playing, he called again to say how much he missed me and wished we could be together. I also had two shows that night, and after the second one I was exhausted. I was in the dressing room getting ready to go back to my hotel when the club owner sent word he wanted me to do a third show. My contract called for two shows, and I didn't feel up to a third, so I told them I wouldn't do it. It was almost 1 A.M. and I knew I wouldn't get away from there until 3 if I went onstage again.

The club owner was a very nice man, and I couldn't understand why he would make such a request. Finally he came into the dressing room and said, "Tammy, *please* go on again—just for a little while. The customers are begging for you, and I would consider it a special favor if you'd do it just this once." He was so sweet about it that I couldn't refuse, but I was so tired I didn't even feel like standing up, so I drug a stool out with me and climbed on to it to open the show sitting down with my guitar. After my second song I noticed the crowd was staring at me. I could hear them "ooohing" and "aahing." I became very self-conscious. Mini dresses were still in style then and I had on a red one. I thought, Can they see up my dress or what? Then I felt someone behind me and turned around to see George standing right by my shoulder. It was such a shock I dropped the little baby Martin guitar he'd given me and broke the neck on it.

I said, "What on earth are you doing here? You're supposed to be in Oklahoma."

He just laughed and said, "Don't ever underestimate Jones. I'll show up when you least expect me." The crowd loved all this of course, and we really put on a show for them.

Afterward I learned George had cut his second show short and hired a Lear Jet to get him to Milwaukee before I finished my last show. But he hadn't reckoned on the time change from Oklahoma, so when he arrived at the Milwaukee airport he realized I'd be gone from the club by the time he got there if he didn't do something drastic. He called the owner and told him to do anything he could to keep me around another few minutes. Then he jumped in a cab and offered the driver a $20 tip if he could get him to the Nickobob Club in twenty minutes. By the time he arrived it was 2 A.M., and we had only a few hours together before he would have to make connections to fly on to Dallas for his show that night.

On the way back to the hotel he noticed a fever blister on my lip and asked, "What have you been doing to get that . . . kissing some of those old boys in the band?"

I said, "Of course not. I get fever blisters all the time."

He said, "Now don't you lie to me. I know you've been kissing one of them old boys." And he pretended to be really upset about it. He carried on for over an hour, teasing me, but acting like he actually believed I'd been kissing someone.

I was beginning to get irritated and I said, "George, I don't believe you. You go to all the trouble and expense of hiring a Lear Jet to bring you here so we can have a few hours together, then you waste half the time acting silly over a dumb fever blister!"

He laughed and said, "You know, you're right!" And then, I'll be damned if he didn't turn over in the bed and go to sleep!

He really got my goat that night and he knew it. But a little while later, when I had to wake him up to go to the airport, we were both laughing about it—that time George was being playful. I didn't see a real outbreak of his temper until about a month later on our first trip to Florida.

George owned a house in Lakeland, Florida, which he leased to his friends Joe and Peggy Asher. He wanted me to see it with the idea that we might consider moving there. I had always loved Florida so the thought appealed to me, especially since we'd been getting so much attention in Nashville. Songwriters were constantly stopping by our home to pitch material, people we didn't even know who would just walk up and knock on the front door. Fans and tourists would actually bring blankets and sit on the lawn, and hardly a day went by that something about us wasn't in the papers. I felt like I was living in a fish bowl. We announced we'd gotten married on August 22, but actually we weren't married at all, and I was afraid sooner or later some reporter in Nashville was going to find that out and print it. Lakeland was far enough away to offer peace and privacy.

The day we arrived to look at the house it was pouring rain, so we checked into the Holiday Inn on Memorial Boulevard and George called Joe and Peggy. He wanted to wait until the rain stopped before we went out to see the house, so he invited them down to the hotel. Joe and George started drinking immediately, and Peggy and I just sat around talking. After a couple of hours she and I were both bored to death, so she kept trying to get Joe to go home with her. He refused and she finally left without him.

By that time George was really drunk, and he soon passed out on the bed. Joe left and I thought, Good. Now George will sleep it off and I can go to bed. I got into my gown and robe and lay down very gently so I wouldn't wake him up. But my head had no sooner hit the pillow than I heard a loud banging on the door. I opened it to find Joe standing there with a tray of Bloody Marys balanced above his head. He pushed past me and set the tray down. I was telling him please to be quiet when he walked over to the bed and woke George up to give him a drink.

I was furious. "Put that drink down and get out of here," I said. "I can't believe you'd wake up a man who's already passed out from too much drinking to give him more!"

I hadn't gotten the words out of my mouth before George was up off that bed swinging. He was like a wild man. He swung at me and missed. That made him so mad he threw a whiskey bottle against the wall and smashed it into a million pieces. Then he came at me again, chasing me around the room yelling, "I'll show you. You don't talk to my friends like that."

I was petrified. All I could think was, I've got to get out of here or he's going to kill me. I ran out of the door and down the hall with him right after me. I was still wearing my robe and gown, but George was fully dressed, boots and all. I ran out onto the fourth floor balcony and down the outside steps toward the parking lot. George was just a step behind me the whole way, still yelling and cursing at the top of his voice. When I reached the parking lot I heard a thud behind me and looked around to see George sprawled in the gravel by the flower bed that bordered the steps. Apparently the sharp toe of his cowboy boot had caught on the bottom step and tripped him. I knew falling down would make him madder than ever, so I ran as fast as I could and didn't look around again until I was across the main highway behind a market.

It was after 10 o'clock at night and the store was closed. No one was around. I couldn't see the hotel parking lot from where I was hiding, so I didn't know if George was still there or not. The rain had stopped but there were puddles everywhere, and my robe and gown had gotten muddy around the hem. I didn't know what I was going to do. I had no money or identification on me, and I didn't know a soul in Lakeland so I couldn't call anyone for help. I was afraid to go back to our room, but I knew I had to get out of that parking lot and off the street. I could just imagine the police cruising by and spotting a bedraggled woman in a flimsy, muddy robe and nightgown. I thought of what nice headlines it would make if I was picked up!

I saw a neon sign down the street that said "Blue Egret Motel." I made my way there like a thief in the night, hiding in the shadows as much as possible and sneaking from the protection of one building to the next. The motel was a dump—one of those places where you can check in without getting out of your car—but I was so desperate I didn't care how bad it looked. A middle-aged lady was sitting inside the drive-up check-in booth. I thought, Lord, what will I say to her?

But I needn't have worried. She was very cool. If she thought it was peculiar that I was checking in wearing a nightgown, she didn't let on. I told her my luggage would be sent over from another hotel later, and that I would pay her when I checked out the next morning. She said, "Take number six," and handed me a key, barely glancing up from her True Romance magazine. Once inside the room I realized I didn't even have a cigarette or money to buy any. I paced the floor and wrung my hands. I was more hurt than angry. I couldn't believe that the same man who could be so gentle and considerate when he was sober could turn into such a madman when he was drunk. I had never been exposed to anything like that in my life because none of the men in my family drank, and certainly none of them ever became violent. My grandfather never even raised his voice to my grandmother, much less his hand, and I was horrified to realize George Jones was quite capable of striking a woman if he was drunk enough.

I cried and worried and wondered what to do. I knew what was facing me back at the hotel, and I wanted to give George time to sober up before I saw him again. About two hours passed before it suddenly occurred to me that he hadn't kept on chasing me after I'd seen him fall down. Had he hurt himself? I started to panic. Suppose he'd broken his leg or something! If he was hurt I had to get back to him.

It was now well after midnight, so I hurried back to the hotel, walking on the darkest streets so I wouldn't be seen, terrified some mugger was going to jump out of the shadows at any moment. I wasn't about to walk through the hotel lobby to ask for a key the way I looked, so I retraced my steps up to the fourth floor balcony, then down the hallway, approaching our room very cautiously. It took me several minutes to get up the nerve to knock on the door, and when I did George called out immediately, "Come on in, it's unlocked." I stepped inside to find him propped up in the bed with his arm resting on a pillow. "Where the hell have you been?" he growled.

"I took a long walk." I tried to sound nonchalant.

"Not dressed like that you didn't," he said in a sarcastic tone.

"Well, I didn't ask to leave like this," I said. "There was no sense in what happened. I just couldn't believe Joe would come back here and wake you up to drink more, and I had to tell him what I thought."

"I don't want to talk about it," George interrupted. "My wrist is killing me. I think it's broken."

I could see that it was swollen and bluish. I thought to myself that if it was broken it served him right, but he looked so pitiful I couldn't help feeling sorry for him. I helped him up and drove him to the Watson Clinic where they x-rayed his wrist and found it was in fact broken. They gave him a shot for pain, then sent us next door to the Lakeland General Hospital where an orthopedic surgeon was called in to set his arm. The painkiller mixed with the liquor that was still in his system made him higher than a kite, but this time he was silly and as limp as a dishrag. He couldn't do anything with one arm in a cast, so when we got back to the hotel I undressed him and put him to bed. When we woke up the next morning George was as sweet as he could be. The night before seemed like a bad dream. If it hadn't been for the cast on his wrist, I would have thought I'd imagined the whole thing.

We drove over to his house, and I fell in love with it immediately. It was a rambling ranch-style house with a swimming pool in the backyard. I've been a sun-worshiper since my childhood when I picked cotton in a bathing suit to get a tan, and I loved the thought of living in a place where you could lie out by the pool all year round. We decided to move to Lakeland as soon as all the arrangements could be made.

Meanwhile we had moved into my house on Old Hickory Lake because it was bigger than George's place in Nashville. He was redecorating from top to bottom and having a ball. I had never known a man to be interested in decorating, and since I knew nothing about it myself I was fascinated to watch him at work. He'd surround himself with samples of wallpaper, fabric, and carpeting, and he knew exactly what he wanted for every room. He'd walk through a furniture showroom and say "I want this and this and this and that," and pick out a truckload in ten minutes. When he got it all home everything fit perfectly in place as though he had worked from a blueprint.

We had fun at the Old Hickory Lake house even though we were looking forward to moving to Lakeland. Bobby Bare and his family lived next door, and friends in the business, like Waylon Jennings, stopped by often to pick and sing with George. Waylon Jennings adored Tina. She'd run to his arms the minute she saw him to be tossed in the air. One time he threw her too high and she split her head open on a ceiling fixture. We had to take her to the emergency hospital to have it sewed up. Waylon was so upset you'd have thought he'd killed her.

In January 1969 George and I were asked to join the Grand Ole Opry. Becoming a member of the Opry is like joining a very exclusive and respected club, and no honor means more to a country music performer. The Opry first went on the air in Nashville's WSM in 1925, and it's been a regular Saturday night feature ever since, making it the longest running program in the history of radio. In the early days country music performers got their bookings through being heard on the Opry, and since they made most of their money on these out-of-town engagements, singing on the show was more important that any other single job. WSM was powerful enough to reach many states even before the show went network in 1937. The performers would go on the road during the week, but they always made it back to town on Saturday night in time to work the Opry. Over the years every great name in country music has appeared on the Opry at one time or another, and standing on the stage of the old Ryman Auditorium where it all happened made me feel both proud and humble.

George more or less took it in stride the night we made our first Opry appearance, but I was very nervous. The radio shows are broadcast before a live audience, and although they're the best audience in the world if they like you, they can also be the coldest if they don't. I kept thinking, Lord, who do I think I am, standing here where Hank Williams and Red Foley and Patsy Cline and all the greats have stood and still stand? It sounds silly, but in the old Ryman the ghosts of those legends always seemed to be present, and the feel of tradition and history was so strong it was almost tangible. My nervousness must have shown because Jeannie Seely, already an Opry star then, walked up to me backstage and said, "Don't worry. We're all scared our first night. You'll do fine."

One of the greatest things about the Opry is that no matter how much competition there is among performers to attain the biggest hits or the best bookings, they're all brothers and sisters on that stage, and everyone is very supportive and helpful. When you're just starting out and still unsure of yourself, nothing makes you feel better than a pat on the back from a performer whose talent you admire. Jeannie's words helped me that night, and as soon as I heard the music and appeared in front of the audience I felt great. George and I did fine, and I'll never forget the thrill of hearing the applause of an Opry audience for the first time. It makes you feel accepted in a very special way.

By the first of the year George and I had just about finished our separate bookings, and Shorty called to say our first date together would be at the Playroom in Atlanta in February. I was thrilled, not only because I was looking forward to working with George all the time, but because I had a sentimental feeling about the Playroom since it had been my very first booking. We worked hard putting together a new show. We hired country comedian Harold Morrison to travel with us, as well as Patsy Sledd, who sang backup with me. Harold opened, then I came out and did my show. George came on next and did his show, then called me back, and we finished together doing several songs that he'd recorded with other singers like Melba Montgomery and my duet number "My Elusive Dreams."

Opening night was terrific. The crowd seemed to love seeing us work together as husband and wife (they thought!), and we both felt an extra excitement knowing the other was there. Some performers work better together than others, and there was always a special chemistry between George and me onstage that the audience sensed and responded to. Professionally we brought out the best in each other. I knew by then that he loved my voice, and nothing on earth made me more proud than that. He once told me that he fell in love with me before he even met me. He said it happened the day he heard "Apartment #9" for the first time on his car radio. And of course he was my all-time favorite singer, and I was in awe of his talent. Unless he was drunk or there had been a bad scene between us, we always had *fun* working together, and it carried from the stage down into the audience and made them have fun too.

The day after opening night at the Playroom I had to fly to Nashville to overdub an album Billy was ready to release. When I got back to Atlanta late that afternoon, George was drunk. I was disappointed, but I thought maybe I could sober him up by showtime if I cooked him a good meal and got some coffee down him. We had a kitchen on the bus, which we had parked behind the club, so I started a big pot of stew. The owner of the club, Buddy McMahon, came on the bus with George, and from their conversation I gathered they'd been drinking all day. When the stew was ready I went to the back of the bus where the kitchen was located to dish it up for them. I'd been back there about five minutes talking to Harold Morrison and a couple of the band members when George came charging down the aisle yelling, "What are you doing back here—trying to make out with these guys?"

I realized he was so drunk he'd forgotten all about my going after the stew. Before I could say anything he grabbed me and literally threw me down the aisle of the bus, sending my slipper flying through the air. We never did find it. One of the boys grabbed George and locked him in our bedroom. I got off the bus and went inside the club to wait for showtime.

After I'd done my forty-five minutes, I introduced George as usual, not certain if he'd come out or not. He walked onstage and glared at me, then took the microphone and started to sing. After one song he looked at the band and said, "Let Tammy Wynette finish the show. I'm leaving." And he walked off.

The crowd started booing and carrying on, so I went out to try to calm them down. But they wanted George. I started singing, but they kept booing and chanting, "We want George, we want George." I had never faced a hostile audience before and it was a terrible experience. I couldn't really blame them because I knew they were disappointed in the way George had just walked off and left them sitting there after one song. But I was doing the best I could and it hurt that they weren't a little more understanding.

I worked another twenty minutes or so, then headed back for the bus, ready to climb all over George for what he'd done. But the bus was empty. Then someone in the club told me George had left with the owner,

Buddy McMahon. No one knew where they'd gone. I had heard that it wasn't unusual for Jones to disappear for days at a time when he was drinking. But he'd never gone off since we'd been together, and I was worried sick about him.

That wasn't the only thing I was worried about. I suspected I was pregnant. When George didn't come back the next day, I went to a doctor and learned my suspicions were true. I thought, Well girl, you've done it now. You're pregnant by a man you're not even married to, and he's gone off God-knows-where and for all you know you may never see him again.

That night I somehow got through two shows by myself, and again the following night I went on and performed alone. No one had heard from Buddy either, so I figured, Well at least we can't be sued for breaking a contract when he's gone off with the club owner. There was also some small comfort in knowing he wasn't alone, lying dead in some alley behind a bar somewhere.

The boys in the band kept assuring me George would turn up sooner or later, and sure enough on the fourth night he arrived in time for the show. He was still drinking and still surly so I kept out of his way between shows. After we finished work I was afraid not to go back to the motel with him, because I knew he was about to get really mean, and I didn't want to do or say anything to set him off. I decided to be as agreeable as possible.

When we got to the room he didn't say anything until he'd gotten into bed. Then he looked at me and said, "You thought I was going to marry you, didn't you? Well I'm not. I've changed my mind and I'm *not* getting married." My heart sank. I loved this man, even at his worst, and I was still convinced he could and would stop drinking.

As calmly as I could, I asked, "What made you decide that?"

"Never mind," he said. "I'm just not going to marry

you; that's all." Then he turned over and went to sleep.

I lay there wondering if he really meant it, or if it was just the liquor talking. After what he'd said I wouldn't have told him I was pregnant for anything.

The next morning George woke up as cheerful as he'd been mean the night before. He acted as though nothing had happened, and when I asked where he'd been for four days he said, "Oh, Buddy and I chartered a Lear and hit the high spots in Vegas." He was as casual about it as though he'd been down to the corner for a pack of cigarettes. "Come on." He was already up getting dressed. "Forget about that. Get out of bed and put on something nice 'cause this is the day we're getting married!"

I thought, What next! First he's not going to marry me, and then he wants to get married immediately. Will I *ever* understand this man? I didn't mention what he'd said the night before and neither did he. I realized he probably didn't even remember it. I knew this was a different man. This was the George Jones I'd fallen in love with, and I believed I could forget the other one even existed.

The only clothes I'd brought with me were casual daytime things and stage clothes, except for a red wool suit. My outfit looked like something you'd wear to a fancy luncheon with the girls. George put on a charcoal gray suit that was exactly right for a daytime wedding; George is fastidious about his clothes, and in all the years we were together I never saw him wear anything that wasn't perfectly matched, exquisitely tailored, and immaculately clean. Even when he was so drunk he couldn't stand up, his pants still held a crease.

We drove to the edge of the state line to Ringgold, Georgia, where you can get married in three hours. We laughed and talked and planned our future the whole way there, and the worry and heartache of the past week was soon forgotten. It was easy to get caught up in his enthusiasm and push any misgivings out of my mind. I believed with all my heart that together we could conquer his drinking problem, and since we always got along beautifully when he was sober, I was certain we could be happy together for the rest of our lives. I knew it wouldn't be easy living with him while he was still trying to stop drinking, but I also knew the end result would be worth it. We had everything going for us: we were in love, we were in the same business; we had the same interests and friends. We could make as much money as anybody needed. He loved my children and they loved him. He had promised me many times that he would stop drinking, and he had gone for longer periods without getting drunk since we'd been together than he had before. I didn't expect him to change overnight, but I knew he would eventually. All we needed was time.

When we got to Ringgold we located the courthouse and it took almost no time to get blood tests and a license and find a judge to marry us. At last I was officially Mrs. Jones! I told him I intended to frame that license and hang it over our bed. It was dated February 16, 1969. He laughed and said, "You can't because if you do everyone will know we've been lying since August."

We drove back to Atlanta, arriving well before showtime. When we got to the hotel George called room service and ordered champagne sent up. Then he called the bass player, James Hollie, and told him to round up the boys and bring them to our suite because he had a surprise for them.

When they were all gathered in the room, he passed around the champagne and said, "Let's toast the new Mrs. Jones. I know we told you boys we got married last summer, but that was a lie. We just got married today and I want you to welcome my bride."

The guys were really sweet and seemed genuinely happy for us. It made me feel good to know they had accepted me so readily because a lot of pickers feel it cramps their style to have a woman on the road. I knew their language and conduct on the bus was a lot different with me around, and some musicians would have resented this. But George's band had been nice to me from the beginning, and in return I felt a great affection for them.

James Hollie, the bass player from Dallas, soon became my rock of Gibraltar, the one I could always depend on to look after things on the road as well as help me take care of George. Freddie Haws, the drummer, also from Dallas, was always coming to my defense against George, and he got himself into trouble over it more than one time. Charlie Justice, the fiddle player I mentioned earlier as being called "Grumpy," was like the Daddy of the group, and we all loved him; he retired from the road in 1977 and we still miss him. Charlie and Sonny Curtis the steel players were from Ohio. Our lead guitar player, Charlie Carter, was a friend of Hollie's from Texas. They had played clubs together down there before James went to work for George. Like me, Carter had grown up a fanatical George Jones fan, so working for his idol was like a dream come true. The only musician George and I hired after we were married was our piano player, Jim Ebert, who was a friend of Sonny's from Ohio.

Jim stayed with me until 1977 when he retired from the road, and the night he left the boys were all crying and so was I. When you've been on the road together for a long time and someone leaves, it's like losing a member of your family because you do become like a family. Most country music bands are with their "road" families more than they're at home, so having a group who gets along well enough to live together in very close quarters is sometimes more important than their musical talent—although George was lucky in that he had both good musicians and good guys. Since Freddie, Carter, and James had all been buddies in Texas, and Ebert, Justice, and Sonny were friends back in Ohio, it made our group even closer. I soon came to feel I had inherited six big brothers when I married George.

A few days after we were married I told George

that I was expecting a baby. He was delighted but our
joy was short-lived. Before he'd had a chance to share
the news with our relatives, I had a miscarriage. We
were both disappointed, but the doctor assured me I
could get pregnant again, so we decided we would
avoid using any type of birth control and hope for the
best.

In March 1969, about a month after our wedding,
we moved to Lakeland to start a new life. We had had
so much notoriety in Nashville that I was looking
forward to a fresh start in a new location.

George immediately went to work redecorating the
Lakeland house and adding on two more bedrooms.
My aunt and uncle from Birmingham, Earleen and
Jack Robbins, came to live with us to take care of the
girls while we were on the road. We were traveling
much less than before, because with two of us working
we were making twice as much money as we had
separately. We were averaging about six days a month
out of town and still making as much as when we were
going out twenty days. The extra time off made it possible for us to have a fairly normal home life, and we
both loved it.

Our next door neighbors, Cliff and Maxine Hyder,
soon became our best friends. Cliff has amyotrophic
lateral sclerosis, commonly known as Lou Gehrig's
disease. When we first met him he hadn't driven a car
in over a year. He had become disgusted with life and
thought himself too disabled to enjoy the activities he
once had. He went out very little; Maxine did all the
driving and family errands. George took to Cliff immediately, and every time he'd leave the house he'd insist
that Cliff come along.

The first time we took them fishing, Cliff had
trouble getting into the boat because he didn't have
full control of his legs. I was afraid he was going to
fall and really hurt himself. I whispered to George,
"Help him," but George shook his head.

"No, I won't. If he falls down I'll pick him up,

but I won't help him until he does. He's got to learn to do more things for himself."

George's attitude gave Cliff the courage to try harder. Cliff had stopped going out to dinner altogether because his hands shook so badly he was afraid he would spill food all down himself in public. George would say, "Now Cliff, we're all going out to dinner tonight and Maxine's going with us. If you don't want to stay home alone and fix your own dinner, then you'd better come along." And Cliff would.

Within a short time the change in him was remarkable. They were going everywhere with us and Cliff acted like a new man. The four of us had many good times together. We used to spend hours playing a game called Aggravation, which is a complicated version of Chinese Checkers. George played as though his very life depended on winning. He absolutely couldn't stand to lose, especially if Cliff beat him several games in a row.

One night we played until 2 or 3 in the morning and George didn't win a single game. He got so mad at one point he accused Cliff of playing with loaded dice. The next morning when I went to take out the kitchen trash, I found the Aggravation board busted to pieces in the garbage. I took it back inside where George was eating breakfast and said, "Well, I wonder how this happened!"

George grinned sheepishly and admitted he'd smashed it against the kitchen counter the night before while I was getting ready for bed. "I just couldn't stand Cliff beating me like that," he said. "But don't worry, I'll make us a new board."

He and Cliff spent the afternoon in Cliff's garage workshop making *ten* Aggravation boards. We gave some of them to friends, but George kept enough so he could break one when he needed to and still have a supply left.

My father's parents Mama and Papa Pugh were getting up in years, and I wanted to do something nice for them. George and I bought a piece of land behind

Cliff and Maxine's property and built a small trailer court. We named it Tammy's Courts and it's still there today. We bought Mama and Papa Pugh a nice new house trailer and moved them down from Alabama. Billy Wilhite, who had replaced Bill Starnes as George's manager, moved into another trailer in the park to oversee things. Then Mother and Foy moved to Lakeland and we bought them a house, so we had a lot of family around. George was always very good to my relatives. He loved Mama Pugh like his own mother, and she thought the world of him. Mother and Foy are still close to George, and even now there are times when he's drunk and needs a shoulder to cry on that he'll call Mother in the middle of the night.

When George's mother Clara Jones came to visit us from Texas, we decided to take her and Mama Pugh to see greyhound racing. Both old ladies were Pentecostals and very religious, and neither of them believed in smoking, drinking, or gambling. George had box seats at the track, and when we got there Mama Jones looked around and said, "Oh, Glen, if the folks from my church back home ever found out I was here they'd kick me out." She always called her son by his middle name because his father's name was also George. George laughed and promised his mother we wouldn't let word get back to Texas that she'd been to the dog track.

Mama Pugh said she was thirsty, so George ordered her a Screwdriver because they didn't serve soft drinks to people in the box seats. She had never had a drink of alcohol in her entire life, and after a few sips of the vodka and orange juice, she tapped George's shoulder and said, "This thing's done got to my head and I feel plumb funny."

He said, "Well, Mama Pugh, maybe you'd better not drink any more of it."

She said, "Why, what do you mean? I *like* it. It's right refreshing." And she drank the whole thing down.

Mama Jones wouldn't bet on the dogs because she considered gambling a sin. But she'd say, "Glen, that number 7 dog in this race sure is a purty thing. I wouldn't be surprised if he could run real fast." So George would go and bet number 7 for her. If she won she wouldn't take all the money. She'd say, "You just give me the money above what it cost you to play that dog, Glen, 'cause I don't believe in gambling."

We laughed at them all afternoon, but the best was yet to come. We'd made arrangements to meet Maxine and Cliff and the rest of the family at the Hawaiian Village restaurant in Tampa. That was George's favorite place to eat out, and we went there so often everyone knew us. Mother and Foy had already gotten a big table when we arrived, and since George had won at the track that day, he suggested we celebrate with some champagne. When it came Mama Jones took one sip; then she made the awfullest face and said in a loud voice, "Glen, this stuff tastes just like vinegar. I don't know how a body could drink it."

The Hawaiian Village was a typical Polynesian restaurant in decor with a dim, candlelight atmosphere. Mama Jones and Mama Pugh had never been anywhere like it and said it was too dark to read the menu, so George ordered for them. When her food came Mama Jones took one look at the Chinese pea pods and said, "This here is nothing in the world but plain old butter bean hulls and I ain't a eatin' it!" Mama Pugh said it was so dark she couldn't see *what* was on her plate, but it sure looked like a mess. They kept the rest of us in stitches throughout the whole meal.

When we got ready to leave, George told Jack and Foy to go get the cars while he paid the bill. There were about twelve of us so the check was over $150. We had all walked up toward the cash register when we heard Mama Jones call out from the table, "Glen. Ooooooh, Glen. You done gone off and left your money laying here." She had two $20 bills in her hand, waving them up above her head. The restaurant was quiet and other customers had turned around to look at her. George was embarrassed to death, trying to answer her as quietly as possible, but she was all the way across the room, hollering loud enough for everyone to hear.

"Mama, I left that there on purpose," he said. "It's the tip." His face was turning red.

"Well, I *never*." Mrs. Jones shook her head in disbelief. She put the money back on the table and looked around at the other customers. "I always tip the little bag boy when he helps me with my groceries," she told the whole restaurant, "but I don't give him but a quarter." The customers were laughing, but she had no idea what she'd said that was so funny. We got the biggest kick out of her.

I really loved George's mother. She was as good as could be, and I was glad we were still together when she died because it would have broken her heart to see us get a divorce. She knew what it was like, living with a man who had a drinking problem, because George's father had been the same way. When George was drinking she always took up for me, and one time when he was acting particularly ugly she said, "Glen, don't do the things to Tammy that your Daddy did to me. I don't want her having to run out the back door with a brown bag under one arm and a bunch of younguns under the other to get away from you like we used to run from your Daddy when he was drunk. That's no way to live. When your Daddy did finally stop drinking a few years before he died, it was too late because we were too old to enjoy life anymore. Don't let the same thing happen to you and Tammy."

When George was drunk he didn't listen to his mother any more than he listened to anyone else, but when he was sober he remembered the things she told him. He always said, "I hated my father for his drinking and for the miserable life he gave my mother, and yet I do the same thing. It just doesn't make any sense."

But George got drunk only a few times that first year in Lakeland. The worst scene took place back in Nashville when we brought Mother and Foy and Cliff and Maxine with us to the 1969 Disc Jockey Convention. I was nominated again for best female vocalist by the Country Music Association, and I was looking forward to us all going to the awards show. George checked us into three rooms at the Monterey Motel, then said he had to go run a few errands. When several hours passed and I hadn't heard from him, I feared the worst because George always called me frequently when he was out—unless he was drinking. The phone finally rang but it wasn't George. It was the hotel switchboard operator saying she had a message for Mr. Jones. "Tell him the young lady is here to pick him up, and she's waiting in her car in front of the hotel lobby."

I hung up really confused. The phone call meant George was still somewhere in the hotel. But Foy had looked for him in the bar and hadn't seen him anywhere. It also meant George intended going somewhere in the company of a young lady. Well, we'll see about that! I thought.

I went to the lobby and saw a car parked by the front door with a pretty girl behind the wheel. I walked outside and asked her if she was waiting for George Jones. She said, "Yes, who are you?"

"I'm *Mrs.* Jones," I said, "and Mr. Jones won't be joining you today."

She got very flustered and said, "Uh . . . well, you see, he didn't call me himself. My boss told me to come pick up Mr. Jones."

I said, "Well, you go tell your boss Mr. Jones isn't going anywhere with you or anyone else."

She was in such a hurry to get out of there she couldn't get the car started, but she finally pulled away, and I went back into the hotel to try to find George. I learned that the girl worked for an old buddy of George's, Shot Jackson, who owned a music store down on Broadway near Tootsie's Lounge. Shot had rented a room at the Monterey for convention week so he would have a place to entertain prospective clients. George had apparently run into him in the lobby and gone to his room to drink.

I went back to my room to wait, and sure enough,

about ten minutes later George burst through the door, drunk and furious. "How dare you tell *anyone* I'm not leaving here," he yelled. "I go where I please with *who* I please, and don't you forget it!" He grabbed me and knocked me against the wall, then tore out of the room.

I could feel my face beginning to swell up almost immediately, and by the time I got ready to dress for the award show, my cheek had turned bluish-black. I covered it as best I could with makeup, then put on a short wig, pulling the hair close around my face so the swelling wouldn't be so noticeable. Mother, Foy, Cliff, Maxine, and I went on to the show at the Ryman Auditorium.

We had no idea where George was. But about halfway through the show I saw him stagger in and sit down. He was really drunk by then, and knowing how unpredictable that would make him, I couldn't pay attention to the show for watching him. I was so upset I didn't even hear them call out my name as winner of the Best Female Vocalist award. Someone had to nudge me to tell me to go onstage to accept the award.

Winning for the second year in a row was a great honor and I was thrilled about it, but George had spoiled the evening for me. I kept worrying about whether people could look at my face and guess what had happened back at the hotel. I remember standing next to Johnny Cash, that year's winner as Best Male Vocalist, while they were taking pictures, thinking, My bruised face will be all over the papers tomorrow and everyone in Nashville will know George is up to his old tricks again. It was important to me for people to think George had "reformed" since our marriage, and for a long time I wouldn't admit differently to anyone. Of course I couldn't keep his drinking a secret from the band or from our family and close friends in Lakeland, but very few people in Nashville knew he was still going off on drunken binges. But I never doubted that George would reform with time. Especially when I learned we were going to have a baby.

George and I were working the night I realized I was pregnant. We got back to the motel after the show and got undressed and into bed to watch television. He lit up a cigarette and all of a sudden I felt very nauseated. I said, "I don't know what's wrong with me, but you've got to put that thing out. It's making me sick."

George said, "That's strange, cigarettes have never made you sick before."

Then it hit me and I smiled. "Oh, yes they have," I said. "With Gwen, with Jackie, and with Tina."

He sat up, "Oh no, Tammy. I can't believe it. I don't want to get my hopes up. Are you sure?"

I said, "I can't be positive because I never have regular periods, but I have gained some weight and now this awful feeling when I smell cigarettes—what else could it be?"

I had been trying to get pregnant for almost a year, since I had had the miscarriage right after our marriage. After all that time George was afraid to let himself believe it had finally happened. The next night at work, however, he grinned the whole time he was onstage. The guys in the band kept saying, "George, what's wrong with you tonight?" But he wouldn't answer. He just kept grinning.

As soon as we got back to Lakeland, George drove me to my doctor's office. I didn't even have an appointment, but he was so anxious to know for certain that he wanted me to go right away. The doctor knew George was in the waiting room, so after he examined me he handed me a little book and said, "Here. Give this to your husband." I looked at the title. It read "What Every Father Should Know About Babies."

I was so excited I could hardly wait to tell George. But I didn't say a word. Instead I just handed him the book. When he read it he let out a whoop and almost knocked me over, he hugged me so hard. He broke the speed laws driving home to tell Cliff and Maxine; then he stayed on the phone for hours, talking to all his relatives in Texas and anyone else he could think of to call. When Billy Sherrill heard, he said he knew the "bloodlines" were good so he wanted the pick of the litter. "And whether it's a girl or a boy I'll have a recording contract waiting to be signed the day it's born," he told George.

I had never seen a prospective father more thrilled. You would have thought George Jones was the first man in history to sire a child. He wasn't around to see his other children grow up because his first wife had divorced him while he was in the service, when their daughter Susan was still an infant. George was only eighteen then, nothing but a kid himself, and he hadn't gotten to know Susan until she was nearly grown. He used to say that his two sons by his second wife Shirley had grown up "behind his back" while he was on the road, so he was looking forward to the experience of being a father as much as a man who'd never had children. The fact that he was almost forty might have had something to do with his excitement too. Having a baby at middle age made him feel young again.

I was just as happy as he was, but for different reasons. I wanted George's baby because I loved him and knew how much he wanted a child. But I also thought a baby would supply the motivation he needed to stop drinking. He was a good father to my children, and I was confident he would be even better with one of his own around. We all waited for the baby with great anticipation.

Meanwhile, George had big plans for the whole family, and as usual his enthusiasm for a new project soon rubbed off on me.

Chapter 7

$\mathcal{L}$ ET'S take a drive. I've got something I want to show you." I was sitting out by the pool behind our house in Lakeland when George called from the back door. I knew my husband well enough to recognize that mysterious tone in his voice. It meant he had found something he wanted to buy—probably something very expensive—and he was after my approval. It's probably another antique car, or a new boat, I thought. He had started collecting old cars, which had become a fun hobby for him, and he'd been talking for some time about wanting to buy a larger fishing boat.

He wouldn't even give me a hint where we were going as we drove toward the outskirts of town, but when we were about twelve miles out, he turned down a long private road, lined on both sides by citrus groves. By this time my curiosity was killing me. Then as we approached a clearing, I could see a huge old colonial house, surrounded by oak trees so enormous they had to be several hundred years old. Their branches were heavy with moss that hung in thick tangles almost to the ground. George pulled up and stopped by the steps leading to a wide veranda where six white columns rose to the overhanging roof. The place looked more like the Civil War South than Florida. You expected to see "Mammie" stick her head out of a second-story window and yell "Miss Scarlet, Miss Scarlet."

I was asking questions a mile a minute, but George just smiled and led the way to the front door. A real estate man was there to show us through sixteen large rooms which included six bedrooms, a study, a formal dining room, a game and recreation room, and an old-fashioned kitchen larger than the entire apartment where I'd lived in Birmingham. The rooms had twenty-foot ceilings and hand-carved woodwork, but the place was dark and gloomy and badly in need of repair. One upstairs bedroom had been painted bright turquoise with orange woodwork, and there were psychedelic drawings all over the walls. The hardwood floors, which were dull and marred, creaked beneath us, and the kitchen had no modern conveniences at all. Although you could tell the old house had once been elegant and majestic, it was now shabby and uninviting.

"We could get this house and five acres for just $100,000," George said hopefully. "Don't you love the old place? Isn't it something? And later on we can buy the thirty-eight surrounding acres."

It's *something,* all right, something that would cost a fortune to fix up, I thought. No, I didn't love it. I didn't even like it. Those big, old, high-ceilinged rooms and the creaky floors gave me the willies. I was perfectly content in our comfortable, smaller house next door to Maxine and Cliff. What did we need with this huge place? Admittedly the outside was impressive, but it was so run down it looked more like Tara *after* the Yankees marched through Georgia.

I said, "George just look at the shape this place is in!"

"Don't think about the way it is now," he said. He was looking around with that gleam in his eye that meant he was dying to get his hands on it. "Use your imagination. You know how I love to decorate. I could make this the most beautiful home you've ever seen in your life."

"And that would cost at least as much as the price of the house," I reminded him.

He smiled as though he'd been waiting to hear that. "You're right," he said, "but I intend to make it pay for itself!"

"George Jones, what have you got up your sleeve now?" I asked, knowing I was about to hear some new scheme of his.

"With this much land I could build a country music park that people from all over the South would come to see." He spoke excitedly. "There's a natural bowl about half a mile from the house that would be a perfect setting for a stage with bleachers going up on three sides. With the warm climate here we could have outdoor shows year round and get the best acts in country music to come here to perform. And I could make the grounds into a tropical park where families would come and bring picnic lunches and spend the whole day. There's nothing like it around Lakeland. It could be a gold mine." I had never seen George more enthusiastic. "And think what a great old house this would be for the kids and the new baby to grow up in. There are stables out back where we could keep ponies, and there are peacocks and chickens and guinea hens running wild all over the place. If I started working on it soon, I could have the house ready to move into by the time the baby comes. What do you think?"

It was hard not to be infected by George's enthusiasm, but the idea of getting involved in such a big project made me uneasy. It would take every dime we could get our hands on to swing it financially. Then, what if the park wasn't the success he thought it would be? We could lose everything!

"Please, George. Let's think about it for a while," I begged.

But I could tell he had already made up his mind.

He told the real estate man we'd be in touch. Then all the way home he kept describing the things he wanted to do with the park. He had once built a rodeo-type arena with bleachers down on his property in Texas where he held country music shows periodically. He had had a lot of fun running it and made some money too, and that had given him the idea for a large scale operation like the one he wanted to build in Lakeland.

I held out for nearly a month, but George was determined to have his park, so I told him to call the realtor and buy the darn thing. If nothing else, I told myself, it would keep him too busy to think about drinking.

When the offer we made was accepted, George was as happy as a kid at the county fair. He named our new homestead Old Plantation Park and immediately threw himself into a dozen projects at once, redecorating the house, landscaping the grounds, building a stage and bleachers. He spent $150,000 on trees and shrubbery alone. He had royal palms imported from South America and planted every three feet along the half-mile path from the house to the park. He planted flower beds; he had two fish ponds built in the shape of guitars with lush foliage all around them; he hung big sturdy swings from the thick branches of the old oak trees and cleared out all the undergrowth that was running wild through the orange groves.

The house itself was a beehive of activity. Workmen were everywhere: tearing out the old kitchen, stripping floors and walls, replastering and painting. The basic structure proved to be sounder than it looked. The house had been built in the 1800s by a millionaire lumberman who used only the best materials available. It had originally stood on Lake Mirror in downtown Lakeland, where it had become a local landmark. Then the city acquired the property and decided to put a new Chamber of Commerce building on it. A local dentist offered to move the old house to land he owned out of town, so they gave it to him just to keep from having to tear it down. It cost the dentist $20,000 to have the house moved. Then he put in all new electrical wiring and plumbing and added a new roof. He had lived in it with his family for several years before financial setbacks had forced him to put it on the market. I prayed the same thing wouldn't happen to us!

George not only had his hands full with redoing the house and grounds; he was also battling local authorities over zoning laws that prevented us from turning the property into a commercial park. He hit one legal snag after another, and he would storm around the house cussing all the officials involved, as well as the residents of the area who didn't want a park there. Then he'd make a little progress and get all enthused and excited all over again, determined not to give up until he'd seen his dream come true. When we went out on the road to work, his heart wasn't in it. He ate, slept, and talked his music park, and anything that kept him away from working on it was an irritation. He was working against a deadline on the house because he wanted it ready for the new baby.

My doctor had told me not to work past my seventh month of pregnancy, and even though George had more than enough to occupy his mind, I was still nervous about leaving him on the road by himself. He had gotten accustomed to having me with him, and I knew my presence was a great deterrent to his drinking, even though he did slip off and get drunk now and then. Since I'd been cooking on the bus for him he hadn't been drinking as much. He hated truck stop food, so he would rather have a drink than eat it unless he was starving to death. After two or three drinks he didn't care about food, just more drinking. But if good home cooking was available he'd fill up on that and drink a lot less.

Sometimes our meals on the road became a real event. On one of my last trips out before the baby, we went to Washington State. We were driving over mountain roads all day, and George had warned me that it would take dried pinto beans much longer to cook in a high altitude. I had put the pintos on early that morning, but they still weren't done until way after dark. We were all starved by the time I had dinner ready, so our driver pulled off into a picnic area by the road, and we sat around and ate ourselves sick. It couldn't have been a simpler meal—fried cornbread, pinto beans, and salad—but it tasted fantastic! The cool mountain air made us so hungry we woke up the next morning ready to stuff ourselves again. There were no roadside restaurants anywhere nearby—by this time we were in Oregon—so I decided to try a first and cook breakfast on the bus. With the band, the driver, Harold, Patsy, George, and myself there were eleven to feed, so I cooked up all the bacon and sausage and eggs we had. I didn't have any bread for toast so I put cheese on top of the fried cornbread left over from the night before and broiled it. Then I fried potatoes and cooked up a pot of grits. We stopped again at a roadside park and had another feast. The boys said it was the best breakfast they'd ever eaten. We all gained about five pounds on that trip!

I knew there wouldn't be any meals like that with me back home in Lakeland, and I was worried about George getting bored and restless, and drinking just to pass the time. When it came close to the first weekend he was supposed to go out without me, he became more and more depressed. He kept coming up with excuses to cancel the shows, and I kept reminding him that we'd be sued if he did.

Two days before he was to leave, I secretly called our lead guitar player Charlie Carter in Texas. I asked if he and our drummer Freddie Haws would fly to Lakeland and spend the night with us, then fly out with George the next day to meet the bus in Iowa where they were booked. I told Charlie that George was down in the dumps, and I was afraid he'd go off and get drunk if I sent him out alone. I guess I was treating George like a baby, but the signs that he was getting ready to tie one on were all there: restlessness, depression, a sour disposition. Charlie agreed to fly in with Freddie the following day. George was genuinely happy to see them and I felt relieved. Now he'd have some company and I knew I could count on the boys to keep an eye on him. When I saw them off at the airport the next morning, it felt strange not to be going with them. But the baby was due in less than a month, and I knew I had to follow the doctor's orders.

About 2 o'clock that afternoon the phone rang. I picked it up expecting to hear George's voice on the line. Instead it was Charlie.

"He's gone," he said flatly.

"What do you mean he's gone?" I asked.

"George is gone," he repeated. "He just disappeared. We had a couple of drinks on the plane but he wasn't anywhere near drunk. When we got off in Chicago to change planes he said he was going to the bathroom, so Freddie and I waited. But he never came out. When I went in to look for him, he was gone."

I could tell Charlie felt bad enough about what had happened without me fussing about it. So I told him to notify Hap Peebles, the promoter, that George was missing and might not show up that night. "You and Freddie go ahead to the date in case he does get there," I said, "and call me if you hear anything."

George didn't show up that night or the next, so the boys went on home Sunday, and I kept a constant vigil by the phone. When Hap Peebles phoned to ask what had happened to George, I begged him not to sue for the broken dates and promised we'd make them up free of charge after the baby came. That marked the beginning of my promising promoters free dates when George skipped out on bookings; it was a practice that continued throughout the rest of our marriage. I couldn't count how many free shows I did during the next four years, and George never once took it seriously. He'd laugh and say, "What the hell do you care if they sue me? It's not you they're suing." But since it was the "George Jones and Tammy

Wynette Show," I felt I had a responsibility to see that the bookers got what they contracted for, and I considered a lawsuit against my husband a reflection on me too.

The first day George was missing I walked the floor and worried myself sick. The second day I got mad. When Carter got back to Texas he called to say he'd heard a rumor George was down there, but he didn't know where. I told him to let me know if he heard anything more.

It was hurricane season in Florida, that muggy, sticky, late September heat when the barometer drops so low you can feel the pressure closing in on you, and the air seems thick enough to cut with a knife. I felt big and clumsy and the weather made me even more miserable. I was feeling more than a little sorry for myself and I was furious with George. How could he do this to me with our baby due at any time? For all I knew he was lying dead in a gutter somewhere. I thought, What if the baby comes early and I have to go to the hospital, and they ask me where my husband can be reached? What could I say? Your guess is as good as mine?

By the fifth night I was a wreck. Still no word from George and having friends check his old familiar haunts in Texas and Nashville failed to turn up anything. I was tossing and turning in bed long after midnight, trying to get comfortable enough to sleep, when the phone rang. A soft-spoken male voice said, "Tammy, I can't tell you who I am, but I'm calling for George. He just wanted me to tell you that he's okay." I could hear music and the sound of men and women talking and laughing in the background. He was obviously calling from a party.

"Where is my husband?" I demanded.

"Oh, I can't tell you that," the man chuckled. "George wouldn't like it if I told you that, but don't you worry. He's just fine."

I said, "I can't believe you would do this to a woman who's lying here ready to have a baby any day and doesn't even know where her husband is or when he'll be home again. How would I reach him if I had to go to the hospital?" By this time I was on the verge of tears.

"Sorry, but I can't say any more." His voice was smug, and I hated him even though I had no idea who he was. "I have to hang up now." The line went dead.

I lay there in the dark, crying one minute, furious the next, until anger and tears had exhausted me, and I could see the first light of dawn coming through my window.

Mother was coming that day to take the girls home with her until after the baby was born, and Jack and Earleen had gone to Birmingham to visit relatives. I knew I'd be more alone than ever with everyone gone. The house seemed deathly quiet that afternoon, and I thought I'd go crazy if I didn't get out of it. Just as I started to go next door to visit Cliff and Maxine, the phone rang. It was George's sister Lois calling from Beaumont, Texas.

"Tammy," she began hesitantly, embarrassed about the circumstances that had hade it necessary to call. "I don't exactly know how to tell you this, but I woke up this morning and found George passed out on my front porch. Evidently someone dropped him off here late last night because there's no car parked outside. I couldn't wake him and I got worried, so I called a doctor to come over. He said George was drugged, but he would probably be okay after he slept it off."

Drugged? I was shocked. George never used drugs. I'd seen him take a diet pill once in a while if he'd had a rough night and couldn't get started the next day, but that was the extent of his involvement with drugs. "How is he now?" I asked.

"He's conscious," she answered. "But he's got a terrible hangover. He wanted me to call you to ask if he can come home, but frankly I don't think he's up to a plane trip. He should probably stay in bed at least one more day. He says someone must have slipped him something in his drinks because he doesn't remember taking any drugs. Do you think I should keep him here or what?"

"Yes, keep him another day," I told her. "Just let me know when you put him on the plane, and I'll pick him up at the airport."

George arrived home late the next afternoon, looking like something the cat drug in. I felt sorry for him in spite of myself. Nothing was mentioned about his escapade. He kept asking how I felt, if I thought the baby had dropped yet, had I been eating right, etc., but he didn't offer any information about where he'd been or with whom, and I didn't ask. I didn't want to start a scene that would have him running off again, and after seven days of worry and very little sleep, I was just too tired to argue. I knew that I would be in the hospital having a baby within a few days, and I didn't want a cloud of tension hanging over us at a time that should be one of the happiest we could possibly share.

I didn't learn what had happened during those seven lost days until months later when we were playing a date in Dallas. Bob and Evelyn Van, a couple I'd met through George, came backstage to see us after the show. When I went out to the bus to change clothes, Evelyn went with me. We were no sooner alone than she started talking about George's spree in Texas. Evelyn is a lot like I am. If she's with somebody she likes, she'll blabber on and on and end up putting her foot in her mouth without even knowing it.

"Tammy," she said, "I'm so sorry about that Houston thing a few months ago."

Female intuition told me I could learn a lot if I kept quiet, so I pretended to know all about it. "Well, don't worry, Evelyn," I answered. "You certainly couldn't have prevented it. I know how George is when he's drinking."

"I'm so relieved to hear you say that," she went on. "I did try. He was with Link Davis when he called us. He said he had run into Link by accident when he was changing planes in the Chicago airport, and they had decided to come to Texas and party. And boy, were they partying!"

I had heard the boys in the band mention Link Davis's name but I had never met him. I remembered someone saying he had been a running buddy of George's. I asked Evelyn to describe this Link to me.

"Oh, he's a heavyset gray-haired man," she said. "He walks with a limp and has a soft voice, almost feminine sounding."

So that was who had called to tell me George was all right!

"George and Link hit all the clubs," she continued, "and every night George would end up inviting the heavy drinkers to come back to the hotel with them. The night Bob and I stopped by to check on him he had half a dozen people in his room, and they were all drunk. That ole girl Fran, who George used to date, was there too. It made me so mad I told Bob he had to stay there all night if necessary to make sure nothing happened. I said, 'You're not going off and leaving George by himself with that girl, and him drunk. Lord, Tammy's at home about to have a baby and I'll bet she doesn't even know where he is.' Bob did stay but he needn't have. He said George passed out cold before the night was half over and the girl went home. The next day Bob tried to get George to come to our house, but he wouldn't do it. Then we called back a few hours later and they had checked out. The next thing we heard someone had dropped George off at his sister's house, so I figured he was safe then."

I didn't tell George about my conversation with Evelyn. What was the point of bringing it up? You can't change the past by stirring up the present. But a few weeks later we were working Panther Hall in Fort Worth, and something happened that made me so mad I brought it up anyway. Before the show George and I were sitting in the front of the bus on the sofa when the door opened, and a man I'd never seen stepped inside. He said, "Hi George," then turned to me. "Well, hello Tammy. How are you?" I recognized his voice immediately. And he fit the description Evelyn had given me. It was Link Davis!

Before he could take another step I stood up and said, "Get off this bus right now. I know who you are, and you'll never again have a chance to call me in the middle of the night and refuse to tell me where my husband is when I need him." George turned ash white. Link Davis didn't say a word. He just backed off the bus with his mouth hanging open. I haven't laid eyes on him since. I was so mad that for once it was George who was concerned about calming *me* down.

"I'm sorry, Tammy. Please forgive me," he pleaded. "You don't know how I regretted what I did when I ran off like that. By the time I got to Texas I wanted to turn around and come home, but I was afraid you'd kick me out if I did, so I just got drunker and drunker to forget about the mess I was in. Please, don't be mad at me now. It was a long time ago and I promise you I'll never do anything like that again."

Later that night George asked me how I'd known Link Davis when I saw him. "I recognized his voice," I said. "You don't forget a voice that calls you in the middle of the night when you're pregnant and worried sick. I promised myself then that if I ever ran into the man behind that voice, I'd tell him what I thought of him." George was amazed. He never knew I'd had a little help from Evelyn.

Since I hadn't nagged George about running off when he got home from Texas, things had smoothed over between us by the time the baby was born a week later. Mild labor pains woke me up around midnight. I lay there timing the contractions for a while, thinking it wasn't necessary to wake George up until they got closer together. Suddenly he rolled over, got up off the bed, and started feeling his way toward the bathroom. He looked so funny. Any time he went to the bathroom in the middle of the night he would grope his way in darkness without opening his eyes, because he said if he opened them and saw light he couldn't get to sleep again. I watched him fumble his way back to bed and sink down into his pillow, knowing he'd be asleep again in two seconds if I didn't start waking him up.

"Don't go back to sleep, George," I said. I nudged him. "My labor has started and we're going to have to go to the hospital soon."

He sat up with his eyes still closed. "What? What? What?"

I laughed. "Open your eyes, George; it's me." He was already lying back down. "Get up now. We have to get dressed." I had half expected George to go to pieces when it came time to go to the hospital because it had been so long since he'd been through the experience of becoming a father, and this baby meant so much to him. But he calmly swung his feet over the side of the bed, then sat there for a minute holding his head in his hands.

"You okay?" he mumbled.

"Yes, I'm fine," I assured him. "Now let's get ready to go. I'll call the doctor and you get your clothes on."

He walked across to the closet and turned on the light. It will hit him any minute, I thought, and he'll panic. But he rummaged around the closet a minute, then called out, "Where's my avocado green pants and the green and white shirt that goes with it?" I laughed to myself, Now that's typical George Jones. Even at a time like this he has to be dressed just right! He was the only man I ever knew who wore coordinated tennis outfits to mow the lawn. I could hear him pushing hangers around.

"They're in there somewhere," I said. "Just keep looking."

He finally found the pants and shirt he wanted. I was ready by the time he got dressed, and he remembered to grab my suitcase on the way out. He drove to the hospital at a slow, steady speed, not rushed or nervous in the least. I thought, Well, he sure fooled me! He talked about the oranges in the groves along the highway being ready to pick and about the dew being so heavy he had to turn on the windshield wipers. He couldn't have been more relaxed if we'd been out for a Sunday drive.

My doctor had alerted the hospital, and since we were the only "celebrities" Lakeland had, we were met at the emergency entrance by half a dozen nurses and a wheelchair. When George jumped out of the car he left it running, windshield wipers and all.

They took me to the labor room and led George to a room right across the hall from me. He called my grandmother and my aunt and uncle and told them to meet him in the father's waiting room one floor down. Meanwhile he started drinking one cup of coffee after another.

My obstetrician, Dr. S. L. Watson, was running between the two rooms, checking on me, then checking on George. "I think he's in worse shape than you are." He laughed. I told him how calm George had been getting there and he said, "Well, the minute you were out of his sight he started coming apart. He's not even sure I can handle the delivery!" Dr. Watson had recently had a heart attack and sometimes, if he was very tired, his hand would shake. George had seen a newspaper rattling in his hand and it scared him to death. "He turned white," Dr. Watson reported, "and wanted to know if I thought we should call in another doctor to assist. I told him I'd been delivering babies for forty years and I thought I could handle this one, but I don't think he's convinced."

About an hour and a half later I was ready to be taken into the delivery room. George grasped my hand for a minute as they wheeled me past him. Then he rushed off to the elevator and down to the next floor to tell my relatives I was about to deliver. By this time he was so excited he was about to explode. He burst into the father's waiting room, jumped in the air, and clicked his heels together. "Hot a 'mighty!" he exclaimed. "She's having it right now!" He looked around grinning, fully expecting to see Earleen and Jack and Mama Pugh sitting there; instead, a room full of strang-

STAND BY YOUR MAN

The house where I was born.

My father and mother, Hollice and Mildred Lee Pugh.

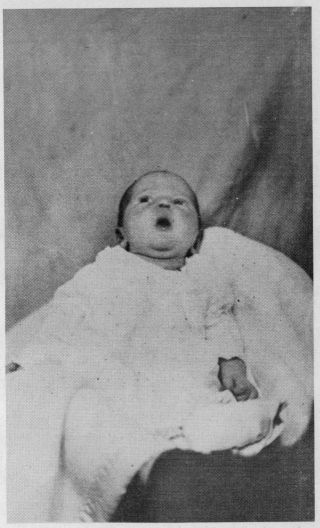

May, 1942. At the age of two weeks—mouth open as usual.

My mother and father (top row), with my grandmother, my aunt,
Carolyn Jetton, and my grandfather, Chester Russell.

With my mother and her sister, Carolyn Jetton. Taken at home by my grandfather.

At 13, with my mother and my stepfather, Foy Lee.

In 1959, when I won all-star basketball honors. With a friend, Era Lee Osburn.

At a talent contest in 1958. We were the Blackwood Bros. Quartet. From left: Margaret Stanphill, Betty Canup, Claudette Russell (my cousin), Imogene Patterson, and me.

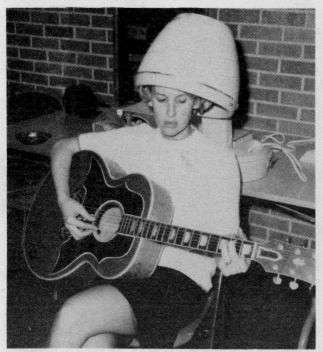
Practicing two weeks after coming to Nashville.

With my producer, Billy Sherrill, recording my second song, "Your Good Girl's Gonna Go Bad."

My home, fifteen years ago. Jackie, my daughter,
was born here.

Before the fireplace where I used to cook.

My house in Nashville.

My living room.

The master bedroom.

Before . . .

and after.
Quite a change!

Performing on stage, eight months pregnant with Georgette.

In 1973, with George Jones at the Grand Ole Opry in Nashville.

My "Greatest Hits" volume one—the first collection by a female country western singer to sell a million copies.

The entrance to
Lakeland Park.

Looking out at the crowd at a Lakeland Park show.

With Burt Reynolds in Atlanta, Ga., at the opening of his restaurant, called "Burt's Place."

In July of 1976, I was invited to perform at the White House for President and Mrs. Ford and all the foreign ambassadors. I performed with Roger Miller and Ella Fitzgerald. By the way, I danced with the President!

My grandparents, Mr. and Mrs. Chester Russell, on their fiftieth anniversary.

My pilot, Bernie Lentz, alongside my plane. This photograph was taken in December, 1977. He lost his life in a plane crash on January 3, 1978. A man we loved and trusted.

With my husband, George Richey, on our wedding day,
July 6, 1978.

With my husband and children, from left: Tina (13), Deirdre (14), Georgette (7), Kelly (12), Jackie (16), and Gwen (17).

My aunt, Carolyn Jetton, and her husband, Gerald. She was the matron of honor at our wedding.

My mother and stepfather, Mr. and Mrs. Foy Lee, taken at home in Jupiter.

My bus, after it burned in July, 1978.

At a news conference on October 6, 1978, at the Carolina Coliseum in Columbia, South Carolina. This was my first appearance after my abduction, and my face shows the bruises.

With my husband, George Richey, record producer and writer.

Our home in Jupiter, Fla. My hideaway is 75 feet from the ocean on an island, and has seven bedrooms and a pool.

Jupiter, Fla. Our house is in the last row on the right, fifth from the bottom.

ers stared back at him. My relatives hadn't arrived yet! George told me later that those expectant fathers looked at him like he was crazy. He said he'd never been so embarrassed in his life, so he just backed out and closed the door behind him!

I desperately wanted a boy because I thought George wanted another son. My delivery was easy compared to what I'd gone through with Jackie, and after that last final push I said, "Is it a boy? Is it a boy?"

Dr. Watson held her up by her heels for me to see. "No honey, it's another girl. But she's a beauty."

"Ooooooooooh," I moaned. "Please don't tell me it's a girl. I *don't want* a girl. I want a boy!" I was half drunk from the medication they'd given me and I started crying. I was so sure George would be disappointed.

I vaguely remember being wheeled to my room after the delivery. George told me later I kept apologizing to him for having a girl. He leaned over the bed and kissed me and said, "Oh, honey, you don't know how happy you've made me. I wanted a girl all along because I wasn't around when Susan was a baby, but I thought *you* didn't want a girl because you already had three. That's why I said I wanted a boy. Wait till you see our daughter. She's the prettiest little thing in the whole nursery."

They made George leave the room when they brought the baby in to be nursed so I had my first good look at her alone. When she opened her little eyes and looked up at me, I laughed out loud with tears running down my face. It was like looking at a miniature George Jones. As the old country saying goes, she was his "spittin' image." There was no mistaking those close-set brown eyes that are a Jones trademark. When George came back into the room I said, "She looks just like her Daddy. And she sure has the Jones eyes."

"Oh, I didn't notice that," he answered in a casual way. "I don't think she looks like me."

But later, when he thought I had dozed off, I heard him talking on the phone to his mother in Texas. "You ought to see her, Mama! She looks just like me! She's a Jones all right. There's no denying that!" You never heard a prouder father.

We named her Tamala Georgette Jones for obvious reasons, and by nightfall she had already become the star of the nursery. In the next few days it seemed as though the entire city of Lakeland turned out to see her. Visitors were lined up outside the nursery window every time it opened, taking flash pictures and pushing at one another to get a better view. The nurses finally had to move Georgette's bassinet way in the back and put up a sign warning people against using flashbulbs in front of the baby's eyes. George and I never could get up to the window to see her together, so they had to let him come in the room when I nursed her even though it was against hospital rules. It was the only way he could see his baby.

Two weeks after we brought Georgette home from the hospital, we moved into the Old Plantation house. George had put the finishing touches on his decorating while I was in the hospital and he had done a fabulous job. The day we moved in I walked from room to room, ooohing and aaahing like Cinderella touring the Prince's palace. Our bedroom was decorated almost exactly like the one we'd slept in the first time we were together back at his home in Nashville. It was done in red, black, and white with a carved mahogany, wooden-canopied, king-sized Spanish bed. When I bent over to lay Georgette down I saw a huge plaque framed in red velvet hanging above the headboard. "That's your homecoming present," George said when he saw my surprise. On it were engraved three love poems he had written for Georgette and me, and I cried before I had finished reading them.

Very few people ever saw the sentimental side of George Jones, and since he's such a private man I knew it hadn't been easy for him to display his deepest feelings on a wall plaque. That gift meant more to me than all the hundreds of thousands of dollars worth of jewelry, furs, and cars he gave me over the years.

No man was ever more generous about buying gifts than George. He was an impulsive spender and never asked the price of anything. His philosophy was "if you have to ask, you can't afford it." He wouldn't have dreamed of quibbling over a price, even when he knew he could get something cheaper if he bargained. Once in Los Angeles he bought me two diamond and emerald dinner rings at an auction because he couldn't decide which one he liked best. He wrote out a check for $36,000 and didn't bat an eye.

But the plaque was something he had put himself into, and I treasured it more than if it had been the Hope diamond. It became a symbol of our marriage, and I couldn't begin to count the times that plaque saved us from a bad argument. We'd go to bed mad with each other over some disagreement, neither one of us talking, and George would lean over and whisper in the dark, "You gonna love me when I'm old, Tammy?" It broke the silence every time! Of course there were other nights when I lay in bed alone, with George out drunk somewhere, thinking bitterly that the damn plaque wasn't worth the wood it was made on.

Georgette had her own nursery at the Plantation House with a door opening into our room, but Daddy didn't want his baby in another room. He moved her baby bed into our room, right beside our bed, but even that didn't suit him. He wanted her in bed with us, and that's where she ended up every night for the first few months. By that time she was spoiled to death, and when I'd try to put her in the crib she'd pull herself up and shake the bars and holler until one of us picked her up. The minute she saw me or George coming to get her, she'd stop crying, hold out her little arms, and giggle and coo. As soon as we'd lay her down on "her place" between us, she'd fall right to sleep with no trouble at all.

Some nights when she fussed from the crib I'd say, "George, just let her cry for a while. If we don't pick her up for two or three nights she'll break the habit of sleeping with us." But he couldn't stand it, and two minutes later he'd be up getting her.

George was never what you'd call a disciplinarian with any of the children. I think he spanked Tina once in the six years we were together, and he never laid a hand on the other girls. When Georgette reached the age where she was into everything, I would sometimes have to spank her little hand and scold her. George would get up and leave the room. He couldn't take it.

Georgette never did move into her own room. When she got older she made the rounds at night, sleeping with us some, or with MeeMaw and PeePaw if they were spending the night, or with Gwen or Jackie or Tina (even today Georgette can't stand to sleep alone). Gwen and Jackie thought the new baby was their own little live doll, and they argued over whose turn it was to change her diapers or give her a bottle. If I had let them, they would have changed her clothes fifty times a day. Tina was a little jealous at first because she had been the baby before Georgette came along, but when she realized she was still going to get her share of attention she got over it.

Tina started school the same year Georgette was born. By that time we knew for certain that the meningitis had not left her mentally retarded in any way. She did have brain damage because skull X rays showed a dark spot the size of a half-dollar behind her left ear, but this affected her nervous system, not her ability to learn.

She was a hyperactive child, impatient and harder to control than the other girls, but the doctor said she would probably outgrow these symptoms in time, and she has. He put her on Ritalin the first year she was in school to calm her down. Hyperactive children respond to amphetamines or "uppers" the way a normal child will respond to a tranquilizer. Ritalin did calm her, but the side effects were not good; she complained of stomach cramps and sometimes would sit around like she was half asleep, so I took her off the medication. Her teachers complained that she would not pay attention in class and said she was disturbing the other children, so I put her into a private school for slow learners, and once she was able to learn at her own pace she was fine. Today she's a normal, healthy, active teenager, a cheerleader at her school and also a member of the basketball team. She's still headstrong and hard to control at times, but then so was I as a teenager.

One of the first things Tina learned in school was how to print her name. Her legal name was Tina Byrd, but she signed everything Tina Jones. One day she came home from school in tears and climbed up on George's lap sobbing. "The teacher says I can't sign my name Jones. She'll give me bad marks if I do, and I don't want to sign my name Byrd because my name is *Jones.*"

George looked at me with a pained expression on his face. Then he petted her and told her not to worry about it anymore. "Your Mama and me will take care of that."

When we were alone he said, "What they're doing to Tina in school is not fair. I can't stand to see her hurt like that. I'm the only Daddy she knows and I feel like your girls are mine anyway, so why don't I just adopt them if Euple Byrd doesn't protest?" When Euple didn't come forth in the allotted time, the judge gave his consent for the adoption.

The day we got the news George couldn't wait for Tina to get home from school so he could tell her. She came bouncing into the kitchen where he was sitting at the table. He called her over and sat her on his lap. "Tina, I've got a surprise for you. Tomorrow you can go to school and write Jones on all your papers because it is legally your name. I'm your Daddy now."

She just looked up at him with those big almond-shaped eyes and said, "I thought you already was."

To Tina the piece of paper didn't make a bit of difference. She had already made up her mind that George was her Daddy. But the older girls did understand "adoption" and they were thrilled to death the day their new birth certificates arrived in the mail.

George and I were scheduled to make our Las Vegas debut on my birthday, and I was really nervous about it. The audiences there are different, more sophisticated, and I didn't know if they'd enjoy a show like ours. And George was even more worried than I was, and started drinking two or three days before we were due to leave. We had been booked for two weeks at the Landmark Hotel, so I wanted to get there ahead of time to make sure the lighting crew had their cues and to let our band rehearse long enough to get used to the sound system.

The day I was supposed to leave, George refused to come with me, but I went on anyway, hoping he would follow in time for opening night. George's daughter Susan was staying with us, and she promised to keep an eye on him. I knew the people who book Vegas hotels wouldn't waste time on acts who didn't show or didn't put on a good show, so I was even more worried than usual about George getting there.

The day before the opening George slipped off and no one knew where he'd gone. I had everybody I could think of out looking for him. Finally Susan called to say she had tracked him down in Tampa. He had agreed to fly to Vegas if she would come with him. I said, "Get him here as quick as you can."

His flight was to arrive at 6 P.M. and we were to go on at 9:30 P.M. But Susan called back at 4 to say he'd given her the slip again. "We got as far as the Tampa airport," she explained. "After he bought the tickets he excused himself to go to the bathroom, and that's the last I saw of him."

I remembered the time he'd run out on Freddie and Charlie in the Chicago airport and ended up in Texas. "He could be anywhere by now," I told her. "Just get on the flight and come on without him."

I don't remember ever being as scared on an opening night as I was on that one. Al Gallico had flown in from New York and Billy Sherrill was there from Nashville, and they were both trying to reassure me that I could carry the show without George, but nothing they could have said at that point would have made me feel any better. The late comedian Jack E. Leonard, whom I had never met, heard about my predicament and volunteered to open the show for me, even though he had his own performance down the Strip at the Riviera later that night. My knees were shaking so hard when they announced my name that I was certain I'd never make it to the center of the stage without falling on my face. What if I opened my mouth and no sound came out? "Oh God, please help me get through the next hour and I'll never ask for another thing," I prayed.

My teeth were chattering; I had chills; I felt like I was going to throw up any second. I would have given everything I owned to be anywhere else in the world. I don't even remember getting through the first number. I think I was in shock. By the middle of the second song I was just beginning to relax enough to be able to focus my eyes and hear the sound of my own voice when all of a sudden the house lights came up. Oh, my God, I thought, what have I done wrong? Is it so bad they're stopping the show *now?* For a moment there was dead silence. Then, as if by a signal, the entire audience stood up. Someone was rolling a giant cake out onstage. My birthday! I had forgotten all about it. The whole room began singing "Happy Birthday," and tears streamed down my face. Then I looked out and saw a tall man stepping across the tops of the tables to reach the stage. It was Jimmy Dean! He jumped onstage, picked me up, twirled me around, and kissed me on the forehead. "I love you even if Jones didn't make it tonight," he said. I thought that was darn nice of a guy I'd never even met before!

Dean agreed to sing a song while I got control of myself, and having him up there for a few minutes helped me get it together enough to finish the show. Afterward he waited backstage with Susan. "You did a great job and they loved you," he told me, "so don't worry about Jones not being here. Come on out with me tonight and let's celebrate your birthday. Maybe George will show up tomorrow." So Jimmy Dean took me and Susan out on the town. We saw two or three shows, including a topless one, which was a new experience for me. I was a little embarrassed, but fascinated nevertheless!

If I'd ever had any doubts about the guys in my band being protective I sure learned that night. Every time I looked around in a casino or at a show I'd spot a couple of my boys nearby. It soon became obvious that they were following us. When Jimmy took us back to our hotel we dropped Susan off at her door first, then walked on down the hall to my door. I heard footsteps behind us and turned around to see Sonny Curtis and Freddie Haws strolling by very casually. I don't know if Jimmy noticed what was going on, but I laughed to myself and pretended not to see them. He said goodnight, then left. I waited about two minutes, then opened my door again and said, "And goodnight to you, too, boys!" Sonny and Freddie had just started to walk away. They turned around and grinned like they thought they'd really put one over.

The next morning I got a call from Shorty Lavender in Nashville. He said he was going to fly to Florida and find George. He called from our house about noon and said George was there, drinking a little, but not too drunk to work. "Look, it's all I can do to get him to agree to come," he said, "because he's scared to death to face that Vegas audience. He says they won't like him because he's so country. So please don't jump on him about last night when we get there, or he'll use that as an excuse to go off and get drunk."

I met them at the airport at 6 P.M., and we went straight back to the hotel so George could rehearse with the band. They worked for three hours and afterward George felt much better about going on. That night he put on a terrific show and the audience loved him, just as we'd all known they would. Afterward he said, "Well, I can't imagine what I was afraid of. It's just like working Texas, except the money's better and we can lay out in the sun all day."

He made every show after that, and things went fine until closing night. We had booked a 7:15 A.M. flight out the next morning so we could get home and get ready to leave for a show in Texas the following day. But George ran into a drinking buddy after the last show and decided to stay out all night.

I found him at 4 A.M. playing blackjack in the Landmark casino. When I walked over to him he yelled, "Get outta here. You're gonna change my luck." By that time he was drunk. When he stood up to push me away, he knocked over his stool. Before he could reach me one of the pit bosses had him in a full nelson. He was struggling, knocking chips and cards all over the place, but the guy was so strong George couldn't shake him off. They kicked him out of the casino and told him not to come back.

I knew he wouldn't show up for the rest of the night, so I told Mother and Foy, who had brought Georgette up with them, to go ahead and take her back on the early flight to Lakeland, and I'd follow later. I waited around for George until after 8 A.M. Then I flew home. I had no idea if I'd see him in Dallas or not. But he did show up. He hadn't been to bed and he was still drinking, but he'd won $16,000 gambling, so nothing could have brought him down that night.

After months of legal hassling back and forth, George finally got permission from the county officials to open a public music park on our property. He erected a $20,000 sign, thirty feet high, with colored lights spelling out "Old Plantation Music Park." When the last shrub had been planted and the last nail hammered into place, we all piled into golf carts and toured George's park—his dream come true. I'll bet Walt Disney wasn't any prouder the first time he showed his family around Disneyland. The natural bowl had been transformed into a beautiful stage with tall white columns (matching the ones on the house) to support the front, a huge chandelier shaped like a wagon wheel, and red carpeting on the floor. George had put in the best sound system he could buy, and backstage there were luxurious dressing rooms, a convenience country music performers rarely ever found at open air dates. Later George added a $40,000 steel roof over the bleachers so audiences could watch the shows in comfort even when it was raining. There was seating for 11,000 people.

The park itself looked like a tropical paradise. Practically every type of flower, fern, and shrub that grows in middle Florida had been planted. There were bright patches of color surrounded by green everywhere, and the fresh sweet smell of orange blossoms from the nearby groves almost took your breath away. Someone told George that if God ever needed another Garden of Eden He should call on George to do the landscaping. There was a fully equipped children's playground and a picnic area with wide, comfortable porch swings hanging from old oak trees. Peacocks and peahens strolled around like they owned the place. George had restored the barn, and we had four shetland ponies, a little palomino he bought for me and some quarter horses.

There was a small three-room house on the property that we fixed up real cute so Mother and Foy could live there while we were building them a bigger house. We also used it as an office. We had moved Mama and Papa Pugh's house trailer to the new property and also bought another trailer for Earleen and Jack, so he could patrol the park for us at night. It was nice having our family around us, and we all felt that the park was a group effort. Foy and Jack both worked there and Cliff and Maxine spent about half their time with us.

When opening day arrived at last, George and I were about to burst with nervous anticipation. We were proud of our park, but we didn't know if the public would like it enough to keep returning after they had satisfied their first curiosity. Would country music shows go over big enough in Lakeland for us to make a profit?

Counting the cost of our home we had invested well over $250,000 in the park, and we knew the next few months would decide whether our investment was going to pay off, or whether George's daydream was going to become a nightmare.

Billy Sherrill and his family and Jan Howard and some other friends from Nashville flew in for the big event, and Al Gallico came down from New York. We had booked Conway Twitty to headline the Sunday afternoon opening show with us, and we were praying we would have a good enough turnout to fill up at least half the bleachers. George and I were up at dawn attending to last minute details, running back and forth between the house and the park in the little golf carts George had bought for that purpose. The kids were as excited as we were. To them it was like having an amusement park in their own backyard and they loved it! Soon Foy came rushing in to tell us that cars were backed up for *six miles* outside the main entrance. The police were going crazy! They'd never had a traffic jam like that in Lakeland.

George tried to act cool about the whole thing, but I squealed and jumped up and down like a kid. We didn't have to worry about empty seats at the bowl. By showtime the bleachers were filled to capacity, and families who couldn't find seats were standing up in the back. We learned that thousands more had to be turned away! People had brought children, grandparents, picnic lunches, coolers filled with beer, playpens for babies—everything they needed to make a day of it—and they seemed to be having a wonderful time.

Charley Pride had called me the night before from Tampa, where he'd just closed a show, to say he was coming over the next day to surprise George at the opening. Even our band didn't know Charley was hiding backstage. James Hollie, our bass player, was singing Charley's current hit "All I Have to Offer You Is Me" during our show, and just as he got to the line, "All I have . . . ," Charley stepped out onstage and sang ". . . to offer you is me." The crowd went wild and James about fainted. So did George! In the end we all gathered onstage for the finale—me and George, Charley and Conway—and the crowd became so excited they broke through the picket fence around the rock garden George had built between the stage and the audience, trampling about $5,000 worth of landscaping. It was such an exciting day we wondered whether the park could ever live up to its opening, but as it soon turned out, our shows became so popular we had to increase them from once a month to once a week. We booked the top names in country music at that time, among them Johnny Cash, Merle Haggard, Charley Pride, the Statler Brothers, and Jack Greene and Jeannie Seely.

Merle Haggard, one of George's favorite singers, performed there a number of times. After his shows he and George would go up to the house, kick off their boots and lie around the floor picking and singing to one another. Sometimes Merle's wife Bonnie and I would go off in a golf cart to find a quiet place in the park where we could swap stories and "woes" about Jones and Haggard. Our husbands were a lot alike—talented, temperamental, difficult men who were hard to understand and impossible to control. Bonnie and I were a lot alike too. No matter what they did, we still loved them and took them back.

Merle used to say to George, "What's wrong with us, Jones? Why do we treat the good women bad and the bad women good?"

George would answer, "I don't know, but if we can't make it with Tammy and Bonnie we can't make it with anybody."

Now that we're all divorced I wonder if George and Merle ever think about that.

If George and I were in town when a show was running at the park, I always invited the performers up to the house for dinner. I'd fix country dishes like ham and dumplings, cornbread, string beans, fried corn, hot biscuits and my specialty, homemade banana pudding.

We had some great times at the house with our friends in the business because normally country music stars never get to see one another except backstage at a television taping or an awards show. We all spend most of our time on the road, and two big acts are almost never in the same town on the same weekend. One night last year I happened to be passing through a town where Loretta Lynn was performing. I had a night off so I surprised her and ended up spending the night in her hotel room. We sat up all night like a couple of teenagers at a slumber party, gossiping and acting silly. Sometimes life on the road makes you hungry for a normal social life, but if any of us had to give it up we'd be itching to head out again within weeks.

One of the biggest attractions at the Old Plantation Park was George's antique car collection, which was continually growing. He'd had a building constructed to display the automobiles and visitors would spend hours looking them over. Among others he had a 1929 Model A Ford, a German Styre that had been one of Hitler's staff cars, a 1936 Chevy, a 1940 Lincoln Zephyr and a 1923 Cadillac that looked like it had just come off the showroom floor.

The flashiest car we owned wasn't an antique, but a brand-new custom-designed Pontiac Bonneville George had bought from the famous country-western clothes designer Mr. Nudie of Hollywood. The car was a white convertible with a plastic dome top to protect the 4,000 silver dollars embedded in the dashboard, door panels, and around the hand-tooled leather seats. The hood emblem was horns from a Texas steer, and rifles had been mounted on the front fenders. The door handles were real pistols and the console between the two front seats was a fancy leather saddle. That's where Georgette sat when we drove the car in parades. The car radio came on by pulling a trigger and the horn sounded like a cow mooing. George even had a tape of a cattle stampede he could play in the tape-deck. It was a dream car for a cowboy with a sense of humor and George loved it.

George was constantly on the lookout to find new additions for his collection, and so was I because it gave me the chance to buy him presents for special occasions that I knew he would like. Once he found a Model T Ford with a rumble seat in Lakeland for only $2500, but I talked him out of buying it and he pouted all the way home. I had taken the owner aside and told him I wanted to get the car for George's birthday, which was a few weeks away, so he had agreed to hold it for me. George called the man back later, and when he was told the car had been sold he was furious. "You made me lose it!" he accused. He fussed and fumed and wouldn't even eat his supper; he was so upset. Later that night I had someone bring the car over to the house, and when he saw it he was so excited he had to take a drive that minute. It was one of the few times I was ever able to surprise him with a gift that he really wanted because he had everything, and when I did come up with a secret gift he would always find me out. If George saw something he liked he bought it for himself, so by the time birthdays, anniversaries, or Christmas came around I could never think of anything he needed or wanted.

That first year after Georgette was born was the happiest I had ever known. George was drinking very little (mostly just beer and wine, which he didn't consider drinking at all); the park was a fantastic success, even though running it was a headache at times; we had our family close by, and the kids were all healthy and happy in their new home. Some mornings I'd wake up so contented I'd almost have to pinch myself to believe my life was going so well.

My career couldn't have been better. "Stand By Your Man" had become a crossover hit, which meant I had a record on the pop charts for the first time. The song, which Billy Sherrill and I wrote in about fifteen minutes one afternoon before a recording session, generated extraordinary interest from members of the press who didn't usually pay attention to country music singers.

Feminists had condemned the song, saying it was typical of the kind of thinking that had kept women down all these years. Magazine and newspaper writers wanted to hear how I felt about their criticism, and I enjoyed the opportunity of being interviewed about something other than my personal life for a change. But I never did understand all the commotion over the lyrics of that song. The title was an idea Billy had been kicking around for some time, and when we started working on it that day before the session, the lines just fell into place naturally, the way they do on good songs. The words are:

> Sometimes it's hard to be a woman
> Giving all your love to just one man
> You'll have bad times,
> And he'll have good times,
> Doin' things you don't understand
> But if you love him
> You'll forgive him
> Even though he's hard to understand
> And if you love him
> Be proud of him,
> *Cause after all he's just a man*
> Stand by your man
> Give him two arms to cling to
> And something warm to come to
> On nights he's cold and lonely
> Stand by your man
> And tell the world you love him
> Keep giving all the love you can
> Stand by your man.

I don't see anything in that song that implies a woman is supposed to sit home and raise babies while a man goes out and raises hell. But that's what women's lib members thought it said. To me it means: be supportive of your man; show him you love him and you're proud of him; and be willing to forgive him if he doesn't always live up to your image of what he should be.

Many articles written about me have pointed out that although my theme song is "Stand By Your Man," I've had four husbands. They insinuate I sing one thing and live another. Well, maybe I do, but it hasn't been by choice. I would much rather have stood by one man for a lifetime than four for a short time, but circumstances didn't work out that way. That doesn't mean I don't believe that's the way it *should* be, or that I've given up hope that someday it can and will be that way for me. Although I consider myself a lot more liberated than many of the "sisters" who criticized the song— especially when it comes to things like financial independence, being the family breadwinner, raising children alone, and running a business—I *am* emotionally dependent on men and I wouldn't want it any other way. I'm happiest when I'm in love, and I'm miserable when I'm not. If they're honest about it, I think most women feel the same way. Fame and success are wonderful, but love is what makes *my* world go around.

That's why it hurt so much when my marriage to George started crumbling. It happened little by little. Our relationship had been stormy from the beginning, but I loved him so much that the good times more than made up for the bad. Then as he broke promise after promise about his drinking I began to lose faith in him. His words didn't have meaning behind them anymore. I wasn't any easier to live with when George was drinking than he was. He'd get drunk, I'd nag, he'd drink more, I'd nag more, and we'd both end up feeling hateful and resentful toward each other. I knew the nagging only made things worse, but I couldn't help myself. There was no way I could sit quietly by and watch my husband kill himself, as well as my love for him.

I told him what was happening. I said, "George, every time you get drunk you kill it a little more. Every time you break a promise something inside me dies.

Please don't do this. Please don't kill the love I have for you."

But he'd just put his arms around me and say, "Awww, honey, that won't happen. We love each other too much for that to happen."

But we didn't. There's no love in the world that can't be killed if you beat it to death long enough.

Chapter 8

OR months after Georgette was born, George appeared to be a changed man. He seemed more at peace with himself, more contented than I'd ever seen him, and he was more in control of his drinking than he'd ever been. Because of this I was totally unprepared for what happened the day all hell broke loose in Lakeland.

Early that morning George left the house to go to the park on business. Instead of taking a golf cart to run down there, as he usually did, he drove his car. That should have been a warning to me, but I wasn't the same suspicious wife I'd been when he was drinking heavily. His months of good behavior had lulled me into a false sense of security. He hadn't been upset or depressed about anything when he left the house, so as far as I knew everything was fine. Still, a feeling of dread started creeping up from the pit of my stomach when he didn't show up for lunch and didn't call. When George was sober he was never gone for more than a few hours without checking in at home. This was his choice, not my request, so any time I didn't hear from him on schedule I suspected the worst.

I called the park office, but they said they hadn't seen George all morning. Cliff and Maxine were visiting Mother and Foy at the guesthouse, so I called them and asked if the men would look around the park to see if George was out with the workmen somewhere. Meanwhile I went to work on the books (I did all the bookkeeping for the park) with one of our employees, Richard. The older girls were in school and Georgette was down at Mother's, so the only people in the house were me, Richard, my live-in housekeeper, Doris McNish, and her sister-in-law, Thelma Brown, who helped out with the cleaning. Richard and I were working at the dining room table when Thelma came running into the room calling, "Miss Tammy, Miss Tammy. I see Mr. George a comin' and he sho' is in bad shape!" Her eyes were as big as saucers.

When I got to the back door George was trying to get out of his car, but he was so drunk he couldn't get the door open. When he finally managed it, he stepped out and fell face down on the ground. Doris ran out and half-carried, half-dragged him to the back porch. Then Richard and I got him into the house and sat him in a chair at the kitchen table. But when we let him go he fell forward, flat on the floor. He seemed barely conscious, but he didn't get the nickname "Possum" for nothing, so I wasn't sure whether he was really as drunk as he was acting. I wasn't about to take any chances on setting off that temper of his. I looked at Richard and winked. "Well, bless his heart, he's passed out," I said as sweetly as I could. "Help me get him up to bed. He'll wake up after a while and eat something, and then he'll feel better." Richard and I started up the stairs with George between us, each supporting one of his arms across our shoulders. There were two landings leading up to our bedroom and George drug his feet all the way, catching those sharp-toed boots on the edge of every step. By the time we got to the top landing, my back was aching and I could have

killed him, but I didn't let on for a second that I was
mad. We laid him down on the bed.

We must have worked fifteen minutes trying to get
those blasted boots off. I knew he was curling his toes
inside to make it harder for us. When they were finally
off I reached up to unzip his pants. As I touched the
snap on his blue jeans, he came up off that bed like a
maniac. He swung at me and missed, then swung at
Richard, who was tall and skinny as a rail, and missed
him too. He grabbed me by the shoulders and started
shaking me, yelling, "Now tell me about it; *tell* me
about it."

This was something he said often when he was
drunk, but in all the years I was married to him I never
did find out what it was he wanted me to tell him
about.

"What, George? *What* do you want me to tell you?"
I tried to remain as calm as possible.

"*You* know. You know what." He started shaking
me harder and his grip was so tight that pain was
shooting down into my arms. I had never seen his eyes
so wild. He tried to swing at Richard again, which
gave me a chance to jerk away. Richard bolted for the
door. He was so scared he jumped from the top landing down one flight of stairs to the second landing. I
was running right behind him. But when I reached the
second landing I looked up behind me, and for an
instant I froze in my tracks. George was standing by
the banister with a 30-30 rifle aimed right at my back.
I heard him say, "You may run out on me, baby. But
you won't run out on this."

I took off down the second flight of stairs as fast as
I could go. Before I reached the bottom step I heard
a loud click, the sound of the safety on the gun being
released. A cold chill ran over me. Even as I was running the flesh was crawling on my back in terrified
anticipation of a shotgun blast that might come at any
second. Doris and Thelma were already hiding outside,
and Richard had just hit the back door at top speed
when he saw Cliff coming up the back steps. It was too

late to stop. He crashed into him with such force that it knocked Cliff off his feet and sent him sprawling halfway down the steps. Cliff landed with his ankle twisted painfully underneath him. (We later learned it was broken. Poor Cliff. His disease made it difficult enough to walk without having to be in cast for six weeks.) As Richard flew past Cliff, who was trying to struggle to his feet, he yelled out, "George has a gun!"

I stopped to help Cliff up, but he waved me on. "Go get help," he said. "I'm all right here. George won't hurt me."

I knew he was right. I was the one George was after, not Richard or Cliff. By the time I reached the backyard George was outside on the porch. I turned just in time to see him raise the gun to his shoulder, aiming it directly at me. A loud blast echoed in my ears as I ran screaming toward Jack and Earleen's trailer, which was several hundred yards from the house.

I knew Jack could help. He weighed over 200 pounds and had biceps bigger than my waist. He was the only man I knew who could single handedly over-power George when he was drinking. But when I got to the trailer Jack wasn't there.

I rushed inside and locked the door, then looked out to see if George was anywhere in sight. He wasn't. I could only hope that he was too drunk to run after me. I called George McClelland, a friend of ours who was a private detective. When I told him what was happening, he said, "Tammy, don't call the police. If you do, this will be all over the papers tomorrow and you don't want that. Let me handle it. I'll be right there."

By the time McClelland arrived, Cliff had crawled down off the steps and was safely hidden behind some bushes next to the house. We could hear George inside the house. It sounded like he was ripping the place apart. "My God, he must have gone crazy," I told Mc-Clelland. "I have never seen him this wild. He loves this house and everything in it. Even at his drunkest he wouldn't try to destroy it."

About that time we heard a loud crash, the sound

of glass shattering everywhere. "If I go in there after George with him this drunk and holding a gun, somebody will get hurt," McClelland said. "I'm going to call an ambulance to come get him."

While he went to the trailer to make the call, I stayed with Cliff, who couldn't stand up because he couldn't put any pressure on his ankle. We could hear horrible noises coming from inside the house—furniture hitting the walls, glass breaking, and things crashing as if six men were in there demolishing the place. I wondered if there would be anything left by the time the ambulance arrived.

We heard the siren as the ambulance turned into the park entrance. With McClelland's help the attendants were able to subdue George and get him into a straitjacket. Most of the fight was gone out of him by then; he looked like a trapped animal. He was dazed and out of his head when they put him into the back of the ambulance and drove off. I was so grateful the children were at school and spared the sight of their Daddy squirming around in a straitjacket.

I went inside the house to look at the damage. When I saw what he'd done I sat down and wept. All the Spanish lanterns that had been hanging in the downstairs rooms were smashed to pieces. He had thrown two dining room chairs into my china cabinet and broken all my china and crystal. One of the chairs was still stuck in the shattered glass door. He had ripped the drapes off the windows, thrown furniture against the walls, leaving huge holes in the plaster, and kicked in three television sets. The wall behind one of the sets was scorched where flames had shot up when he smashed in the screen. Glass figurines had been thrown against walls and windows, and broken glass was scattered everywhere. I felt as shattered as the debris around me, and I made up my mind that when George sobered up he was going to see what he'd done to our home. Any other time he'd made a mess or broken things while he was drinking, I had always made sure it was all cleaned up before he sobered up. But this time I wanted him to see it just as he'd left it.

George's doctor called me later that day to say he had put George in a padded cell and planned to leave him there until he was completely dried out. He couldn't understand George's sudden outburst of violence anymore than I could, but he suspected it might have been caused by a mixture of diet pills and alcohol. George had put on quite a bit of weight in the year that he'd been drinking less and eating more, so his doctor had given him a prescription for an appetite suppressant ("uppers"), warning him not to drink when he took the pills. Mixing amphetamines with alcohol can cause serious side effects, including psychotic behavior, and his doctor told me he was certain George had been temporarily out of his mind when he went after me with a gun and wrecked the house. He didn't want George to have any visitors while he was at the sanatorium, including me. "I want him to have time to get his head clear, as well as his body," he told me.

The next day, I had to leave for a two week tour of Canada. The children were going to stay with Mother while I was gone, and I instructed her not to allow the maids to touch the mess George had made until after he'd been home to see for himself what he'd done. I called Mother and George's doctor every day while I was away. George was kept in a padded cell for ten days. The doctor said George didn't remember anything about his violent outburst, except that he thought he recalled our getting into some kind of argument. We hadn't.

I was still in Canada when the doctor released George, but Mother described his homecoming to me as one of the most pathetic sights she'd ever seen. He didn't call anyone to come pick him up, so he came home in a taxi. Mother looked out the window of the guest house in time to see him pay the cab, then walk across the backyard of the big house with his head down and his hands in his pockets. He went up the back steps and in the kitchen door. A few minutes later he came out and sat down on the top step and held his head in his hands and cried like a baby. I don't know what he thought when he saw what he'd done to the house, but it must have made an impression on him because when I got home a few days later, it was all back in order and most of the broken things had been replaced. That was the last time George ever demolished a house when he was drunk.

Little by little George's old patterns of drinking and disappearing returned. He'd be fine for a month or a few weeks; then for no apparent reason he'd slip off and get roaring drunk. Sometimes he'd stay out all night; other times he'd be gone for several days. Sometimes he'd get violent; other times he'd go quietly to bed and sleep it off. But I never knew what to expect, and the fear of violence was always there. He never showed that side of himself in front of the children, but there were many times when he'd tell me to send them upstairs because he could feel himself losing control. Some nights I took them and went to a motel to sleep because I didn't want them to see him stumbling around drunk. Other times I'd drive around all night looking for him, hoping I could get him home before he passed out.

At times when I was away, George would get Mama Pugh to come up to the house and play gospel songs on the piano for him, and he'd sing all the old hymns and pray and cry and say, "Oh, Mama, Mama, why do I do it? I love Tammy so much. What makes me do these things?" She'd try to comfort him, telling him to put his trust in the Lord, and the Lord would give him the strength to stop drinking. He'd promise to give it up. Then, the next day, he'd get drunk all over again.

If George went on a really big bender, he usually ended up in Nashville or Texas, where he could always find drinking buddies. Once he started drinking, there was no way I could keep him from running off because he could always outsmart me. I'll never forget one of those occasions. He came home so drunk I couldn't imagine how he'd driven the car. Foy and I put him to bed and I was determined he was not going out again that night. I was sure he'd kill himself trying to drive. I hid his car keys and mine; then I went down to the office and took the keys to every vehicle we had off the board and told Mother to hide them in her purse under her bed. I also went through George's pants and took all his money and credits cards. I was confident I had him down for the night because he was too drunk to walk, he didn't have keys to a car, and he didn't like to leave the house unless he had at least a few hundred dollars in his pockets. I got in bed beside him and went to sleep.

But about 1 A.M. I woke up and looked over to discover he was gone. I thought, Well, he's downstairs searching for something to drink. (I had stopped keeping liquor in the house.) I tiptoed down to the kitchen, but he was nowhere in the house. His car was still parked in the backyard where we'd left it. I called Mother and asked if he'd been down there to get keys, but she said he hadn't. Then I remembered how he sometimes hid vodka in the orange groves so he could chug out there in a golf cart and mix himself a Screwdriver with fresh orange juice when he wanted it. (George was always ingenious about hiding liquor. One of his favorite tricks was to keep a miniature bottle tucked down in the side of each of his cowboy boots!) I went to the shed where we kept the golf carts, but they were all there. Then I noticed an empty space. Something *was* missing! The riding lawnmower was gone!

I couldn't imagine he would actually drive that contraption anywhere, but after looking around the grounds, I had to assume he'd taken it someplace. I got in the car and drove to the nearest bar, which was ten miles away. When I pulled into the parking lot, there sat our lawnmower right by the entrance. He'd driven that mower down a main highway to get there, and it must have taken him over an hour to go that far. I walked into the bar absolutely fuming, but when I saw him sitting there, just as smug as you can imagine, I almost laughed in spite of my anger. He looked up and saw me and said, "Well, fellas, here she is now. My little wife. I told you she'd come after me." He was laughing and having a grand old time. I could have choked him! But he let me lead him to the car and take him home. Any other time if I'd tried that, he might have knocked me across the room. You just never knew.

Our marriage wasn't the only thing suffering from George's drinking. He was having problems with his liver and he had a puffy, bloated look about him that worried me. I insisted that he see his doctor for a checkup. The doctor told him that his liver was scarred from so much drinking. "Now, every time you take another drink the alcohol goes to those scars first," the doctor said. "If you don't give it up you're going to spit your liver out through your mouth before you die."

After hearing that news, George drank more than ever. His theory was, "If I'm dying I may as well have fun while I can." For the first time he started turning the bottle up to his mouth and drinking it straight, which often made him gag. If he vomited he'd turn the bottle up again and drink more. When he'd gone about six weeks without drawing a sober breath, I went to see his doctor alone.

"George is killing himself just as sure as if he'd taken a gun to his head," I told him. "What can I do to make him stop it?"

We talked it over for a long time and decided that if George thought I was going to divorce him, it might shock him enough to straighten him up. So I called my attorney and told him what to do. Then, while George was out getting drunk, I packed up the kids and flew to Nashville. I didn't leave a note or anything. I wanted him to be completely surprised when my attorney served papers on him.

I had no intention of going through with the divorce because I was still in love with George. I didn't know what made him drink and I knew he didn't know either, but I did know he had gone for long periods before without it, and if he really wanted to he could do it again. I knew George loved me, but I wasn't sure if he loved me enough to give up drinking.

Suddenly I was afraid. Suppose when he got the divorce papers he said, "Well that's fine with me. Let her have her divorce!" What would I do then?

I called my attorney in Lakeland and warned him not to let things go too far. "Remember I don't want this divorce," I said. "I want to save my marriage, not lose my husband."

I hadn't been in Nashville a week when the news that I'd filed for divorce hit the papers. The filing was a matter of public record so I couldn't deny it, but I couldn't tell the press *why* I'd left George either. I knew if he ever found out I wasn't serious about wanting a divorce he'd be so mad he'd keep on drinking just for spite. I didn't want to talk to him because I was afraid I'd weaken, but he managed to track me down at the apartment we kept near the airport. When he called he was drunk. He wanted to know why I was doing this. Didn't I realize he loved me and we belonged together?

I was so furious that he was still drunk that I hung up on him, but he got on a plane and flew to Nashville and showed up at the door. He was fairly sober when he arrived, but he had been drinking some so I told him I couldn't live with him any longer. It was the hardest thing I'd ever had to say to him because my heart wasn't in it.

"It's either me or the liquor," I said. "If you can't give it up, then I'm giving up on you. I won't live this way any longer, and I won't sit by and watch you kill yourself."

He said, "I'm ready to try, I really am." But I told him "trying" wasn't good enough, and that made him so mad he left.

I packed up the girls and went back to Lakeland, not knowing whether my big show of strength had shaken George up or not. Then I heard he was making the rounds of all the bars in Nashville, drunk out of his mind, and I thought, Well, this is it. I can't go back to him if he won't stop drinking and he obviously doesn't care enough about me to give it up. I was heartsick.

I felt hurt, rejected, and furious all at the same time. I had worked myself into such a state by the time George showed up at home in Lakeland a few days later that I didn't even give him a chance to open his mouth. "Get your things packed up and get out right now," I said. "It's over." Then I realized he was stone cold sober.

"Please, Tammy," he said. He looked so sad and beaten I wanted to fall into his arms, but I stood firm. "I'm here because I've had too many days of drinking and thinking, and I know now that you are right and my doctor is right. I'm ready to give it up. You mean more to me than anything in the world and I can't lose you. *Please* give me another chance. You won't regret it. I promise you."

That was all I needed to hear. I knew George would live up to his promise this time because he had been shocked that I would go as far as filing for divorce, and he was scared. My gamble had paid off!

For the next year George Jones was a different man. He even looked different. He put on nearly forty pounds! His waist went from a twenty-nine to a thirty-six, which irked his male vanity no end, but he had never felt better in his life. George had been a heavy drinker since his teens, and his system had never been without alcohol in all that time. He did continue to sip beer or wine once in a while, but for the most part he stayed away from anything alcoholic.

It was the best time of our marriage. George's sons Bryan and Jeff came to visit that summer, and with all the other relatives in Lakeland we had a houseful. The park was going great and showing a profit every month. With the extra income we didn't have to work the road as much, so we did a lot of traveling, taking the whole family, including MeeMaw and PeePaw, and sometimes Maxine and Cliff, along with us. We went to Hawaii, Mexico, the Bahamas, and we had a ball.

When we worked the road we took Georgette with us, and it was really fun having a toddler along. She wanted to be right up there in the spotlight with us, and she loved to come out onstage and take a bow. All the guys in the band petted her and made a fuss over her, but she never acted bratty. Instead she constantly did things that kept us laughing.

I remember one time when something she did was funny, but not funny. We were playing Roanoke, Virginia, and we had come in on the bus early enough to check into a motel and rest before showtime. George and I were lying down to watch television and Georgette was playing around the room. I got engrossed in the movie on TV, but after a few minutes I noticed Georgette wasn't in sight, and she was being awfully quiet. Then I heard splashing noises coming from the bathroom. I looked in to find her just as busy as she could be—washing my wig in the toilet! She was so proud of herself for helping Mama out that way!

Georgette is eight years old now, and she still loves going on the road with me. I take her often during the summer when she's out of school. The first time she sang onstage by herself she was just three years old. She *loved* it! She walks out there now like an old trouper and belts out "Delta Dawn" with more power than some adult singers have. She has my lungs and her father's phrasing, so I don't have any doubts that she'll end up in the business. Billy Sherrill says he's still holding that contract for her! (Tina had a hit record with George at the age of eight. She sings beautifully too.)

After three years of running a successful country music park, George began to get bored with it. The newness had worn off and he was losing interest fast. He had proven he could do it and make a profit, so it was no longer a challenge. George had always been easily bored—nothing ever kept his attention for long—so I really wasn't surprised when he began to show impatience with the demands the park made on our time.

Since George had signed with Epic, we had started recording duet albums, with Billy producing us, so we were needed in Nashville more often than before. We were also more in demand than ever for bookings, having reached the height of our popularity as "Mr. and Mrs. Country Music." Between road work and flying into Nashville to record, we had very little time to spend in Lakeland. This also meant we were away from the children more than we wanted to be. After giving it a lot of thought we finally decided the best thing to do was to sell Old Plantation Park and move back to Nashville where we'd be close to the industry.

It was a difficult decision because we all loved our old antebellum home. It had been the scene of many wonderful memories for both George and myself—as well as some pretty awful ones—and I didn't think we'd ever find another house we loved as much as that one. It still breaks my heart to go back to Lakeland and see what it looks like today. The acreage that was once so beautifully landscaped is now a subdivision just like thousands of other subdivisions. The theater has been torn down and the park is gone.

We moved back into the house on Old Hickory Lake in Hendersonville in late 1972. We also bought a 340-acre farm in Springfield, Tennessee, about twenty-eight miles from Nashville. We needed an investment for the profit we'd made selling the park, and the farm gave George a new "toy." He enjoyed running back and forth out there to play farmer. It was a working farm with 160 head of black angus cattle. Mother and Foy moved into the big old colonial home on the property, and we had a trailer put out there for George's daughter Susan and her husband Harmon Smith. Harmon helped out on the farm and Foy was the overseer.

We soon realized the Old Hickory Lake house was too far from town for convenience to Music Row. Any time we had business in Nashville we had to drive more than an hour each way. So we bought a French regency house above Tyne Boulevard on one of the highest hills in Nashville. Again George went to work decorating, a project that always kept him happily occupied for at least a couple of months. He still wasn't drinking anything except a little beer and wine now and then, and I was really proud of him. He even celebrated his fortieth birthday without getting drunk! I gave him a party and our friends brought silly, gag gifts which we piled into a child's red wagon.

During this period I decided it would make life a lot easier for me if I had someone along on the road to help with my hair and wardrobe. I spent so much time waiting on George and Georgette that I didn't have enough time left to take care of my own needs. I asked Jan Smith, a Nashville hairdresser who had traveled on the road with Connie Francis, if she'd like to try going out with us.

I had met Jan a year earlier at the 1971 Disc Jockey Convention under very unhappy circumstances. At that time she had been the hairdresser for the Johnny Cash TV show, so she was backstage the night of the Columbia Records show to set June Carter's hair. As artists on the label, Johnny and June were there to perform for disc jockeys as well as the Columbia, CBS, and Epic executives who had come in from all over the country. George and I were featured on the show, too.

The Nashville Epic people had been really looking forward to presenting George because he was a new artist on the label, and many of the executives from out of town had never seen him perform in person. George and I had gone to the Columbia offices that afternoon to rehearse for the show, but instead of singing he had spent the afternoon going from one office to another getting drunk. Most of the executives were watching the World Series on television, and George got all involved in that while he was partying. He still hadn't rehearsed when it was time for us to leave for the Ryman Auditorium. I found him in one of the producer's offices so drunk he could hardly stand up.

"I'm not going with you," he said. "You go do the show by yourself."

"Come on, George," I said. "You can't let all these people down."

"Don't you start on me," he yelled. "I'll do what I want to do," and he picked up a whiskey bottle and threw it across the room at me.

Having appeared at one Disc Jockey Convention with my face bruised from his knocking me around, I decided I wasn't going to give him a chance to do the same thing again, so I left. But he had our car keys, so I had to call Shorty Lavender to come pick me up and drive me to the Ryman. It was pouring rain and I was soaking wet when we got to the auditorium.

By the time I'd arrived backstage my eyes were puffy from crying, my hair was a stringy mess, my wet clothes were sticking to me, and I looked like the last place I belonged was on a stage. Jan Smith saw me come in and followed me into one of the dressing rooms. I had seen her backstage often because she worked almost every television show that was recorded in Nashville but we had never talked. She said, "Hi, I'm Jan Smith. What on earth happened to you? You look like you've been run over by a Mack truck!" I couldn't answer her. I knew if I opened my mouth I'd start bawling again. All I could think about was those Epic people out there waiting excitedly to present their newest artist, the great George Jones, and he was so drunk he could hardly stand up, much less give them a good show. Jan said, "You wait here. I'm going to borrow June's heat rollers, and I'll come back and see if we can't do something to fix you up a little bit."

It was a sweet thing for her to have done, and I appreciated it. It was also nice of June to have let Jan come work on me when she'd been hired to come there for the Cash family. Jan did such a good job that night that I started using her to fix my hair for all my album covers, and we became close friends. Her son Cannon was the same age as Georgette, so we had a lot in common to talk about. George never did make it for the Columbia show that night. He was back at the apartment, drunk when I got there, and he became so violent I had to sleep outside in the car to get away from him.

Jan accepted my offer to go on the road, and she had been with me for several months when George began showing signs that he was leading up to a big drunk. We were returning home from a tour where he had been as restless as a caged animal the whole time out. The boys knew something was up because he had been so short-tempered with them. George's doctor had prescribed Librium to help calm him down during these nervous, restless moods, and he had begun taking the medication constantly until he was up to eight or ten pills a day. Along with this he would also drink a few beers. He didn't get drunk, but he didn't act like the sober George either. On this particular day he'd had even more Librium than usual, and as the bus got closer to home he seemed to sink deeper and deeper into depression. We all sensed what was coming, although I really couldn't let myself believe George would fall off the wagon for no reason after nearly a year without drinking. He didn't have anything to be depressed about. It was just a black mood that would hit him periodically, almost like a woman going through her monthly cycle. He would pace the floor, jam his fists in and out of his pockets, such air through his teeth, snap off anybody's head who tried to talk to him, and make the people around him as miserable as he was.

We were all sitting up front in the bus and the tension was getting heavier by the minute. The guys in the band were doing their best to cheer George up, so they began telling Jan old "George Jones" road stories about crazy things he'd done over the years.

They told her about the time Webb Pierce, a country music star known for his ego, was bragging to George about how much money he had. They'd both been drinking. Webb was saying he had paid so-and-so for his new car, and so-and-so for his bus, etc., and George just got fed up with him. So he said, "Hell, Webb. I flush more'n that down the toilet every week." And with that he walked over to the bathroom door and stood where Webb could see him. He pulled a roll of hundred dollar bills out of his pocket and flushed twenty of them down the toilet. The boys said Webb's eyes almost fell out, and after that he shut up about money.

They'd been telling stories like this for over an hour when Jan said, "George, do you realize I'm the only person on this bus who's never seen you drunk?"

For a moment there was dead silence. Then George looked her in the eye and said, "Then your skinny ass better hit Tyne Boulevard at a fast lope when we pull in, 'cause if you don't run, you're sure gonna see it!"

By then I had gone to our bedroom in the back of the bus, and I didn't hear his threat. But a few minutes later when we pulled up on Tyne he got into his car and left. He stayed drunk for two weeks.

I felt like my world had come crashing down around me. I guess it was naive of me to believe that love could keep an alcoholic from drinking, but I knew there was no bad habit I wouldn't have broken for George, and I couldn't help but feel if he loved me enough he would do the same for me. I knew he *could* do without it when he wanted to because he'd stopped twice before for months each time. That made his falling off the wagon hurt even more. It was like his telling me that I didn't mean as much to him as the bottle. When we'd gotten back together after I'd filed for divorce, I'd told him if he started drinking again I would leave him for good. Now he'd done it and I was still with him. I knew I couldn't put up with his drinking, but I wasn't ready to put him out, either. It was that old story of not being able to live with someone, yet not wanting to live without him.

Therefore I decided if I couldn't leave him at least one thing was going to be different. I was no longer going to pretend nothing had happened when he came home from a spree. I had always kept my mouth shut to avoid a scene for fear it would make him run off and get drunk again. But now I was determined to make him face up to what he was doing to himself and to us. I knew if I continued to keep quiet I wouldn't be able to face myself.

When he tried to apologize after his two-week drunk, I said, *"Don't* George. Every time you get drunk you tell me three things afterward, and two of those have lost all meaning. 'I'm sorry' doesn't mean a thing to me anymore; 'I promise I won't do it again' has become a joke because it's a promise you never keep; and 'I love you' means less and less every day. If you don't stop what you're doing the day will come when I won't care whether you love me or not."

George didn't pay much attention to my words because he was convinced he could always talk me into giving him another chance. But he did notice the change in my attitude after he went on a week-long binge with his friends Charlene and Peanut (Earl) Montgomery. That time I did something so out of character he had to pay attention.

George and Peanut were doing a lot of writing together. They'd written a number of hits, including "We're Gonna Hold On," which was our first duet release after I filed for divorce and we got back together. Peanut and his wife Charlene lived in Florence, Alabama, and every time they'd come to Nashville to see George there was trouble. I don't think Peanut and Charlene ever came with the intention of taking George out and getting him drunk, but somehow that's always the way it worked out. They were his friends and they weren't going to take the chance of getting him mad by refusing to party with him when he was in the mood. And when they came around, he was always in the mood.

On this particular day they came to the house with songwriter-musician "Wild Bill" Emerson. As soon as they arrived George started making drinks. When they left to buy more liquor I decided I didn't want to be there when they got back, so I took the kids and drove out to the farm. But Mother told me George and his friends had just been there. They had decided to go buy some food and come back there to party for two or three days. I knew that meant a real rip-roarer, so I brought Mother and Foy back with me to Tyne Boulevard. Then I decided I didn't want to take a chance on George changing his mind and coming home that night. I knew if he did he'd bring that whole gang with him and I was not up to facing that. So I took Mother, Foy and girls and checked into a motel.

The next day I wanted to know whether it was safer to go home or to the farmhouse, so I called a private detective we knew and asked him to find out where George and his friends were. Sure enough, they had all come back to the Tyne Boulevard house and were still partying. The detective advised me to stay away until they had cleared out.

Three days passed before he called to say the group had left in George's car, apparently all still drunk. Meanwhile Mother and Foy had gone back to the farm, so I took the kids and went home. When I walked into my kitchen I could have died. Food had been left sitting out so long it was moldy, the sink was piled high with dirty dishes, the stove was greasy and filthy, and the garbage hadn't been taken out since I left. The smell alone was enough to make you gag. The rest of the house wasn't much better. I counted seventeen empty whiskey bottles lying around in three different rooms. Ashtrays were overflowing onto the living room carpet, record albums were strewn everywhere, table tops were littered with dirty glasses and cigarette butts, and a lamp was turned over on the floor. I couldn't imagine adults going off and leaving a house in such a filthy mess.

George came home while the older girls and I were trying to clean up. I needed only one look at his face to know how sick he was. He had a grayish pallor and the expression of a whipped puppy. There were deep circles under his eyes, which were puffy and bloodshot. He brought his hand from behind his back and handed me a dozen red roses.

"I'm sorry, honey. It won't happen again, I promise," he said.

I was tempted to tell him what he could do with his roses, but instead I took them and laid them down on the cluttered counter. He tried to mix himself a Bloody Mary, but his hand was shaking so bad he spilled more vodka than he got into the glass.

"Who's been cooking, Charlene?" I asked, trying to keep the rage out of my voice.

He just nodded meekly. But when he took a good look around the kitchen and saw the mess, he had to cover his mouth and run for the bathroom. A while later he came back to the kitchen and asked timidly if I would fix him something to eat. "I'm so sick," he said, "I've got to have something to settle my stomach."

I told him to go back to bed and I would call him when it was ready. I put his roses in a crystal vase and set it on the table; I got out my best silver and china and a linen tablecloth. The table looked elegant. Then I dished up a big plate of the food that had been sitting there for days—soured potatoes, moldy beans, rotten meat, and cold, stale cornbread. "It's ready," I called. "Come and get it."

He came down the hall still holding his head with his eyes half shut. He sat down at the table and picked up a forkful of food before he realized what was on the plate. He let out a moan, then started gagging and backing away from the table. "Oh, Tammy, please don't do this to me," he pleaded.

"If it was good enough for you to eat the other day when Charlene cooked it, it's good enough for you now," I said. "It's the only supper you're getting in this house, so if you don't want it, you can do without. This time, I'm *not* cooking for you."

He turned without a word and started back down the hall. When he got about halfway to the bedroom he looked back with a sheepish grin and said, "You know, Tammy, I don't blame you."

It's strange how your mind (or is it your heart?) plays tricks on you when you love someone. Deep down I guess I knew George would never stop drinking, and that it was just a matter of time before I'd have to leave him. But then he'd be okay for a month or six weeks, and I'd start to believe in him all over again. A part of me simply refused to give up hope. To outsiders we seemed like the perfect couple. *Mr. and Mrs. Country Music!* We had a following of devoted, almost fanatical fans, unlike any married couple had ever had in country music. We were by far the most in-demand duet on the road and wherever we appeared crowds were so enthusiastic you could feel the waves of affection pouring out from them. We had captured their imagination in a special way. I don't know why —maybe because George was a legend, *the king,* who had romantically run off with his queen, sired a beautiful princess and was now living happily ever after in a glamorous, fairytale world. How sad that we couldn't live up to their sweet fantasies! The fans knew about George's drinking problem, but that didn't matter. Stories of his wild escapades only added to the Jones legend and made him seem that much more exciting. When you're in love, it's hard enough to get over an ordinary man. It's almost impossible to get over a legend.

But I knew I was beginning to get over George early in 1974. Looking back, I guess we both realized when we moved from Tyne Boulevard that we were giving our marriage one last chance. We probably wouldn't have admitted it then, even to ourselves, but there had been a subtle change in our relationship. We made an almost desperate attempt to keep up appearances for our fans and friends. When we were nice to one another, we were overly polite, like you'd be to a stranger. When we fought it was no longer the passionate battles that lovers have, but more the cruel kind of picking at one another that comes with resentment.

Later friends told me that our effort to pretend nothing had changed between us didn't fool them for a minute. Jan and her sister Nanette Nichols, who is also a hairdresser, Billy Sherrill and his wife Charlene, producer-songwriter George Richey and his wife Sheila, all knew the situation between me and George had reached the breaking point.

Even our real estate lady, Betty Bernow, knew something was up by the way we told her we wanted her to find us our dream house. We wanted lots of space inside with big grounds outside so George could work in the yard when he got the urge, but we wanted it no further out than a few minutes from Music Row. One winter on the mountaintop above Tyne Boulevard had convinced us we weren't in a practical location unless we wanted to build a ski lift to take us back and forth when it snowed. We had either been snowed in or snowed out half a dozen times, and even on good days our bus couldn't get up the hill because it was too steep.

As silly as it sounds, George and I both thought another move, a new setting, would improve things between us. I guess we figured if we found the perfect house our marriage would live up to it. Betty searched Nashville until she came up with what did indeed seem perfect. The house was huge—17,600 square feet, twelve bedrooms (including a five-bedroom children's wing), fifteen baths, an office, two huge dens, an enormous L-shaped living room, a formal dining room and another dining area off the kitchen. There was also an outdoor covered patio as large as a one-bedroom apartment, an Olympic-sized swimming pool with a bathhouse, a bar, a tennis court, a playground area the size of a schoolyard with park swings, slides, teeter-totter, merry-go-rounds, and trampoline, and nine-and-a-half acres of beautiful grounds. All this was located on Franklin Road, just ten minutes from the CBS studios where we did all our recording. The owner had built the place four years earlier at a cost of $1,400,000. But he had gone bankrupt and was desperate to sell.

The house had been on the market for months and the price had dropped to $500,000. We had sold the farm so we knew we could swing the $100,000 down payment.

We debated for about a week; then when we learned another buyer was interested we decided to take it. But the day we were to sign the papers George disappeared and I couldn't find him anywhere. He didn't show up until our bus was already pulling out of town headed for our weekend dates. He had to flag us down to get on. He'd been drinking and had forgotten all about our appointment with the owner of the house. The next day I called Betty from the road to learn the other buyer had given the owner a $50,000 check to hold the house. I was heartbroken. I was also furious with George for causing us to lose the deal.

When we got back to town, Betty called all excited to say the other buyer's check had bounced. If we could close the deal before he made the check good, the owner said we could have the house. Again, George was out drinking and I didn't know when he would show up, so I asked Betty if the owner would let me sign the papers alone. When he agreed, Betty and I went to meet him. I gave him a check and told him to put only my name on the deed because I didn't know if George and I would ever live in that house together. "Well, I'll leave a blank space for his name, just in case," he said.

George came home two days later apologizing for messing up the deal on the house again.

"You didn't mess it up," I told him. "I went ahead and bought it without you."

"You did *what?*" He was surprised.

"I got the extra money I needed from CBS to add to what I had in my account, and I bought the house," I explained.

George was furious! "I can just imagine what the owner must think of me," he complained, "my wife having to go out and buy her own house! I won't live there! You've embarrassed me and I don't want the house!"

He fussed for three days, but the more he thought about it the more he did want the house, so by the time I went to sign the final papers the following week, he went along to make sure his name was added to the deed. When the owner saw him he just smiled and said, "George, you don't have to say a thing. I've already added your name to the papers. We men have to stick together." That made George feel like he'd put one over on me, so he was very happy about the house after that.

The minute the place was ours George went to work redecorating inside and out. He didn't like the black brick exterior so he spent $15,000 having it stuccoed over. He decided to use decorative wrought iron for burglar bars across the windows; then he got the idea of having it designed in the musical notes of "Stand By Your Man." Billy laughed and told George that some of the melody was from a PD (public domain) Strauss waltz, so if we ever decided to sell the house to people who didn't like country music, we could tell them the windows were decorated with a classical song.

By the middle of June the house was almost ready, but not quite. We were leaving on tour and we were determined to sleep there at least one night before we went out of town, so we "camped out" in a million-dollar mansion, sleeping on mattresses on the floor.

When we got back off the road we had a recording session for a duet album. We went into the studio on the afternoon of July 3. We hadn't finished one song before Peanut and Charlene showed up. It had gotten to the point where it upset me any time they came around because it always meant another drinking spree for George. I'm sure George knew I was upset, but he didn't let on. Between each take he'd go over in the corner and talk to them while I listened to the play-backs with Billy.

As soon as the session was over George tossed me

his keys and said, "Here, wait for me in the car. I'll be right out."

I waited. Five minutes, ten, then thirty passed and George didn't come out. And when I went back inside to find him, I was told he had left by another exit with Peanut and Charlene just as soon as I was out of sight.

The more I thought about him sneaking off with them the madder I got. We had planned to do something special with Georgette the next day for the Fourth of July because the older girls were in Mississippi visiting relatives. I knew now George would never show up. I drove home and called Nanette.

"George has gone off with Peanut and Charlene again," I told her, "and I know he won't be home tonight. I've decided to take Georgette and drive to Florida. Wanna come?"

She had been going on the road with me when Jan couldn't leave Cannon, so we had become very close. Nan didn't hesitate. "I'll be packed by the time you get here," she said.

Meanwhile Jan had decided she wanted to go, too. Her husband, news photographer John Smith, was off in Argentina on a CBS-TV assignment, so she was going to be home alone for the holiday with Cannon.

We piled the kids in the back of the limousine and took off. Nan drove as far as Atlanta; then I took over. There was no point in stopping. The kids were sound asleep by then, and we were wide awake, giggling like schoolgirls. It was one of those nights when everything that happened was funny. I said "Let's hit every town between Jacksonville and Miami. We can take the kids to every tourist attraction we see." And we did exactly that, falling into motels at night exhausted, then sitting up for hours longer, talking ourselves weak. The kids had a ball. They saw everything from alligator wrestling to trained seals, and they ran our legs off. After a few days I realized this was the first time I'd been free of tension and strain in so long I couldn't remember when I'd felt so relaxed. Even at my happiest times with

George there was always some tension because I never knew when one of those black, restless moods would strike him.

When we returned to Nashville a week later I felt like a new woman. Even though we had covered a lot of ground I was rested. Nan, Jan, and I had had long conversations about my situation with George, and just talking about it to two women who knew firsthand from traveling with me what he could be like helped clear my mind. I had finally admitted to myself that the new house wasn't going to improve my marriage.

George didn't show up at home until several days after we returned from Florida. He came in with that same whipped puppy look, begging forgiveness and promising not to do it again. I'd heard it all so many times before it was beginning to sound like a broken record. He didn't say where he'd been and I didn't ask. At that point, I didn't much care.

It's strange that through all those years of living with a disappearing husband, I'd never suspected him of being with another woman. I'm jealous and possessive when I'm in love, and the thought of my man out with someone else brings out my green-eyed monster in a second. Women make themselves readily available to men like George Jones (there's a show business saying: "Being a star means never having to sleep alone"), but somehow I always knew my competition came in a bottle, not a skirt. Only once did I think he'd been with someone else, and it had scared me to death.

We were still living in Lakeland at the time and George had been out all night. I heard him come into our bedroom just after daylight. He sat down on the bed and gently asked if I was awake. Then he took my hand in his. When I looked at him, I saw that he was about to cry. I don't know why, but the thought flashed through my mind that he was about to tell me he had spent the night with another woman.

"You know I love you, don't you?" he began.

I answered, "Yes, I know you do," thinking, Oh

Lord, that's exactly what he's about to tell me, and I don't want to hear it!

He was so choked up he could hardly speak. "I have to tell you something. . . . I've done something so awful, I don't even know how to tell you about it." Everything he said convinced me that my intuition was right.

"What is it, George? Please tell me."

"I just . . . just don't know how I can say it," he stammered. Tears were brimming over his eyes. "I was with another woman tonight," he sobbed, "but you've got to believe me. Nothing happened."

Then he explained he'd been playing poker at the Holiday Inn with some men he'd met in the bar. He had been drinking heavily and losing heavily. When he ran out of cash they gave him counter checks to use so he could stay in the game. Before it was over he had written $8000 worth of checks! When the game ended three women arrived, and they passed around more drinks. Then everyone left except one girl, who stayed behind with George.

When she started coming on strong to him he realized he'd been set up. "It sobered me up in a second," he said, "and all I could think of was getting out of there. I knew they planned to have that girl keep me busy until after the banks opened so they could cash those checks. We've got to do something to stop them."

The next morning I got to the bank just ten minutes after it had opened, but I was already too late. They had been the first customers when the doors opened. Our attorney advised me not to press charges because it would get George into trouble for illegal gambling, so we just let it drop and wrote it off to experience. George threw away more money than most men earn anyway. Almost every time he got drunk he'd either sell something, like a new car, at a great loss, or he'd give away something valuable, like a piece of his jewelry. He always picked up the tab for his drinking buddies, and if they decided to fly to another city to party, he paid for that too. He carried a big wad of hundred-dollar bills everywhere he went, even if he was only going to the corner for a pack of cigarettes, and I used to worry constantly that someone would knock him in the head to steal his cash.

The summer and fall of 1974, after we'd moved into the Franklin Road house, was a time of constant turmoil and tension. George would go for short periods without drinking, and we'd both try to pretend everything was okay. Then he'd fall off the wagon again and disappear for days at a time. He had begun staying away from the house when he was drunk, mainly I think because he didn't want to face my temper. I had stuck to my word about not letting things slide by to avoid an unpleasant scene. If he drank I fussed and fumed. I knew it wasn't helping things between us, but it made me feel better to get it out of my system instead of keeping it inside the way I had before. He'd say, "The trouble with you is you don't trust me to have just a couple of drinks and enjoy myself. You always expect me to get drunk." Then I'd say something sarcastic like, "Yes, and you always live up to my expectations, don't you?" That would start it, and we'd end up in a bitter argument.

I knew it wasn't just his drinking that was causing our problems. It was my reaction to it, too. But I couldn't help it. I *hated* it. I hated what it did to him, and I hated the nagging wife it had made me. I felt like a failure both as a wife and lover. Secretly, I blamed myself for not being able to keep him happy and satisfied at home. I thought if I were just smarter, or prettier, or sexier, or a better companion, he wouldn't want to escape by drinking. In my mind I knew alcoholism is considered a disease, and that no one can help an alcoholic unless he first wants to help himself, but in my heart I still felt inadequate.

We didn't book any dates for December 1974, with the intention of taking the whole month off to be with our family. The girls and I had talked for weeks about making this a special Christmas. We were all going to Acapulco for a fabulous vacation! I started my shopping early in the month, and even George seemed to be catching the Christmas spirit. I thought, If we can all have a good holiday together and start 1975 off on the right foot, maybe—just maybe—.

Billy called and suggested we take advantage of some of the time off to do another duet session. He wanted us to record the old song "Near You," so we set a date for December 12. The first part of the session didn't go well because we were using a different studio at CBS and just weren't getting the sound we had always gotten in Studio B. I was already edgy about that when I looked up into the control booth to see Charlene and Peanut standing there smiling. That was all I needed! In the next break I went into the ladies room and bawled. I knew there was no way George would stay sober with them in town. After the session was over George started toward the control booth to see them, then turned back and handed me the car keys. "I'll meet you outside," he said. I remembered what had happened the last time he'd said that, so I really didn't expect him to come home with me. But to my surprise he came out a few minutes later and we drove to the house.

It was almost midnight by the time we got home, so we went right to bed. I had fallen into a deep depression that I couldn't shake off. It wasn't just the worry that George would go on a bender with Peanut and Charlene in town. It was everything. It suddenly all seemed so hopeless, and I started crying. George asked me what was wrong, but I didn't want to tell him I was afraid something was going to happen to spoil our holiday, so I gave him other excuses for being depressed—problems with my housekeeper, a legal hassle with the label over royalties—things I usually could take in stride.

This was the one time during my years with George that I tried to lay my burdens on him. Normally I didn't confide worries or fears to him because I didn't want to say anything to make him depressed, knowing depression always brought on drinking. But this time

I poured my heart out and told him everything that was bothering me, except how I felt about Peanut and Charlene being in town. The last thing he said to me before we went to sleep was, "Tammy I know a lot of things have piled up that look bad right now, but you have attorneys to handle the legal matters, and we can always hire a new housekeeper. We're settled in our new home and we're about to start a new year. Everything's going to be fine. Just don't worry."

I went to sleep thinking it felt good to be the one who was being comforted for a change. I told myself I had been wrong to worry about what George would do with Peanut and Charlene in town. After all, he had come home with me from the session, hadn't he? I was being unfair, always expecting the worst. I resolved to give George the benefit of the doubt more often.

Jackie and I both had dental appointments the next morning, so I planned on taking her downtown with me. George wanted to go by the building we'd bought for our booking agency to see how they were doing on reconstruction and decorating. (After Hubert Long died Shorty Lavender started his own agency, and George and I had gone in with him as partners.) Before I left the house I brought George his coffee to the bedroom as I always did. He was still in his pajamas, sitting on the side of the bed. I asked him if he wanted me to wait until he got dressed so I could comb his hair for him. He always liked me to fix it when he was going out. "No," he answered. "I think I'll mess around the yard a while before I go down to the agency, so don't bother fooling with it." I reminded him of a business meeting we had that afternoon at the house at 1:00. He said, "I'll meet you back here." Then he kissed me goodbye and I left.

By noon I could see we were running late at the dentist's office, so I called home to leave word for George in case he got there before I did. Mother answered the phone. She and Foy had spent the night to babysit while we recorded. She told me George had come into the kitchen shortly after I left, already dressed to go out. "He acted funny," she said. "He stood by the kitchen window for a couple of minutes watching Foy working out by the pool. Then he said the strangest thing. He said, 'It's just not gonna work. It'll never work out, not any way.' When I asked him what he meant he said, 'Oh nothin'. Tammy was just a little depressed last night and I guess I've still got it on my mind.' Then he went outside and backed his car out. But he stopped and came back inside to get something out of ya'll's bedroom before he drove off. He didn't say when he'd be back."

My mother adored George Jones. They were close enough that she had a kind of a sixth sense about him, about his moods and feelings. I knew by the tone of her voice that she was worried. But after my resolution of the night before, I refused to let myself fall into the old trap of assuming the worst.

I made it home in time for our 1 o'clock appointment. When George hadn't called or shown up by 1:30 I started getting that sick feeling in my stomach in spite of myself. I called the agency, but they said he had left there several hours earlier. Then I remembered George's "getaway" bag. That's what he called the leather shaving kit where he kept his overnight things. He always took it with him if he left with the intention of staying away overnight. I ran into his bathroom and looked in the cabinet where he kept it. Sure enough, the "getaway" bag was gone.

At that moment something inside me seemed to slip away. I had an actual physical sensation of a heaviness being lifted from inside me. I knew then that George had walked out on me for the last time. For a fraction of a second I felt relief. Then an overwhelming sadness flooded through me, the kind that makes your limbs ache and your heart feel heavy. It was like the sensation you feel after someone you love has suffered terrible pain for a long time before dying. There's a sense of relief that it's finally over, but at the same time you don't know how you'll ever live with the loss. I didn't get hysterical. But silent tears I couldn't stop began streaming down my face.

Nan and Jan Smith sat up with me most of the night. I never did stop crying. Why couldn't my heart accept what my head knew was true? *It was over.* Mark it down in your mind, I told myself. On December 13, 1974, George Jones walked out of your life for good.

Three days later Shorty called to say he'd heard from George. "He's down in Franklin (a little town about twenty minutes from our home) and he wants to come home." I told him he'd better call George and tell him he didn't have a home to come to anymore. Shorty didn't believe me for a minute. George had run off so often it was accepted as standard practice. Shorty said, "Well, I think that's something you'd better tell him yourself."

A short while later the phone rang.

"I'm coming home," George said.

"No, you're not coming home," I answered very calmly. Then I hung up.

For the sake of the children I was determined not to let what had happened spoil Christmas. We had already made plans to take the family to Acapulco, including George's daughter Susan and her husband Harmon. On December 18 we flew to Mexico as arranged. Mother and Foy were with us and we had beautiful accommodations at the Princess Hotel. The weather was perfect. The children enjoyed the beach and the sun while the grownups tried to pretend nothing was wrong.

We'd been there only two days when I got a call from the Metropolitan Trustee of Nashville, Glenn Ferguson. He was a close friend of the family and someone I often turned to for advice. Glenn warned me that George had put our home on the market and that he already had an interested buyer. I didn't see how he could sell the house out from under me since my name was also on the deed, but I decided I'd better go home and see about it anyway. I didn't want strangers walking through my house with real estate agents while I was gone. I told Glenn I was going to give the family at least one more full day in Acapulco before we returned home.

When we got back to Nashville I learned that George was trying to file papers to keep me from having anything to do with the house. I called John Lentz, an attorney we'd met through Glenn who had been handling a lot of business for us. He reassured me that George couldn't sell the house unless I deeded my interest over to him. "Don't worry about it until after Christmas," he advised. "Try to enjoy the holiday; then you can decide what you want to do about the house." Some holiday!

We hadn't planned on being in Nashville for Christmas, so we had no tree or decorations, and the big house seemed lonely and devoid of holiday spirit. I knew we couldn't have fun without some kind of celebration, and being at home with George gone was just too depressing. I called Glenn Ferguson and asked if he thought he could find us a chalet in Gatlinburg, a beautiful resort high in the Smokies, about 230 miles from Nashville. Since it's a famous ski resort the chalets are usually booked up by fall, but Glenn had contacts and I knew that if anyone could locate a place for us to rent during Christmas, he could. He called back in a few hours to say he'd found something. We all got excited and hurriedly unpacked our sun clothes and packed our snow clothes.

It was early Christmas Eve day when the children and I got into the car and took off for the mountains. Mother and Foy were following later in their car. The mountain roads were icy and treacherous, but when we got there the hard drive was well worth it. Our chalet overlooked the ski slopes with a magnificent view of snow-covered mountains. There was a sunken living room with a huge fireplace designed so you could sit in it and warm your hands and toes. The children loved it! But the nicest surprise was a shiny, beautifully decorated Christmas tree, with a gift for each of us underneath! But in this case, Santa's name

was Glenn Ferguson. He had thoughtfully arranged
for a friend in Gatlinburg to set up the tree and deliver
the presents, so at least the children would have a
happy holiday.

The older girls knew George was gone, but we didn't
talk about it because we didn't want to upset Georgette
and Tina. I told them he'd had to go out of town on
business. Christmas day Mother and I cooked turkey
and dressing and all the trimmings, and under the
circumstances we had a surprisingly good time. By the
time we drove back to Nashville just before New Year's
I felt much stronger emotionally, and I was ready to
face what had to be done. I called John Lentz and told
him to file for divorce. This time it was the real thing.
He advised me to get the property settlement out of
the way first and hold off the actual filing as long as
possible. "Once it goes on record we can't keep it from
the press," he pointed out. "And when they hear the
news, you'll be bombarded with phone calls and questions."

I told John to send word to George to decide what
he wanted in the property settlement; then we could
go from there. But George couldn't make up his mind.
One day his attorney would say he wanted the bus
and the Tyne Boulevard house; then we'd hear he'd
changed his mind and wanted the Franklin Road house
and the houseboat we kept out on Old Hickory Lake.
It had been agreed that our savings would be divided
and we would each keep our own cars.

Finally it was worked out so that he took the Tyne
Boulevard house and the houseboat, and I kept the
Franklin Road house (on which I had made the down
payment anyway) and the bus. I had fully expected
to have to go out and buy a bus, but George sent word
that he didn't need it because he didn't plan on working
for a while. I assumed responsibility for the balance
owed on both the house and the bus, which came to
more than $250,000. I bought out his part of the book-
ing agency and I kept my publishing company, and he
kept his. I didn't ask for alimony and I didn't ask for

support for Tina, Jackie, and Gwen, although I could
have because he had legally adopted them. But I did
ask for $1,000 per month child support for Georgette.
(He made exactly one payment after our divorce was
final in March 1975. By the summer of 1978 he owed
$40,000 in back child support and I finally had to sue
him for it.)

The first few months following George's departure
were the most miserable I can remember. I was glad
when Euple and Don were out of my life, but with
George gone I felt utterly lost and lonely and so
depressed I couldn't imagine ever being happy again.
More than a marriage had ended. A country music
legend had died too. George and I had worked together
for so long that promoters around the country thought
of us as one act, not two separate entertainers, and I
had come to think of us that way too. Except for the
times George was too drunk to make a show, I hadn't
worked alone in six years because we both refused to
accept a booking without the other. I had turned
down numerous television offers for that reason, and
George had turned down offers, too. So in a way we
had both hurt our careers. But we'd had the best duo
act in the business and we knew it, so we didn't feel
we needed to work alone.

I had never lost my awe of George onstage and
had depended on him to carry me through our shows
because he was more at ease with the audiences than
I was. As a team we had been booked solid for 1975,
but when Shorty started calling promoters to tell them
they could have one or the other of us but not both,
most of them canceled out. I didn't work more than
seven or eight days in January and February, and I
was scared to death. I began to wonder if my career
had left with George. If my bookings were going to
fall off, how would I meet all my financial obligations
and support my family? I worried constantly. I had
no appetite and I couldn't sleep. I was too tired to
think, and yet my brain wouldn't shut down long
enough to let me rest. Weeks passed when I didn't get

more than two or three hours sleep a night. Finally, it wore me down.

One night I was determined I was going to get some sleep, no matter what. I took two sleeping pills the doctor had prescribed and lay down to wait for them to take effect. Thirty minutes later I still felt wide awake, so I took two more sleeping pills. Still nothing happened, so I took two Valiums thinking that would relax me enough to give the sleeping pills a chance to work. By this time I'm sure I was high on the pills and didn't know it. That's what's so dangerous about pills. You can be stoned and not even realize it. Then you forget how many you've taken, so you take more. I don't know how many pills I ended up taking that night, but the next morning I was found unconscious on the bedroom floor. I don't remember anything clearly after that until the next afternoon.

I have a vague recollection of being put into an ambulance, a tube being forced down into my stomach, and then coming out of it enough in the hospital to recognize George Richey bending over me with a worried look on his face. I was told later that I had come very close to dying, but at the time I honestly had no thought of committing suicide. I just wanted to *sleep,* to rest long enough to get everything off my mind for a little while. The aftereffects of the pills made me more depressed than ever. I began thinking, Maybe it would have been better if no one had found me. Maybe I'd be better off dead. I felt utterly hopeless, which was totally unlike me, because I believe no matter how bad things look "Where there's a will, there's a way." This time, however, I had lost my will and I told Richey how I felt. I remember him saying, "Tammy, Tammy, *nothing* is worth this. There are four little girls out there on Franklin Road who have *got* to have a mother because they don't have a father. You're all they've got. You have to think of them." I felt so ashamed after it was all over that I swore I'd never fool around with pills again, even if I had to stay awake the rest of my life.

The insomnia didn't improve. Night after night after the children were asleep, I'd walk alone through the rooms of that huge house. Everywhere I looked there was something to remind me of George.

Late one night I couldn't stand it any longer. I called Nan and said, "Come on over here and let's change this place around so I won't see George Jones in every room." She brought her two roommates, Martha Turrell and Denise Shriner, and we began moving furniture, taking down pictures, packing up old mementoes, and gathering up all George's personal things. Richey and Sheila stopped by and they pitched in to help. We decided to break out a bottle of wine and make a party out of it.

Someone put a stack of George Jones records on the stereo just to prove I could take it. But when we got to the trophy room we all just stood there looking at the walls. There wasn't one space the size of your hand that didn't have some award or plaque hanging on it. We didn't know where to start. I said, "Let's put all of George's awards in the hall so I can pack them up for him, then we can rearrange mine on the walls." We started taking his down, one by one. By this time both Nanette and I were crying. Then she came to one that said "Tammy Wynette and George Jones; Vocal Duo of the Year, as voted by *Billboard* magazine." "What do I do with ones like this that are for both of you?" she asked. I said, "We'll just have to divide them up between us." It was horrible. I felt like I was dividing up something far more important than material possessions. It was like giving him the ring finger and keeping the thumb.

We came to the master bedroom last. By this time Richey had had to leave to go to a late recording session, so us girls were working alone. I wanted to change the whole room around but Sheila said, "Tammy, we'll never be able to move your bed by ourselves. It weighs a ton." Nanette, who is five-foot tall and weighs all of 95 pounds, said, "Oh yes we will!" The bed was solid mahogany, a king-sized four-poster with a wooden canopy that was lined with mirrors underneath. First we got the mattresses off and leaned them up against the steps that led down into the sunken master bedroom suite. We were all tired and had drunk enough wine to be silly by then, so we started sliding down the mattresses like a sliding board. We laughed about how ridiculous five grown women looked sliding down a mattress. Then we all stared at the bed, then at each other, as if to say, who are we kidding? We'll never move that thing! But we did. I'll never know how we managed it, because it had taken four strong men to get it in there, but we strained and struggled until we had it across the room. We flopped down to get our breath; then I looked across to the wall where the bed had been. It was empty except for one thing—the plaque George had given me when Georgette was born.

I knew it had to come down, but I couldn't bring myself to do it. Finally I went to the kitchen and came back with three screwdrivers. We started loosening the screws. No one said a word. We all knew we'd start bawling if we tried to talk. When it was down I put a sheet over it and carried it upstairs to a closet. I wanted to save it for Georgette. It was much too precious to throw away, but much too painful to keep around. We took all of George's clothes out of the closet and packed up box after box of his personal belongings. I put his favorite reading chair, which was worn almost threadbare, out in the garage to be sent out and recovered. We didn't stop until almost dawn, when everything that reminded me of George was at last out of sight.

I didn't know it at the time, but that night inspired a song that I featured in my show for a long time, always telling the audience that every line in it actually happened. I didn't write it until months later when I was working in England. I was back in the hotel after my show and I started thinking about how that night had finalized George's leaving, had made it a reality, and how I had started sleeping better after that. I knew I would never forget how hard it had been to put George's memory to rest. So I wrote the song:

> Your picture's in the closet
> Covered with a sheet that used to drape our bed
> And I can't find your glasses
> On the table where you often sat and read
> Your car's down at the station
> And your clothes are in the cleaners being pressed
> That's why the house is empty
> Oh thank God your memory's finally gone to rest
> Your chair is being covered
> It had finally seen the best of better days
> The kids put up your tennis racket
> Now nobody hardly ever plays
> Your coffee mug is gone
> And by mistake the Goodwill people took your desk
> That's why the house is empty
> Oh thank God your memory's finally gone to rest

> *Bridge:*
> Your memory's gone away from home
> Finally it's leaving me alone
> There's nothin' left to think about
> Nothin' to remember or regret
> Now the house is empty
> Oh thank God, *your memory's finally gone to rest*

Chapter 9

I HAD worked my last date with our band "The Jones Boys" in December, right after George left. On the way out of town on the bus, I told them that it was over between me and George, and that they should check with him to find out when they would be working again. I naturally assumed they would stay with him because, with the exception of our piano player, Jim Ebert, they had all been Jones Boys long before I came into the picture. I knew their loyalty was to George. I dreaded the idea of putting together a new band because it takes a long time for everyone to adjust to working and living together on the road, but I realized I had no choice.

The guys didn't ask questions about what I planned to do. They told me later they hadn't believed for a minute that it was *really* all over between me and George. Why should they? This certainly wasn't the first fight I'd had with him about his drinking; it wasn't the first time he'd left home, and it was far from the the first show he'd missed. So they figured I'd cool

down as usual, and we'd get back together. But it broke
my heart to say goodbye to them after that last show
because *I* knew it was over, even if they didn't. And
that meant I wouldn't be working with "my boys"
again.

They all went home for Christmas and I started
worrying about forming a new band. I waited until
after the holidays, then called Buddy Church, one of
the best young guitar players I'd ever heard. He was
then working for Freddie Hart. I asked if he wanted to
come with me as my lead guitar player. He said,
"Tammy have you talked with your group about this?"
I said, "Buddy, I don't have a group. The Jones Boys
are George's band, not mine. I'm sure they'll stay with
him."

"I think you'd better check with them on that,"
Buddy answered. "I wouldn't want to take a job somebody else still wanted. I have a feeling some of the
guys will ask to stay with you."

I didn't make any more phone calls after the conversation with Buddy. I decided I'd just wait and see
what happened. I didn't think it would be fair to call
The Jones Boys and offer them jobs because that would
be like asking them to choose between me and George.
But if they wanted to come on their own I sure wanted
them.

The first call came in late January from James
Hollie. He said, "Tammy, I've talked to George and
he says he's not going to work for the next four or five
months. I don't know whether he really means it or
not, and I may be doing the wrong thing after being
with him so long, but I have a family and I have to
make a living. I want to come with you. Will you take
me?" James Hollie is one of the most loyal men I've
ever met, so I knew he had wrestled with his conscience
before making his decision.

Freddie Haws called next. Freddie is like me, very
sentimental. I appreciate that in a man because I don't
believe in the old-fashioned idea that men should be
too tough to cry. I like to see people not afraid to

show emotion. I could tell from Freddie's voice that he was all choked up and I almost started crying. All he said was, "Tammy, can I come to work for you?" I said, "Freddie, I'd *love* it!"

Charlie Carter called that same day. Then the next day I heard from Sonny Curtis and Charlie Justice, all wanting to work with me. The strange thing is they hadn't gotten together and talked it over. Except for Freddie and James, who saw a lot of one another at home in Dallas, none of the rest of them knew the others were going to call me. I heard from Jim Ebert last. George and I had hired him shortly after we married. He said, "Tammy, do you need a piano player?"

I laughed and said, "Lord, yes, Jim. Do you want the job?"

He said, "I sure do!" Jim is quiet and shy. He paused for a minute then said, "Uhhhh, by the way, do I know anyone else who'll be working with us?"

I said, "I think so, Jim. I believe you know James Hollie and Freddie Haws and Sonny Curtis, Charlie Justice and Charlie Carter."

"Ohhhhh, great," I could hear him let out a sigh of relief. "When do we start?"

Harold Morrison and Patsy Sledd stayed with me too, and it made things easier having the same group with me on the road. But I was still apprehensive about facing audiences without George. Learning to work alone was even harder than learning to live alone.

My first show was in the high school auditorium in Dothan, Alabama. I'll never forget it. I wasn't halfway through the second song before someone yelled from the audience, "Where's George?" I went stiff all over. What could I say? I didn't know how to talk directly back and forth to an audience. In our show George would ask me questions or tease me, and I'd talk to him; then he would talk to the audience. He was the go-between. Without him there onstage to fend off questions or handle overzealous fans who wanted to get into the act, I felt vulnerable, exposed and *very* unsure of myself. I ignored the man's questions, but he wouldn't let up. Finally James Hollie answered him: "She doesn't know where George is. Even *George* doesn't know where George is." The audience laughed and I was able to carry on without interruption. But I knew I was going to have to learn to handle the situation myself if I was ever going to be in full command of my own show.

I soon learned that my audiences were all alike in one respect: they were curious. They wanted to know if it was *really* over between me and George and how I felt about it. Their curiosity was understandable. They had heard and read so much about us while we were married that they felt like we were members of their family. There's an intimacy between country music stars and their followers that goes beyond the usual performer/fan relationship. I knew my fans felt they had a right to know what was going on between me and George, and even though one part of me wanted desperately to guard my privacy, another side said, They're only interested because you've meant something special in their lives. Without their interest you'd still be standing behind a beautician's chair.

I decided the best way to deal with it was to answer their questions before they asked. I kept it as light as possible. I introduced the band as the "former Jones Boys," now the "Country Gentlemen." Then I'd point to them and say, "This is my half of the property settlement." That would break the ice and I could feel the audience relax. Then I'd say, "No, George is not here. I don't know where he is, but then I didn't know where he was half the time when we were married either." That always got a laugh and left the door open for me to tell them that even though I couldn't live with George I still thought he was the greatest singer in country music. That seemed to clear any tension left in the air, and I could go on with my show.

Billy Sherrill came to see me work soon after George left. Afterward we had a long talk. He said, "Tammy, I know how much you enjoy working with Harold and

Patsy, but you've got to change the format of your show. You have to let them go and get new people. The dialogue you've added is good, but as far as the show itself goes, it's the same George Jones/Tammy Wynette Show, only without George Jones. You've got to make it brand new and all yours." He was right, of course, and I knew it, but I put off telling Patsy and Harold. I had never dreaded anything more. When I finally broke the news Patsy and I both cried and Harold looked like he wanted to. They understood my predicament, but in a way that made it even worse.

Patsy said, "Well, I'm thirty years old and I've never had children, so if I'm ever going to start a family I guess now is the time." As it turned out she had a baby the next year, and she still designs and makes stage clothes for performers, including some of mine, so she has a nice little business going at home. And Harold, who had three beautiful and talented daughters, now has his own show with them. So it worked out all right for everyone. But the night we did our last show together I didn't think we'd get through it. Every time Patsy and I looked at each other we'd start to choke up. Then I'd look around at the boys and they'd be misty-eyed too. I knew we were all thinking the same thing. First George was gone from the show; now Patsy and Harold would be gone, too. We'd worked together for over five years, but it had to come to an end. It was one of the hardest adjustments I've ever had to make.

Rather than hiring one girl to sing harmony with me, as Patsy had done, I decided I wanted a singing group who could back me up and also do some numbers on their own. I looked for the right group for nearly four months, and during that time my show was so disorganized I was miserable. I knew what we were capable of doing, but we couldn't seem to get it together. There were times when I wondered if we ever would. At home, when I wasn't auditioning groups, I stayed in seclusion. I didn't even go out to dinner with friends because everywhere I went there were

questions about me and George. The press called
constantly for interviews. I hid at home to avoid having
to talk about it. Also I knew that George was in and
out of town, usually drunk, and I didn't want to take
a chance on running into him anyplace. So the girls
and I spent a lot of nights at home in front of the
television set.

One day Larry Gatlin called. Larry wasn't yet the
star that he is now, but he was well known around
Nashville as an upcoming young talent and a superb
songwriter. I had been one of the first singers to record
his material, and I had great admiration for him. "I
hear you're looking for a good backup group," he
said, "and I know where you can get one that's great."

"Well, who are they?" I wanted to know.

"My brothers and sister," Larry answered proudly.
"They're here from Texas and they sing the best
harmony you ever heard. We started singing together
in church before we started to school so they've had
a lot of practice. I want them to get road experience
because one of these days, when I make it big enough,
I want them out there with me." I had to laugh at
Larry's bold confidence about his own future.

We arranged for them to come over the next day,
and even before I heard them sing I thought, What a
good-looking family! Larry's sister LaDonna Johnson
is pretty enough to be a model. His brother Steve, who
was then teaching school, is darkly handsome, and his
youngest brother Rudy is tall, slim, and clean-cut
looking. LaDonna's husband Tim Johnson, a classical
pianist with a degree in music, accompanied them and
sang too. They didn't finish one song before I knew
this was the group I wanted. They had a unique sound
and Larry was right. It was some of the best harmony
I'd ever heard.

LaDonna had a beautiful voice, Rudy sang great
tenor, and Steve sang strong bass, but they could all
sing any part. They had their own musical sign language; LaDonna would hold up a finger in the middle
of a song and they'd all switch parts. When they sang

with me, Rudy and LaDonna would find their parts, and then Steve would find the fill-in notes that made the sound so different, so *good*. My band took to the Gatlins as quickly as I did, an important consideration when you have to live together in such close quarters. I named them "Young Country" and they went out with us on the very next tour. We redesigned the back bedroom of the bus, the room I had shared with George, into sleeping quarters for four. Including the Gatlins, my bus driver Steve Morse and Nanette, we had thirteen traveling on a bus designed to sleep ten comfortably. But someone usually sat up with the driver, and we'd switch off sleeping on the couch up front, so we never felt overcrowded. In fact, with George gone and the cheerful, spirited Gatlins along, the atmosphere on the bus was so much more relaxed and tension-free that going out was almost like going to a party.

Little by little I was beginning to gain confidence in my ability to carry a show without George. Bookings were picking up, and with the addition of the Gatlins and some new dialogue I worked out with my band, I knew I had put together a good show. I was proud of it and proud of myself for not being as dependent on George as I'd thought I was.

I was also gaining confidence in another area—my writing. During those first few months after George left, I think I would have gone crazy if I hadn't been able to go to the piano or pick up a guitar and pour out in music everything that was bottled up inside. Until then I had rarely ever written a song alone, but I suddenly found ideas almost as fast as I could write them on paper. I even wrote songs for George, because I knew he was going through a time as rough as my own. "These Days I Barely Get By" and "I Just Drove By to See If I Was Really Gone" were two I wrote that he recorded. Every time I wrote a song that expressed my own feelings, like "Slightly Used Woman," "The Bottle" or " 'Til I Can Make It on My Own" (which I wrote with Sherrill and George Richey), I would add it to my act, telling the audiences how and when it was written and what it meant to my life at that time. This made my show more intimate than it had ever been. The fans felt I was sharing my innermost feelings with them, and I was.

Often an almost mystical exchange would happen during this part of the show. The audience responded to me with an equal intimacy, and I would come off stage feeling I had actually known or experienced these people in such a close way it's difficult to put into words. It was almost like the sudden familiarity that sweeps over acquaintances who've just become lovers. I knew I was growing as a performer, but I also felt I was learning to open up as a human being. I liked the feeling but it was also a little frightening.

Putting together a new show and working the road kept me too busy to think about a social life for months after George left. Dating was the last thing on my mind when I went to Montgomery near the end of April to do a benefit show called "Stars Over Alabama." It's an annual event sponsored by Governor Wallace to raise money for state programs for handicapped and retarded children. George and I had worked the show for the Governor every year we'd been together; this was to be my first appearance there without him and I was a little apprehensive about that. There was always a big celebrity turnout for the benefit, and the Governor was especially proud about showing off native Alabamians who had become well known. (He considered me in this category even though I was born across the state line in Mississippi; he called that a "mere technicality.")

At the reception at the Governor's Mansion before the show, he greeted me with outstretched arms and pulled me down on his lap. He was lively and vigorous for a man in a wheelchair, and he started teasing me about being his favorite girl. Then he said, "Tammy, I want you to meet a Montgomery boy who does a lot to help us out on this program for retarded children." He was looking up behind me, and I turned around

and let my eyes follow the direction of his. I thought
my eyes would never reach the top of the man; he was
the biggest thing I'd ever seen in my life. When I
finally got to his face he winked and I thought, Well,
now aren't you something! He was dark complected,
with jet black curly hair and a "bad-little-boy" smile.
He was wearing an expensively tailored off-white suit
that made him look even darker, and I thought he was
the best looking thing I'd seen in a long time. When
I stood up my face barely reached the middle of his
chest. I found out later that he was six-foot-six and
weighed about 265 pounds, but there wasn't an ounce
of fat on him.

Governor Wallace said, "This is Tommy Neville. He
plays football for the New England Patriots. He stays
in Boston half the year, but Alabama is still his home."
Tommy grinned and I felt a little weak in the knees.
We exchanged "hellos" and chatted for a minute before I moved on down the reception line, but I kept
looking at him out of the corner of my eye all evening.
It was easy to keep track of him because he was a
head taller than anyone else in the room. Every time
I glanced his way, I'd catch him looking at me, but
we never had a chance to talk. I had been seated at
dinner with Trini Lopez, Dale Robertson, and Ken
Stabler, the quarterback for the Oakland Raiders, but
I wanted to be at Tommy's table.

After dinner all the performers had to rush over
to the auditorium. Backstage I caught sight of Tommy
once when I was talking to Roy Clark and Wayne
Rogers of "M*A*S*H," but I couldn't break away
to go over to him. After the show I started out to my
bus which was parked by the auditorium door. Suddenly I felt a hand on my shoulder and turned to see
Tommy looming above me. He wanted to know if I
was going to the breakfast that had been arranged for
the entertainers at the Legion Hall. I hadn't planned
to, but I changed my mind quick. It had been a long
time since I'd met a man whose gaze made me feel
tingly, and I wanted a chance to get to know Tommy

Neville. During breakfast I discovered that he had a good sense of humor; he was confident but not arrogant; and he knew how to keep a conversation going. That was important to me because I've always been shy around strangers. When there's an awkward silence I feel like it's my fault so I usually react nervously and say something silly or dumb. But by the time breakfast was over, I was very impressed with this gentle giant who made me feel at ease in his company. When he asked where I was staying in town I told him I wasn't. "We have to drive on tonight," I lied. "The bus is pulling out as soon as we finish breakfast." I didn't know why I was lying. We were headed back to Nashville, but we didn't have a date until the next weekend, so we weren't on any time schedule. I guess I didn't want to face the possibility of not knowing how to handle the situation if we ended up alone. I didn't think I was ready for romance even though I had enjoyed the evening's flirtation. Tommy walked me to my bus, then leaned down and gave me a light kiss, just barely touching his lip to mine. Before I was fifty miles out of Montgomery I was ready to turn around and go back, but of course I couldn't do that. I told myself I was going to have to date sooner or later, even though the idea scared me. I hadn't even liked it in high school. I had always preferred one steady boyfriend. But I knew that if I didn't learn to like dating, I'd have to learn to like being alone. As for Tommy Neville, I thought, Well, I've seen the last of him. But I made up my mind that the next time I met an attractive man I'd go out with him, even if I did feel uneasy.

When I came off the road the following weekend Jackie said, "Mama, Tommy Neville called you." He had told her to tell me he had called, but he hadn't left a number where I could reach him. Then in May he called again. This time he caught me at home. He told me he had some time off in June before he started training in Boston and asked if we could spend a few days together. I checked my bookings and found al-

most a week free during that time, so we decided I'd
fly to Montgomery rather than him coming to Nashville. The minute he hung up I was dialing Nanette to
tell her all about our plans. I was excited and eager to
see him again but very nervous about it. Nanette kept
saying, "Don't worry. You'll have a great time," but
her encouragement didn't stop the butterflies in my
stomach.

Tommy met me at the Montgomery airport wearing
levis and a tee shirt. He looked even bigger than I remembered. I felt like a fourteen year old out with the
senior football star. He took me by the arm and led
me to the baggage claim area, chatting along the way
like an old friend. I was so thankful he was doing all
the talking. My mouth was dry and I couldn't think of
a thing to say. He suggested we go by his apartment so
he could pick up his bags, then drive down to Panama
City where he had friends who had a place on the
ocean. I knew he sensed my apprehension and nervousness, and he was very understanding about it. For the
next couple of days he did everything possible to make
me feel at ease with him. His friends in Panama City
welcomed me warmly and I soon began to unwind. We
sunned on the beach and swam in the Gulf, rode all
the rides at the amusement park, went to romantic
places for dinner and spent hours talking. Tommy
made it clear that he enjoyed being with me whether
anything happened between us or not. That did won-
ders to help me feel comfortable and relaxed, and
when we finally made love it was because I wanted to,
not because I thought he expected it of me.

I know this helped me get over my fear of reaching
out to touch someone again. Before George came into
my life I had never really been in love, so I had always held something back, always kept a little barrier
between myself and the man in my life. But I had loved
George too much to hold back. I had no choice but
to let go completely, so when he hurt me, he hurt me
with all my defenses down. He got to my core and
caused something there to close up so tight it might

have stayed that way if I'd had a bad experience the
first time I wanted to be with a man again. I'll always
be grateful to Tommy Neville for having the sensitivity
to let things happen between us at my pace, not his.
We dated off and on for the next year and I loved his
company, but our schedules never allowed us to be in
the same place very often or for more than a day or
two at a time, so there was no chance for a real love
affair to develop.

Surprisingly, the person I loved being with the most
during this time was Rudy Gatlin. I say surprisingly
because it certainly surprised me. I would never have
expected myself to become involved with a man ten
years younger than I. If anything I'd always been attracted to men a little older, or at least my own age.
Rudy was only twenty-four, just barely grown up, but
I had more fun with him than I'd ever had with anyone before. Our dating was just a natural thing that
happened, starting very casually at first because we
were the only two single people on the bus. If we had
a night off on the road we'd go to a movie or go
bowling, anything to get out of the motel. Or if we
were riding all night, Rudy and I would often sit up
after everyone else but our driver Steve had gone to
bed, talking and listening to Mickey Newberry tapes.
It was the kind of atmosphere that coaxes thoughts to
come out. The rest of the group on the bus would be
fast asleep, and the drone of the big engines cutting
through the black night made you feel suspended in
time, with blackout curtains and Mickey's soft, sweet,
sad music shutting out the rest of the world.

Rudy was also the comedian of the Gatlin family,
and he kept the rest of us on the bus entertained. I
loved his sense of humor, and I had never known a
man who could make me laugh so often and so easily.
Dating him made me feel almost like a kid again—
carefree and happy-go-lucky. It was good for me because my own early twenties had been nothing but
poverty, hard work, and unhappiness.

With Rudy I felt twenty again and it was like having

a chance to go back and relive those years with a happier attitude. The difference in our ages didn't make either of us feel strange. In fact, sometimes I felt younger than Rudy. We had some wonderful times together with LaDonna and Tim, Steve and his wife Cynthia (who stayed at my house to supervise the girls while we were on the road). We went snow skiing in Colorado, water skiing in Acapulco, and once we took a Caribbean cruise together. When we stopped in Nassau we rented motor scooters on Paradise Island and rode all over the place. The last night out on the ship was so beautiful that Rudy and I decided to sleep up on the top deck in lounge chairs by the pool. Jackie had brought a girl friend along on the cruise so they joined us, and we talked half the night away, looking up at a full moon with a million stars so close you felt you could almost reach out and touch them.

Rudy knew that I was also seeing Tommy Neville, and later Burt Reynolds, but that didn't cause any problems between us because there was never any question of our relationship being an exclusive one. Rudy was good for me; he made me get out and do things. Before I got into the business there hadn't been any money for entertainment, and afterward my life was divided between being on the road and being a homemaker.

The road has a way of making you want to stay at home when you're there. After a tour, cooking a big pot of beans for supper and watching television in the comfort of your own home can seem like a luxury. The dating life was new to me, and I was beginning to enjoy it more than I ever thought I would. But my basic instinct to share life with one man was always just beneath the surface, and I knew it was only a matter of time before I would again be longing for the solid, steady kind of relationship I could never expect to have with Rudy. Nevertheless the fun times with him were by far the most carefree and relaxed I had during that first year and a half after George left.

From the day he walked out of the Franklin Road

house I didn't see George Jones again until the next
fall at the annual Deejay Convention in Nashville. (He
left on December 13, 1974, our divorce was final
March 13, 1975, and I first saw him again on October
13 that same year. I wonder if the three thirteens were
significant!) The night of our first meeting was traumatic for me in more ways than one.

The month before I had been in Los Angeles ending
a tour with Johnny Rodriguez. My old friend Mac
Davis called and invited me to have dinner at his house.
I naturally assumed his wife Sarah would be there, but
when I arrived he was alone. He explained that Sarah
had gone to visit her mother. Then he made a point
of mentioning that they had been having a few minor
problems; he blamed it on his heavy work schedule.

Anyone who knew Mac Davis knew that he worshiped the beautiful teenage wife he had married a few
years earlier. They lived in a cute little house tucked
away in one of the canyons between Hollywood and
the San Fernando Valley, and it had the atmosphere of
a cozy love nest. Sarah had decorated it with interest-
ing and whimsical antiques, and there were pictures of
her or the two of them together hanging everywhere. I
especially remember one. It showed Mac and Sarah
facing one another, standing in the rain. He had his
hand gently cupped under her chin, turning her face
up toward his as though he were about to kiss her.
There were drops of water on his hair and the expression on his face was so full of love it made you want
to cry. When I commented on it he said, "Yes, isn't
she beautiful?" That night he barbecued steaks and
we played guitars and sang and talked about the business. It was a nice, pleasant evening and I remember
thinking that Sarah was a lucky girl. When I left he
was watering plants which hung everywhere, remarking
that they were Sarah's pride and joy. "I have to take
good care of them while she's gone, or she'll kill me,"
he said.

Two nights later Johny Rodriguez asked me to go
with him to a party at the home of a woman who did

publicity work for him and a lot of other celebrities, including Mac Davis and Glen Campbell. A group of us were sitting around drinking wine and listening to records when she said, "I just finished making arrangements for a Glen Campbell tour and you won't believe who's going with him." We all knew Glen had recently moved out on his wife Billie, but we hadn't heard he was already seeing someone else.

"Who? Tell us who he's taking!" we asked.

"Sarah Davis," she answered.

I was stunned. I said, "You don't mean *the* Sarah Davis, Mac's wife?"

She said, "Yes, I do. She's living with Glen right now and Glen is supposed to be Mac's best friend. But Mac has no idea what's going on."

We all just looked at one another, shocked. I said, "Why don't they at least tell Mac? He thinks Sarah is visiting her mother."

"I know, and it makes me feel terrible," the woman said. "I'm caught in the middle. I don't feel it's my place to tell Mac, but I feel guilty that I know and he doesn't."

After I got back to the hotel that night I thought about Mac's situation for a long time. I wondered if I should call him, but I knew I couldn't. If what the woman said was true I certainly didn't want to be the one to wound Mac with such heartbreaking news. Besides, there was always the chance that she was mistaken. I told myself that it was none of my business anyway. If it was true, Sarah and Glen would eventually be forced to tell Mac, and he should hear it from them, not an outsider. Furthermore, I had considered Glen and his wife Billie my friends, too. I decided to put what I'd heard out of my mind.

A few days later the tour was over and I flew back to Nashville to be a presenter for the Country Music Association TV Awards Show. George and I were up for "Best Duet of the Year," which was ironic under the circumstances, and I was a nervous wreck about the prospect of seeing him again. I didn't know if he'd come drunk and act obnoxious, if he'd be sober and nice, or if he wouldn't show at all. After ten months I had no idea what his reaction to me would be if we did see one another. But the first person I saw backstage at rehearsal was Mac Davis. He was hosting part of the show and Glen Campbell was doing the rest. Mac waved as he went onstage to do a runthrough and I noticed he was wearing a tee shirt that said, "The Glen Campbell Open." I thought, "Lord, he still hasn't heard anything or he wouldn't be wearing that shirt!"

I soon discovered that the main topic of discussion backstage was Sarah, Glen, and Mac. Apparently everyone knew but Mac. Glen wasn't scheduled to come in until later that afternoon for rehearsal, but he and Mac had played golf together that very morning in Glen's tournament, and Mac had been joking and carrying on with his buddy like always. He had no suspicion that his wife and his best friend had become lovers, or that she was back in Los Angeles that very minute waiting for Glen to return. It shows what love does to people, because Glen is just not the kind of guy to steal another man's wife. I felt sick for Mac and angry at the way he was being treated.

I think at that moment I might have told him, but before he came offstage I looked up to see George Jones walking toward me. He had on a blue tux for dress rehearsal and he really looked good. As he walked toward me I could feel my stomach and my throat tighten up. He stopped just a few feet away, and for a minute we both just stood there and looked at one another. Then he said, "Can't we at least talk? Can't we be friends?"

I said, "Of course we can." And I turned and led the way into my dressing room so we could have some privacy. Being with him wasn't as strained as I had thought it would be, but it wasn't comfortable either. He was so familiar to me that looking at his face was almost like looking in the mirror, but at the same time he was a stranger too. For a moment it was like we were still married—just there to do a show the way we'd done so many other times. But that feeling of oneness we'd shared was gone. We were both wary and on guard. We talked about Georgette and the other girls, and I invited him to come to the house for dinner when he had some time. We had a very civilized conversation but I knew we were both aching inside from the sadness of what we'd lost.

Before I went onstage to rehearse I heard my name called over the loudspeaker, "Telephone call for Tammy Wynette." It was Tommy Neville's answering service. They said he'd been trying to reach me and had left this message: "I believe you could use some support tonight. My plane arrives in Nashville at 7:30 P.M. Could you have someone pick me up and arrange for me to see the awards show?" I thought, What a sweet thing for him to do. He knew that George was scheduled to be there and that I was very apprehensive about it. I was delighted he was coming but a little nervous at the thought of George seeing me backstage with another man. But I knew he had to see me with someone else sooner or later, so I might as well face it.

When I finished my rehearsal Mac was already gone. I went home to change and get ready for the show, then to the airport to pick up Tommy. I stayed in my dressing room until I was called on camera as a presenter, so I didn't see Mac at all that night except on the television monitor. George and I lost out as "Duo of the Year" so I didn't have to go onstage but once. When the show was over Tommy came back to the dressing room with me to get my things, and the first person we ran into was George. He knew who Tommy was because he'd heard we'd been dating. He extended his hand and said, "I'm George Jones. It's nice to meet you." Tommy was more flustered than George, who seemed to be in complete control of the situation. They acknowledged one another, then there was an awkward moment when there was nothing left to say. But there was so much noise and confusion backstage that no one noticed it but us. We said goodnight and went our separate ways.

Tommy's plane left the next morning, so I took him to the airport, then went back home to get ready for the BMI Awards dinner that night. I hadn't wanted to take a date, so I had asked Nanette to go with me. The BMI banquet is traditionally one of the highlight events of Deejay week. Hundreds of guests come to the cocktail party and dinner to see BMI Vice President and Regional Manager Frances Preston give out awards to songwriters whose tunes have been performed the most during the previous year.

Nanette and I spotted Mac Davis as soon as we stepped inside the crowded tent which had been erected behind the BMI building on Music Row. I knew instantly by the expression on his face that Mac had heard about Sarah and Glen. He worked his way through the crowd to me. His first words were, "Why didn't you tell me, Tammy?" He'd been drinking and he was understandably bitter.

I said, "Mac, I couldn't. I just couldn't."

"I thought I had a lot of friends in Nashville," he said, "and now I find out they were all laughing behind my back."

I said, "Oh, Mac. No one was laughing. The people who knew felt terrible for you, but no one wanted to come up to you and say, 'Guess what, Mac,' about something as painful as this. I'm so sorry. Please don't be mad at me."

We talked for a few minutes longer, then he asked me if I'd come across the street to his suite at the Spence Manor after the banquet. I said I would.

The BMI awards presentation always goes on late into the night, and Nanette went home as soon as it was over. When I arrived at Mac's suite Frances and her husband E. J. Preston were there with Roger Sovine, also of BMI, and his wife Shirley. Apparently Mac had gotten drunk during the long evening and had gone wild. He had thrown things around the suite and cursed and carried on, and they were just calming him down and sobering him up.

I learned that someone backstage at the CMA show

had told Mac about Sarah and Glen the night before. Mac heard the story while Glen was onstage. He was so hurt and outraged he would have probably hit Glen if he could have gotten his hands on him, but he had to go on camera the minute Glen came off. Then while Mac was onstage someone warned Glen, so he got out of there fast and Mac never could find him after the show. The next day Glen was already on his way back to Los Angeles, where Sarah was waiting. Mac had finally contacted her a few minutes before I came to his suite, and she had told him everything. I had never seen a man so down in my life.

After the Prestons and the Sovines left, I sat up with Mac all night while he talked (as much to himself as to me) trying to understand why it had happened. Before dawn he started working on a song . . . "Every now and then a blind squirrel finds an acorn, and every now and then a crippled sparrow learns to fly. . . ." The words were so touching I wanted to cry. It was Mac's way of saying I've been a fool, but I won't let it destroy me.

Three weeks later I had to have surgery for adhesions and I was really depressed about it. I had already had three operations in as many years—an appendectomy, a hysterectomy, and surgery to remove adhesions that had formed as a result of those two. I was sick of hospitals and resentful of the physical problems I'd been having. I was feeling sorry for myself when the phone rang next to my hospital bed. It was Mac calling from Los Angeles. He had finished his song and wanted me to hear it. It was so sad that I told him it made me even more depressed. He said, "If I've got a friend in Nashville, it's you. I want you to know that I love you and if you ever need a friend please call me." When I got home from the hospital there was a beautiful bouquet of flowers waiting for me. The card read "Love from the Blind Squirrel to the Crippled Sparrow."

Mac and I have crossed paths only a few times since

then, but I'll always feel close to him. When he was hurting he wasn't ashamed to let it show, and that takes a lot of courage for a proud man like Mac. Life is so uncertain. Just a few months before George and I split up, we were in Los Angeles and had dinner with Mac and Sarah, Billie and Glen Campbell, and Leah and Roger Miller. It was a fun evening and we all teased about being "old married couples." Less than a year later we were all divorced.

George started dropping by the house once in a while when he was in town. The girls were delighted to see him and I was hopeful that we could have a good relationship for their sake. Billy wanted us to start recording together again, and frankly I missed singing with George, so we agreed. Our first single, "Golden Rings," which was written for us by Billy and George Richey, went to number one on the charts, as did our second release, "Near You."

We appeared onstage together a few times, and the audience response was always overwhelming. They loved seeing us together again, but I'm afraid it gave some fans false hope. A lot of them still had (and still have today) romantic notions about George and I getting back together. Fans don't give up easy when they've loved you as a couple, as well as individually. It was the same with Sonny and Cher and Richard Burton and Elizabeth Taylor. Nobody wanted to believe they were really through forever. Even now after nearly four years, I hardly ever do a show when someone doesn't ask "Where's George?" or "When are you and George getting back together?" I have even had fans try to get me to sign *his* autograph along beside mine. It doesn't seem to matter how many times I tell audiences or reporters that George and I will *never* get back together; they don't want to believe it, so they don't listen. But it's true.

If there is one thing in life I am sure of, it's that I will never live with George Jones again. He will always be my favorite singer and I certainly don't regret the time we had together. If I had it to do all over again I'd still marry him, even knowing what I know now. But once was enough.

For a time after the divorce I thought we could be friends. Now I'm uncertain even about that. He's called the house, drunk, and said ugly things a few times, and I guess having to sue him for Georgette's child support has made me bitter. I didn't want to be forced to put pressure on him. But for her sake I would like to be able to have a civil relationship with George. I know it would be better for everybody if we could.

By the end of 1975 I was beginning to feel secure in my career again, and I was also enjoying my first real experience with a single social life. But things had begun to happen around my home that were becoming more and more terrifying, and I often found myself wishing there was a man in the house.

It started in the spring of 1975, not long after my divorce from George was final. At first it was just little annoyances, like mysterious phone calls. There would be someone at the other end of the line because you could hear them breathing, but they wouldn't say a word. Sometimes we'd get twenty or thirty of these calls in a night. I had my number changed so frequently the phone company thought I was crazy, but everytime I got a new unlisted number the calls would begin again within a few hours, as if to say I know everything that's going on at your house.

I also received threats on my life several times when I was on the road. Once in Evansville, Indiana, the caller even threatened the hotel switchboard operator. She was petrified.

Then the break-ins began at home. Even though my house is on a main thoroughfare, it is very secluded because it sits way back from the road and is surrounded by twelve acres of land. The roof on the house is flat and it's easy to climb up on it. Several times when there was evidence of a break-in, the police found the skylight open and cigarette butts left lying on the roof. On these occasions the burglar alarm wires had been cut in the basement.

Whoever was doing it wanted me to know they'd been in the house. They never stole anything. But they'd leave unmistakable evidence that they'd been there— like the kitchen faucet running full force with the sink plugged up. That time two rooms of the house were flooded. Another time all the windows on one side of the house were broken. One night two windows in my bedroom were smashed in with rocks while Tina and I were lying in my bed watching television. She got little cuts all over her legs from the shattered glass.

Another night, after we'd all gone to bed, Jackie went to the kitchen to get something to drink. The house was dark so she couldn't be seen from the outside. She was standing by the kitchen window when she heard the voices of two men outside. They were debating about which side of the house to break into. She couldn't see them in the dark shadows, but she heard them distinctly. She ran to my room to get me, and just as I got back to the kitchen with her a big boulder came smashing through the window where she'd been standing a few seconds earlier.

But the most terrifying of the incidents started one Sunday afternoon when George Richey had taken all the girls to the roller rink. His wife Sheila had stayed at home with me, but whoever was watching the house evidently thought we'd all left when they saw George's big Lincoln pull out full of people. It was starting to get dark, but Sheila and I were just sitting around talking, so we hadn't turned on the lights. Suddenly we heard noise upstairs on the roof.

It was the sound of someone walking. We figured they were headed for the skylight. We were two women alone in a twenty-two-room house that was growing darker by the minute, and we were scared! Sheila picked up a fire poker and I picked up a butcher knife—we didn't have a gun in the house because I was afraid of them—and we huddled by the back door not knowing whether to run out and try to get to the car in the garage, or to stay put and hope we wouldn't be discovered.

Just then the phone rang. It was Gwen calling from the skating rink to give me a message for a girl friend who was going to call. I whispered what was happening and told her to tell Richey to come as fast as he could By the time he got there ten minutes later the noise had stopped. But when he drove up outside, he saw dirty words like "slut," "whore" and "pig" written on doors, the side of the house, and on windows in both lipstick and red paint. After that I wasn't about to spend the night there alone with the girls, so I packed some nightclothes for all of us, and we went back to the roller rink to pick them up. We spent the night with Richey and Sheila.

The next morning, after the girls had been taken to school, Richey drove me home. I had locked the house securely and set the burglar alarm before leaving the night before. We entered the house through the back door and walked down the hall to the kitchen. As you come into the room from that direction you are facing a brick wall surrounding a fireplace. There, written all over the bricks in white chalk, were the same words we'd seen outside—"pig," "whore" and "slut." We rushed from room to room and discovered that every mirror, every television set and some of the walls had the same words scrawled across them in bold print. We called the police (we had also notified them the night before), and after they'd looked around and found nothing—no evidence of a break-in, and yet the burglar alarm had been disconnected—Richey and I cleaned the walls and mirrors so the girls wouldn't see the words when they came home from school.

By the time he left I was emotionally drained and physically tired from not having slept well the night before. I decided to try to take a nap. I lay down on my bed and started to close my eyes. For some reason I glanced up at the mirror under the wooden canopy above my head. "YOU SLUT," printed in bright red lipstick, stared back at me through my own reflection.

Someone had crawled on my bed to write those words above me. I screamed and jumped up. It was terrifying to realize that whoever was responsible for this harassment knew my household well enough to know there was a mirror underneath the canopy over the bed where I slept.

I also began receiving notes in my mailbox that had been pasted together from letters cut out of magazines and newspapers. They said things like "Tammy Wynette you will soon die" or "Death isn't so bad. You'll soon find out."

All together there were fifteen break-ins at the house in nine months. I called the police so many times they got tired of coming. They would find small clues like trampled shrubbery or a discarded cigarette, but they never caught anyone on the grounds, and they never even came up with a good lead as to who was doing all this. It was impossible for the police to patrol grounds as large as mine continually, so I hired security guards to keep watch. During that period not one incident occurred. But after three months I let them go, and the breaks-ins started again.

The strangest part is that nothing frightening or suspicious ever happened at the house while I was on the road. It would always take place when I was at home, as though the intention was not to frighten my children but to scare me! And they did a good job! I became so jumpy that the least noise outside at night would suddenly wake me up, and I'd end up walking the floor for hours before I could sleep again. Many times I called Rudy to bring his gun and come over to spend the night, just so I could get some rest. Other nights we'd all pile in the car and drive to Richey and Sheila's house to sleep.

I had grown closer and closer to Rudy during this time, even though I occasionally dated other men. I saw much more of him than anyone else because we were on the road together in addition to seeing one another in Nashville; the kids always had fun with Rudy and he was around the house often. But little by little word began getting back to me that his brother Larry was very upset about our relationship.

By this time items had been printed in gossip columns linking my name with Rudy's, and Larry had told people he didn't like the kind of publicity his "little brother" was getting. He began putting pressure on Rudy to stop dating me, even though he knew how difficult that would be since we were on the road together more than twenty days a month. As the oldest, Larry had been the undisputed leader of his brothers and sister since they were small children. What he considered a "protective" interest in their lives often seemed more like demanding interference to outsiders. Larry wanted Steve and LaDonna to help him persuade Rudy to end our relationship. This caused tension in the whole group. Rudy was torn between loyalty to his family and his desire to continue seeing me. I don't think Steve and LaDonna wanted to take sides, but when Larry pushed they didn't have much choice.

If you're living in close quarters with someone you're dating, as when Rudy and I were on the road, there's bound to be friction now and then. But the least little thing that happened between me and Rudy was blown up all out of proportion because of Larry's desire to break us up. I don't know why he felt so threatened. Rudy and I were just two people who sincerely cared for one another and enjoyed good times together—he with an older woman, me with a younger man. But Larry tried to make it seem evil and ugly. It wasn't. And no one knew that better than Rudy and I.

Larry was always nice to my face, but the unkind things he was saying about me around Nashville kept filtering back, and I was really hurt. The pressure got so heavy at one point that Rudy and I did try to stop dating. But the strain of trying to stay apart while working together was just too much, especially when there was no good reason *not* to date, so we started seeing one another again. By this time, however, I knew that Larry wanted his brothers and sister out of my show as well as out of my life. He had often tried to convince Rudy that an involvement with me would eventually hurt him, not help him. As it turned out, circumstances proved Larry right. Larry got his chance to say "I told you so." But it came about in a way none of us could ever have predicted.

The night that ended my relationship with Rudy started off as a fun family evening. Mama Pugh and Aunt Athalene were visiting me from Alabama, and I was determined not to let my worry and preoccupation over the break-ins at the house keep me from enjoying what little time we had together. That night Rudy took us all to see *One Flew Over the Cuckoo's Nest* at the Melrose Theater (Georgette had gone to Mississippi for the weekend with MeeMaw and PeePaw; Tina was spending the night out; and Jackie and Gwen each had a girl friend over for the night). We sat around talking about the movie for a little while after we got home; then I began to get a stomach ache, so Rudy went home and I went to bed. A little while later I got up and went into the kitchen to get some Pepto Bismol. Athalene was sitting at the kitchen table drinking a beer. Everyone else had gone to bed, and Mama Pugh was already asleep. I sat down with Athalene, hoping my stomach ache would ease up so I could go to sleep.

We were talking quietly when we suddenly heard noises outside by the kitchen windows. It was raining softly, but we could distinguish sounds of someone running, then low voices. I immediately called Rudy and asked him to come over and bring his gun. I also called Richey and Sheila and told them that we just might all end up spending the night over there. They said to bring sleeping bags for the girls and come over. When Rudy arrived he searched all around the outside of the house, but he couldn't find anything. It had begun raining harder, but after Rudy came back inside the house and things settled down, we began to hear the noises again. First it sounded like someone out by the poolhouse. Then it sounded like someone was trying to get into the basement. I decided we were definitely going to Richey and Sheila's. By this time the girls were already out of bed, so we woke Mama Pugh up, got our things together, and started to leave.

Just as we were about to go out the back door Rudy said he smelled something burning. He ran down the hall and saw smoke coming from under the office door, which was two doors away from my bedroom. We called the fire department and everybody ran outside to wait under the covered patio by the pool. It was still raining, and the actual flames hadn't spread beyond the office when the fire engines arrived, so they were able to put out the fire quickly.

After they left we checked on the damage. The office had been gutted by fire and what hadn't been burned had been ruined by water. We gathered everything together again to go to Richey and Sheila's. But before we could get out the back door Jackie said, "Mama, I smell smoke again." I thought she was still smelling the burnt-out office, but when Rudy and I walked down the hall to look, smoke was billowing out from under the door to the trophy room, which was between the office and my bedroom. We didn't want to open the door and take a chance on flames leaping into the hallway and across to the living room, so we ran outside to look through the window. Flames were shooting ten feet into the air from that room, even though it was raining hard. We could see the fire was spreading fast this time, so we rushed to call the fire department again. But the phone lines were dead.

Rudy was about to jump in a car and drive for help when someone pulled into the driveway. It was a reporter from one of the local TV stations who had come by to check on the report of the first fire. Luckily he had a mobile phone in his car, so he called the fire department and the police. Meanwhile Rudy, myself, and the older girls grabbed buckets from the garage and began hauling water from the pool to pour on the fire. That must have looked ridiculous in the pouring rain, but we didn't know what else to do.

Nothing can make you feel more helpless than a

raging fire, and this one was moving faster by the second. We were all drenched to the skin and our water brigade wasn't affecting the fire, but we kept it up for more than fifteen minutes, until the fire department arrived. We thought they were never going to get there, but we found out later there had been a mix-up about the call. They had thought the reporter was talking about the first fire, and they tried to tell him they had already been there and put it out. By the time they hooked up their hoses, the master bedroom wing of the house was completely destroyed, another section was badly burned, and smoke and water had damaged most of the other rooms on the front side of the house. Newsmen on the scene estimated the damage at more than $300,000.

My bedroom was nothing but a smoldering shell with charred beams where the roof had been and a partially burnt wall on two sides. My dressing room area, where many of my show clothes and all my furs and personal wardrobe were kept, was a heap of smoking rubble. The trophy room where I kept all my awards, gold albums, and career mementoes, was in ashes. The office where my important business papers and personal records were stored was gone. The whole house reeked of smoke and that awful smell of burned-out debris.

When it was over I was limp with fatigue and sick with fear. If they would go this far, what wouldn't they do? I was relieved that we were all safe, but the thought of what could have happened still frightened me! I knew I could easily have been killed. The house is laid out so that the master bedroom suite is far enough away from the other bedroom wings for complete privacy. If I hadn't gotten up with a stomach ache, and if Athalene had already gone to bed, I could have been overcome by smoke from the first fire before anyone discovered it. But the sense of loss I felt over all my precious mementoes and personal items that had been destroyed was even greater than my fear.

What I didn't know was that the worst was yet to come.

We spent the night with Sheila and Richey, then moved the next day to an apartment while the fire investigators took over and the mess was cleaned up.

You see shows on television where the victim of some crime ends up being treated like a criminal, but you don't think anything like that could ever happen to you—until it does.

Before the arson investigators had finished with us my entire family had been interrogated like criminals, and Rudy Gatlin had been put through so much hell it brought about the end of our relationship. The strain and tension on all of us was such that we agreed it would be better if the Gatlins found other employment. (Rudy and Steve are now on the road with Larry, and LaDonna and her husband Tim work for an evangelist whose ministry is aimed at young people.)

The investigators said evidence showed the fire had been deliberately set. Reporters were *constantly* calling them to see if they had any leads, and they named Rudy as a suspect, even though they had absolutely nothing to base it on. A story was actually printed in the paper naming him as the possible arsonist. It was horrible for him. They put him through hours and hours of questions, grilling, and harassment. He volunteered to take a lie detector test, which he passed, and they finally had to admit he was innocent. The newspaper did print a retraction of the first story implicating him, but as so often happens in those cases, the retraction was buried deep inside the paper whereas the story naming him as a suspect had been in the first section.

Even though the investigators knew there were fifteen police reports on file of break-ins at my house, they insisted that the fire was an unrelated incident and an "inside" job.

After they gave up on Rudy, they turned to Gwen. They said she had wanted to burn the house down because she was afraid I was going to move the family to a house I'd bought in Florida, and she didn't want to leave her school friends behind. I told them I thought their reasoning was very bizarre. If she didn't want to leave Nashville why would she burn down her home and take a chance on forcing me to make a decision to move to the beach house?

After Gwen passed her lie detector test they went to work on her girl friend, who had been at the house that night. They asked her where she'd been sleeping. When she said "with Gwen" they tried to make something dirty out of girl friends sleeping in the same bed. Then they went to work on Jackie and her girl friend. They put them all through hours and hours of questioning. Through all this, I insisted on being present with my attorney, John Lentz. I was helpless to stop the ordeal because I knew we all had to be officially cleared before the insurance claim could be settled.

When they were satisfied that none of them had set the fire, the next suspect on their list was my Aunt Athalene. After she was cleared they were really desperate, so they decided the fire had been started by my Mama Pugh. That's when I put my foot down. I sent her back to Mississippi and absolutely refused to let them put her through the same harassment they'd put the rest of us through. The insurance company naturally didn't want to pay off a claim as big as mine, so they were determined to try to prove the fire had been started by one of us.

I believed I knew how the fire was started and I told them so repeatedly. I think someone got into the house while we were at the movies, then waited until we returned home to set the first fire. He thought we were all in bed because Athalene hadn't turned on the kitchen light when she came in to sit down. When the fire department came the first time I think the arsonist was still hiding in the house. There are 17,600 square feet and plenty of places to hide. When the first fire didn't do as much damage as he wanted it to, he went out through the broken windows, cut the wires, came back in, and set the second one, then escaped in all the confusion. But the investigators wouldn't listen to my idea. They continued to insist it had been an inside job, although every one of us had been cleared.

The fire department and insurance people boarded up and sealed off the burned-out section of the house. They wouldn't let me get in there to begin repairs until their "investigation" was finished. Months passed, and my attorney John Lentz had to go through hassle after hassle with them. Every time it rained that wing of the house would be left standing in water because there was no roof over it; at night you could hear rats running around in there. *Seventeen* months later they finally settled the claim for much less than it would cost to rebuild my house, and they concluded that the fire was caused by "person or persons unknown." My fire insurance more than quadrupled, and I now pay more money in annual premiums than most families make in a year.

After the fire, the break-ins and mysterious telephone calls stopped as suddenly as they'd started. But maybe that has something to do with the fact that by the time I moved back into the house three months later, I was married. I've always felt whoever was responsible for all the trouble was too cowardly to continue it after a man moved into the house.

All the months of harassment I'd gone through, with the fire as a final straw, had a lot to do with my marrying Michael Tomlin so suddenly. But Burt Reynolds had a little something to do with it, too.

Naturally, I was flattered. What woman in her right mind wouldn't want to have dinner with Black-eyes— I had seen all his movies and been a fan of his

306

Chapter 10

❧

I FIRST met Burt Reynolds in September of 1975 when he came to Nashville to tape a syndicated television talk show hosted by our mutual friend, Jerry Reed. When I agreed to appear on Jerry's show I had no idea who the other guests would be. Imagine my surprise when Jerry called the day before the show to ask if I'd like to have dinner with Burt Reynolds.

"Burt Reynolds? Are you kidding me?" I asked.

Jerry laughed and said, "No, I'm not. He's here to do my show, too. He flew in with his friend Jim Best, the actor-producer, so we're all going out together tonight." Jerry went on to explain that he and his wife Priscilla, Ray Stevens, who was also on the show, his wife Penny, and the producers of the show had planned to meet that night for dinner with Burt and Jim. "Burt wanted to know if you could be persuaded to join us," Jerry said.

Naturally, I was flattered. What woman in her right mind wouldn't want to have dinner with Burt Reynolds? I had seen all his movies and been a fan of his since he played "Dan August" on TV. But I had never dreamed of meeting him, much less going out with him. What would I say to Burt Reynolds?

"I'd love to go," I told Jerry, hoping I sounded a lot more confident than I felt. "I have a recording session this afternoon, so call me at Studio B and let me know what time to be ready."

About 4:30 that afternoon I was in the middle of a song when the engineer hit the talk-back to tell me I had a phone call. "Take a message and say I'll call back," I said. "I want to finish this number before I stop." His voice came back over the speaker, "Tammy, I don't think I'd tell Burt Reynolds to call back if I were you." All the musicians started laughing and making cat-calls, and I could feel myself blushing in embarrassment. I went into the control booth and picked up the phone.

"Tammy, this is Burt Reynolds." His voice sounded huskier and sexier than it does in movies.

"Hi," I said. My own voice came out like a squeak.

"I understand Jerry mentioned something to you this morning about going out to dinner with us tonight," he went on. "I feel really bad about someone else asking you. I would have called you myself, but since we've never met, I didn't know what you'd think. So I just thought I'd call now and make sure you're coming, 'cause I'd really love to have dinner with you. I've been a fan of yours for a long time."

I thanked him and said I'd be home by 6, so they could let me know then when they'd be coming by. I started to say goodbye, but he said, "Hey, I think I'll stop by the studio and watch you record." That petrified me. I knew I wouldn't be able to sing a note with Burt Reynolds there, so I made excuses and said we'd better wait and meet that evening.

Prissy called after I got home to say they would pick me up at 7 P.M. I didn't know if she meant Burt would be with them or not. I put on a simple long dress and took extra care with my hair and makeup. My girls were as excited as I was; they must have stayed on the phone an hour telling their girl friends that Mama had a date with Burt Reynolds.

By the time Prissy and Jerry arrived it had started to snow. The weather had taken a sudden cold turn —unusual for September—and Prissy had on a warm pants suit. They explained that Burt was waiting at the Spence Manor with his friend Jim Best. Neither of them had brought a warm coat, so Jerry was taking them something to wear. I decided to change into a warmer and more comfortable outfit too, so I put on pants, a silk blouse, and my fur coat. All the way to the Spence Manor Jerry kept telling me that Burt was a really nice guy, not stuck on himself at all. He said, "You know me well enough to know if he wasn't down to earth I wouldn't be going out with him no matter how big a star he is. You'll like him. Now don't be nervous." But Lord, was I nervous!

Jerry knocked on the door of Burt's suite and called out, "Hey, it's me. Open up." I was behind Jerry and Priscilla. Burt opened the door, and I just stood there and stared. He was even better-looking in person. Jerry and Prissy went on in and left me face to face with Burt. He stepped closer and said, "Well, I knew you were gonna look good, but I didn't know you'd look this damn good!" That broke the ice and we all laughed. Jim Best came in from the bedroom of the suite and Burt introduced him to me. I hadn't known him by name, but when I saw him I realized he was one of my favorite character actors. I couldn't count the movies and TV shows I've seen him in. We hit it off right away because he's from Mississippi too.

Burt didn't have a car in Nashville, so we all rode with Jerry to Mario's for dinner. When we got there Ray and Penny Stevens and Jerry's producers and their wives were waiting. The place was really crowded and word spread fast that Burt Reynolds was there. I slid into a corner of the booth where a long table had been pulled up to accommodate us all, and Burt sat beside me. Mario the owner came over to introduce himself to Burt and Jim, and of course he couldn't do enough for us. He brought us fresh melon, boiled shrimp, crab legs and other kinds of good things for hors d'oeuvres. We drank champagne and ate and talked and laughed. We laughed a lot primarily because Jerry Reed is crazy and it's catching.

We were there for several hours, during which time someone took a picture of me with Burt—it showed up in the Nashville *Tennessean* the next morning. The caption said we had been out to dinner together, but it failed to mention there had been nine other people with us. I was mad when I saw it because it made our dinner date seem like much more than it was. I thought I'd had problems in the past with my personal life being overpublicized because of my relationship with George Jones, but I hadn't seen anything until I got around Burt Reynolds. That poor man can't even go into a restroom without someone trying to follow him to get a picture.

When we left the restaurant Jerry said, "Let's go by my house for a drink, then if y'all want to go someplace else I'll run you over to Tammy's to pick up her car." Jerry's property bordered mine on Franklin Road, so he wasn't even a block away. We stayed at Jerry and Prissy's for a little while and talked before he took us to my house. By then it was a little after 10 o'clock. Burt said he'd like to come in and meet my daughters. Mother and Foy were there, too. Tina and Foy were the only ones still up when we walked in. I introduced them and of course they were surprised and thrilled. I asked PeePaw if Mother had gone to bed, and he said she was lying down with Georgette back in the nursery, but that she still had on her housecoat. Burt was determined to meet her. We knocked on the door and when we opened it Georgette was lying there on Mee-Maw's arm sucking her thumb. I said, "Mother, I'd like you to meet Burt Reynolds." She had no idea he was in the house, and she almost died!

She was reading the *National Enquirer,* and Burt said, "Oh, MeeMaw, don't tell me you read that trashy magazine too. My mother does the same thing. I caught her reading a story in there about me last week and I said, 'Mama you know those stories aren't true.' And she said, 'Yes, but it's a good picture, son.' " I think Mother fell in love with Burt right then.

After he talked to Georgette for a minute he started out the door, then he turned back and said, "MeeMaw, what is that I smell in the kitchen? Do I smell beans?"

"Yes," she said, "I cooked pinto beans and corn-bread tonight."

He said, "Oh God, I wish I'd known that. We would have eaten here instead of Mario's."

Then we went upstairs and knocked on Gwen's door. She was propped up in bed reading and when she saw who I had with me she turned ash white. I thought she was going to faint! Jackie was sound asleep across the hall. I went in and touched her and said, "Come on Jackie, wake up. There's someone here I want you to meet." She sat up in bed, rubbing her eyes, and when she opened them and saw Burt she gasped out loud and turned beet-red. The next day she said to me, "Mama, how *could* you do that to me. There I was in an old tee shirt, looking horrible and half asleep, meeting *the* Burt Reynolds!"

When we left the house it had started snowing again. We hadn't driven a mile when Burt looked up and saw blue lights flashing in the rear view mirror. "I don't believe this," he said. "The first time we've ever been out together and we get stopped by the cops!" He pulled off to the side of the road and rolled down the window.

A man in street clothes walked up and said, "Mr. Reynolds, I'm sorry about this. But I'm an off-duty policeman, and my wife and I saw you and Miss Wynette at Mario's. This was the only way we knew how to get an autograph." We laughed and wrote our names on the piece of paper he gave us.

Then we drove to the Spence Manor and sat in Burt's suite and talked for about an hour. He asked me all about recordings and I asked him about movies. He told me he had made one album, and he joked

about it; then he asked me if I'd ever thought about
making movies. I said, "Definitely not. I don't even
like television and I would hate movies. I'm not an
actress and cameras make me nervous." He said he
believed you have to know how to act to put across a
song, and we talked back and forth like that for about
an hour. He was just as down-to-earth as Jerry had
said he would be, and I found conversation with him
as easy as if we'd known one another for a long time.
I drove him back to Jerry's house so he could borrow
a car for the next day; then I went on home.

We were scheduled to start rehearsing for the show
at 11 A.M. the next morning at the Opry House. They
had assigned me a dressing room right next to Burt's.
I stepped outside my dressing room and saw Burt
standing in the doorway to his. He smiled and said,
"Come here a minute. Would you fix my tie?" I
laughed and walked over to straighten his tie. He
looked down and said, "You're the prettiest valet I've
ever had." Immediately somebody was snapping pictures around us, and those shots turned up in newspapers too.

All during rehearsal Jerry Reed kept looking over
at me and laughing. Or he'd shake his finger at me
like I'd been bad. I knew I was supposed to sing on
the show, but I had no idea what Jerry intended to ask
me on the "talk" portion. I kept begging him to tell
me what questions he had in mind, but he just shook
his head and said, "You'll see." He spent the whole
afternoon teasing me and by the time we were ready
to tape I was a nervous wreck.

Ray Stevens was already out there with him when
I went on. Burt was waiting backstage for his call.
Jerry and Ray had been kidding around and the audience was in a good mood, laughing with them. Jerry
asked me to tell them the story of the time I set the
cotton gin on fire. The minute I finished he said, "Now
what's this I hear about you going out with old Burt
Reynolds last night?"

I could have *died*. I didn't know what he was going

to say next. I said, "We had dinner, that's all." I know I sounded panicked. Just at that moment the director motioned to break for a commercial.

Jerry said, "Well, we'll get into *that* when we come back."

"Oh *no* we won't," I said, just as they cut away. When we were off camera I told Jerry Reed he'd better not *dare* say anymore about my date with Burt. He just kept laughing. The whole show went like that, with one crazy thing happening after another. Everything Ray Stevens did was funny, and then Burt fell asleep backstage and woke up thinking he'd missed his cue. We were running behind schedule, but he didn't know that, and he was afraid they'd forgotten to call him. So he stood behind the curtain doing cattle calls to get Jerry's attention. Then he started talking through the curtain in a low tone so the audience couldn't hear. He said, "I have a feeling this is all a put-on and you're gonna do this whole show without me. I've already been waiting back here for a week." Jerry brought him out and then they all started trying to outdo one another. When the show was over my sides hurt from laughing so much.

I knew without Burt saying a word about it that we would be going out that night. When the show was over Jerry said, "Well, we can't end the night like this. Let's all go over to Ray's house." Burt, Jim Best, and I took my limousine. Burt wanted to drive, so I got in front with him and Jim got in the back, as though we were chauffeuring him.

When we got to Ray and Penny's, which was just a few blocks away, Jerry and Prissy weren't there yet. Penny said, "I'm so embarrassed. We've been on a health food kick lately and I haven't been out shopping, so all we have in the house to eat is cheese, peanut butter, and cereal." Burt said, "I knew I should have eaten some of MeeMaw's leftover beans." We settled on cereal. But when Jerry got there the first thing he said was, "I'm starved. What's to eat?" Penny showed him and he said, "No way. I'm going home for bologna and bread." He came back with sandwich makings, and we all sat by the fire and ate and talked. They had a beautiful home, very cozy and comfortable, and the fire felt good after being in the freezing cold outside. We stayed until about 2 A.M.

Then Burt said goodbye to everyone because his plane left early the next morning, and we drove back to the Spence Manor. Jim went into his room right away, leaving us alone in the living room of the suite. By this time I felt really comfortable and at ease with Burt, and I no longer thought of him as a movie star or *the* Burt Reynolds. He's such a regular person that you forget who he is after being with him just a short time. Burt would have been successful, had a lot of friends, and been very popular with the ladies even if he'd never left West Palm Beach. He just has that kind of personality. Naturally I felt a strong physical attraction to him. But I couldn't help thinking the old-fashioned way: This is only the second time I've ever been out with him.

While these thoughts were running through my mind we were talking about everything from our families to the show we'd done that night. I learned that Burt has a deep love and respect for his mother and father, a real affection for them that you don't often see in grown men. He told me that he and his father hadn't been close when he was growing up, that he'd actually been afraid of him. Mr. Reynolds was the Sheriff of Palm Beach County, and he made Burt toe the line. But after Burt's marriage to Judy Carne broke up he turned to his family for comfort, and his father was so understanding and sympathetic they've been close ever since. "I never greet him or leave him that we don't hug and kiss," Burt told me, and it was obvious that the relationship meant a great deal to him.

Burt has a deep respect for women. He isn't the kind of man who would think wrong of a woman for following her feelings, even on the first date. But the last thing on earth I wanted was to be one of Burt Reynolds's one-night stands. It's surprising that thinking about it didn't spoil our experience for me, because I knew that if I didn't see him again I would always wonder if I would have been better off remaining his friend instead of becoming his lover. But my uncertainties disappeared in his arms and when we were close I was beyond caring about anything but the pleasure of being with him. It was a unique experience for me, and one that has never happened since.

When I got home the next morning at 6 I discovered he'd left some clothes there when he changed the night before after the show. I called him quickly at the hotel to remind him of them, but he didn't seem concerned. All he said was, "Good, that will give me an excuse to come back and get them." I thought, Well, maybe I will see him again after all, but I didn't let myself plan on it.

More than a month passed and I didn't hear from him. I wasn't depressed about it; in fact, I had more or less pushed him out of my mind. Yet I never passed a newsstand that I didn't buy every magazine that had an article about Burt Reynolds in it. Rudy was still the number one man in my life, and Burt was a fantasy.

About two months later I had to go to California with my band to do "The Dinah Shore Show" and "The Merv Griffin Show." We had some business to negotiate while we were there, so my attorney John Lentz went with me. Normally when I go to California to do television I go alone, or just with Nanette, and I prefer to stay at either the Beverly Wilshire, the Beverly Hills, or the Beverly Hilton hotels. But on the road we always stay at Holiday Inns, and the one in Hollywood was more convenient for the band because they could get out and walk around and see things.

The morning after we checked in, John and Rudy and I were having breakfast in the Holiday Inn coffee shop before going to "Dinah's Place" for rehearsal. I heard my name called over the intercom; the operator asked me to come to the nearest paging phone. My breakfast had just arrived so I asked John to get the call. I assumed it was someone calling from Dinah's show because no one else knew where we were staying. When John came back to the table he was grinning. "I think you'd better answer your own page," he said.

"Why, who is it?" I asked.

"Just go on to the phone," he urged. With Rudy sitting there he didn't want to say more.

I knew who it was the minute I heard his voice. There's no mistaking that low, husky tone. He answered my "hello" with, "You didn't think I'd find you, did you?"

I laughed and said, "What do you mean?"

"You told me you always stay at one of the hotels in Beverly Hills," he answered, "so I called the Beverly Wilshire, then I checked the Beverly Hilton. When you weren't at either of those I knew you had to be at the Beverly Hills, so I drove over, but you weren't there either. But I found you anyway!" He gloated like a little boy. "What are you doing today?" he asked.

I told him I had to do Dinah's and Merv Griffin's show. He wanted to know when I'd be finished. "I really don't know how long it will take to do Merv's show," I answered.

"You aren't putting me off, are you?" he asked.

I assured him that I wasn't; then he asked what I was doing after I finished work. I said, "Well, I'm supposed to have dinner with John Lentz and my publisher Al Gallico."

"And I suppose you have to get back on the road tomorrow?" he said.

"Yes, I'm leaving early in the morning," I answered.

"Well, at least I found you." He sounded genuinely disappointed that I was leaving so soon. "I just wanted you to know I've been thinking about you. I know how busy you are, but I did at least want to talk to you for a minute. Let me have your number in Nashville again, and I'll talk to you later."

I wondered if he'd lost my home number, or if it just hadn't been important enough to him to keep it the last time he'd asked for it. But I gave it to him again and we said goodbye.

I was very apprehensive about doing Dinah's show because at least one of the pictures of Burt and me taken in Nashville had made the wire services, and I knew she had probably seen it. I didn't know exactly what the status of their romance was at the time because Burt didn't talk about it, and I certainly wasn't going to ask him. I had read that they were no longer "steady dating," although they were still "close friends," but I had learned from personal experience that you can't often believe what you read. I was very concerned that Dinah might have ill feelings toward me if she knew I'd been out with Burt, and that was the last thing I wanted.

I have never known any woman in show business I respect and love more than Dinah Shore; she is one of the finest people I've ever met anywhere. I had always felt more comfortable doing her TV show than any other because we're both Southern, and she has the talent to make you feel relaxed even with that "red-eyed" camera pointing at you. All the way to the studio that morning I kept telling John, "If Dinah acts strained or different toward me it will break my heart." But as soon as we got there she came running to meet me and gave me a big hug. I was so relieved I almost cried. I still don't know if she'd heard about my dates with Burt at that point because it was never mentioned, and she treated me with the same warmth she always had. But knowing Dinah, I imagine she was aware we had been out to dinner and wise enough to know that it hadn't meant any more to Burt that a fun evening with a girl singer he admired.

Burt did not call again before I left the next morning and I thought about it all the way home. I wondered if I should have offered to break my dinner date with John and Al Gallico. But I decided I had done the right thing. The way I was brought up in Mississippi girls just don't chase after boys—at least not so the boys can notice it—and I knew I couldn't change some of my habits from my old Southern Baptist upbringing, even for Burt Reynolds.

The next week I had a couple of days off. I was at home with my girls and a friend of theirs who was spending the night. When the phone rang their little friend answered it. Then she came running and screaming through the house like it was on fire. "It's Burt Reynolds! Oh my God, it's Burt Reynolds. I don't believe it, it's Burt Reynolds!" We all started laughing, and I had to pull myself together before I picked up the extension.

We chatted for a while and he asked if I was going to be in Los Angeles any time soon. I said I had no plans, but if anything came up I'd let him know. After that he began calling every couple of weeks, and once in a while I'd call him from the road. We began to really get to know one another through our long phone conversations. I saw him a couple of times in Los Angeles during that period, but we kept in touch mostly by telephone. By this time my house had burned and Rudy was no longer working for me, so there was no steady man in my life and I began to look forward more and more to Burt's calls.

Being with him was always wonderful even though he almost scared me to death once during that time. I was in Los Angeles to be a presenter on an awards show, and Burt was there filming "Nickelodeon." He was shooting at night so we planned to meet at my suite at the Beverly Wilshire hotel after he finished. I went out to a friend's house that day and used her kitchen to cook up a big Southern meal—stuffed pork chops, fresh string beans, creamed corn, cornbread, and homemade coconut pie. Then my friend helped me get all the food back to the hotel, and I borrowed restaurant warmers from the kitchen to keep it hot until he finished work. He thought he'd be off by 9 P.M., but he called about 7:30 to say they were running behind schedule and he might be working as late as midnight. "I'll let you know how it's going," he promised. During the evening he called or had someone else call four or five times to let me know they were still behind schedule.

He finally arrived about 3 A.M. and he looked exhausted. I had had sixteen candles brought up for the food warmers, and the last one went out just as he walked in the door. I had fixed a very romantic setting for our dinner, with candlelight, pretty china, and crystal, courtesy of the hotel. The suite was decorated in Spanish decor and looked more like a real living room than a hotel room. We sat down to eat, but it was obvious that he was extremely tired even though he was making every effort to be cheerful and witty. He complimented the dinner, exclaiming, "Oh, it's so good. It tastes just like Mama's," and he was eating really fast. I laughed about him wolfing down his food. He had gone on a diet since I first met him and had lost thirty pounds. But now he was off the diet and still losing weight, and he was concerned about it.

When he finished I told him I was going to rinse out my friend's pots and pans so she could pick them up the next day. He said, "Well, I think I'll just sit here on the couch a minute and relax." I was busying myself at the table when suddenly I saw him slump over on the sofa. I rushed over to him and asked what was wrong. He was holding his chest. I thought, "My God, he's having a heart attack!" His heart was beating so hard you could see his hand moving up and down over it, and he was having great difficulty breathing; he had turned as white as a sheet. By this time he had fallen to the floor. I kept saying, "What's wrong, what can I do?" But he just put his finger to his lips as if to say, "Don't ask me. I can't talk right now."

Finally he gasped, "Paper bag," and I knew what he wanted. But I didn't have a paper bag anywhere in the suite. I didn't want to call the desk, so I ran out the door, praying I'd see someone who could help.

I was lucky. Just three doors down there was a maid in a laundry room, something you'd never expect to find at 4 in the morning. She gave me a large paper laundry bag and I ran back to the suite. I put it over his head and within two or three minutes his breathing was easier. He managed to say, "If I pass out, don't worry. It's the best thing that could happen to me because it will make me relax totally and this will pass over." He did lose consciousness for a couple of minutes and I was absolutely petrified. I could see the headlines: "Burt Reynolds Has Heart Attack in Tammy Wynette's Hotel Room." Before he passed out I asked if he wanted me to call a doctor and he shook his head, "No." But I thought, If he doesn't come around any second I'm going to call one anyway. Then he opened his eyes and stood up slowly. "I feel better now," he said. "But I'd really like to lie down." I followed him into the bedroom and lay down beside him.

For the first time since I'd known him he talked about his health. He said he hadn't been feeling right for some time, and that on several occasions he had hyperventilated and passed out, just as he'd done a few minutes before. He had been to several doctors but they said it was overwork and exhaustion. He was angry about it. He told me he had always been healthy and taken good care of himself—he does not drink or smoke—and now that he was supposed to be in the prime of his life he couldn't understand why long days on the set should make him feel so totally exhausted. "I know there has to be more to it than hard work," he said, "and I probably make it worse by letting it worry me and make me nervous."

He didn't get up the next day until about 10 o'clock. I had one more night off before I had to return to the road, so I had planned on spending it in Los Angeles. When Burt got dressed he said, "I have to leave now because I have to go talk to Dinah about something. I hope you understand that it's important—something I have to do. But I'll check back with you later and we'll do something tonight."

As soon as he left I started feeling really depressed, I guess more about Dinah than anything else. I still didn't know what their situation was, but I knew I felt like the intruder and I didn't like it. I decided I wanted to go home. I made a reservation on a 1 P.M. flight, then rushed like mad to get packed and to the airport. Burt had left his watch in the suite, and I didn't want to ask the hotel clerk to keep it for him at the desk, advertising that he'd been there, so I took it with me. I checked out without leaving him any message. I realize now that I was being inconsiderate, but at the time I was thinking, I am just one more girl in this man's life and I am not going to chase him. I don't belong here. I belong at home.

Late that night after I arrived in Nashville, Burt called. "Thanks a lot for leaving a note telling me you were going home," he said. "Boy, when you decide to split, you split, don't you?" Without revealing my real feelings I tried to explain to him that I had simply felt it was time to come home. He wasn't as angry as he was puzzled, but he accepted my explanation, and he continued calling me.

Meanwhile Burt had been responsible for my buying a house in Jupiter Beach, Florida. From the time that George and I divorced, I had intended to buy another house in Florida as a "getaway" place. The Florida climate is my favorite because I love the sun so much, and I don't really get a lot of rest when I'm at home in Nashville. There are always things that have to be done like recording sessions, interviews, photosessions, and business meetings. I knew if I had a place to go where I could find complete rest and relaxation when I had three days off, I could go back on the road feeling like I'd had a week off. But I had intended to buy a house around the Lakeland area or on the west coast of Florida. When I mentioned this to Burt he said, "Oh, please, before you buy anywhere check out the beach at Jupiter. My ranch is near there and it's the only unspoiled area left in Florida. My attorney down there, Wally Colbath, will be glad to look around for you and find out if there are any houses available on the beach."

I put John Lentz in touch with Wally Colbath, and they arranged for me to see several houses in Jupiter. John flew down with me and Wally met us at the airport. I had never been to that part of Florida and I fell in love with it immediately, especially the beaches. The houses we looked at were all right, but nothing really knocked me out until we drove up to the last one we were scheduled to see.

It's in Jupiter Inlet Colony, a small peninsula that's separated from the mainland by the Intra-Coastal Waterway on one side and by an inlet running from the Intra-Coastal to the Atlantic on another. The house is pale yellow stucco trimmed in white. It's a two-story, French regency style, with a circular drive and court-yard facing the street. On the other side is a beautiful golden beach stretching down to meet the Atlantic.

The minute I saw the house from the outside I said, "Oh, John, I just know this is the one I'm going to want and I'll bet it costs more than any other house we've looked at." I had planned on buying a simple beach house, not something this elegant.

"You're right, it does," John smiled.

Wally opened the front door and led the way up a short flight of steps to the most unusual and exotic interior I'd ever seen. The house is built around an indoor swimming pool, covered by a screen roof two stories high. The area around the pool is like a tropical garden with lush green plants hanging everywhere. The structure is square so that all the rooms (except two downstairs bedrooms which I added later) open onto this pool-patio area, giving the whole house a wonderful outdoor, open, airy feeling. The living room, master bedroom, and dining room have spectacular views of the Atlantic on one side, and the jungle garden setting of the pool on the other. I was over-whelmed by the restful beauty of the place before I'd even seen all the rooms. I told John I really wanted to buy it.

Wally said Burt had told him not to let me leave Jupiter without meeting his parents, so he drove us to the ranch. Burt's father is a tall, rawboned man who looks more like a farmer than a former sheriff. His mother is a tall, willowy woman with a gracious manner and bubbly personality. I liked them both immensely. They showed me around the ranch and drove me out to Burt's treehouse, a circular apartment built on cement stilts by a small man-made lake. It's all glass so that you look out into the foliage of the surrounding Florida pines from every room. They also introduced me to Logan and Katherine Fleming while I was there. Logan is Burt's ranch manager and in charge of training his thoroughbreds. His wife Katherine is the kind of person you feel you've known all your life after five minutes of conversation. We hit it off immediately and have since become close friends. I always see them when I go to the Florida house, and we've had a lot of fun going to the races, out to dinner, or just hanging out at the beach or the ranch.

As soon as the papers were signed on the house, I started going down there as often as possible to buy furniture and redecorate. Everytime I went I'd see Mr. and Mrs. Reynolds and Logan and Katherine, and of course that made me think about Burt all the more. Our schedules—his moviemaking and my road work—had been so hectic for several months that we hadn't been able to see one another. But we stayed in touch by phone.

I knew I was letting myself slip toward falling in love with him, and I was anything but happy about it. The last thing I needed was to be in love with a movie star so recognizable he can't even be in public without causing enough commotion to disrupt everything around. And it was foolish to get hung up on a man whose career was even more demanding than my own, a man whose commitments kept him thousands of miles away. I knew that I was just another girl in Burt's life, and I was determined not to become carried away and make a fool of myself.

Meanwhile I was also worried about moving back into my home in Nashville. The girls and I were still living in the large apartment we'd rented until the house was ready for occupancy again. The burned-out wing had been boarded up and closed off, but it still smelled like fire throughout the rest of the house, and I was in the process of repainting and replacing drapes and carpets before we moved back in. I was in no rush to have it finished because in the back of my mind I dreaded moving back home. I was afraid the harassment and break-ins would start all over again.

In Nashville I had had a few dates with a short-time acquaintance, Michael Tomlin, a young real estate executive. Michael was one of the most dashing men I'd ever dated—dark curly hair, handsome features, and a confident manner with women that made me feel I was out with a real man of the world. He wore tasteful, expensive clothes, drove a Mercedes, had his own business, lived in a luxury apartment, and ran around with a wealthy young crowd of Nashville socialites. His world was entirely foreign to me, and although I had nothing in common with his friends, I thought it was fun seeing how the "other half" lived.

From our first date Michael courted me like a princess. We went to the best restaurants; he ordered the most expensive wines on the menu; he held my hand and whispered romantic things; he sent flowers. On our third or fourth date he asked me to marry him. I was flattered, of course, but I knew I wasn't in love with him, so I told him we didn't know one another well enough to talk about marriage. He insisted that he knew all he needed to know about me and asked me to think about it.

A few weeks later, when I was down in Florida working on furnishing my new house, I did start thinking about it. Burt had just finished a long, hard movie and had gone off to Mexico to rest for a few weeks. He called before he left to tell me his doctor had ordered the vacation. "But when I get back from Mexico I want to see you," he said. "Can you meet me in Florida? I want to see your new house and it would be fun to spend some time together there."

I told him I would try to arrange to take a week off. But the more I thought about it, the more I thought how foolish it was. Every time something like this happens I think more and more of wanting to be with him, comparing other men to him, and wishing for things that will never be, I said to myself. He's leading me on without even knowing it, and if it doesn't stop soon I'm just begging to be hurt. I knew Burt was not nearly as involved with me as I was with him. I could tell he enjoyed being with me because we always had a lot of fun, but my feelings were running away from me and his weren't the same. I told myself I was a fool to brood over something that could never be when I had a man back in Nashville who was eager to marry me, a man who was one of the most eligible, attractive bachelors in town.

The newness of the dating experience had worn off in the year and a half since George left, and I longed for a solid, steady relationship with one man. I guess it's strange that marriage represented such security to me since it had never actually worked out that way in my life, but I was convinced I *needed* to be married. Unconsciously I felt if I were married I'd be safe—safe from an emotional involvement with a sex symbol who obviously wasn't ready to settle down with one woman; safe from the harassment and fear I'd lived in at home for the past year; safe from the insecurity of dating strangers.

These were the thoughts that were running through my mind as I sat on the floor of the Holiday Inn in Jupiter talking to Sheila Richey about arrangements for movers to deliver some furniture from Nashville. Sheila had come down to Florida with me to see the house. The phone interrupted our conversation. It was Logan calling from the ranch to say Burt had sent word he wanted me to use one of his cars while I was there getting moved into the house. I thought, That's it. This has got to stop, *now*. If I let myself get any further involved, it will just hurt too much when the time comes to pull back!

I hung up the phone and said, "Sheila, I'm going to marry Michael Tomlin."

She looked shocked. "Are you *sure* that's what you want?" she asked.

I said, "Yes, I am."

"But aren't you supposed to meet Burt down here soon? What will you do about that?"

"Nothing," I said. "I'll be married by then."

She said, "You mean you aren't even going to discuss it with Burt first? You aren't even going to tell him?"

"No, I don't trust myself to talk to him because I might change my mind, and I know this is what is best for me."

I called Michael that night and told him I had decided to accept his proposal. He sounded delighted and told me he was sure we'd be happy. Then I called Mother. I said, "I'm getting married." She knew I was in Florida and that Burt had a home nearby, so she assumed he was there.

"Who?" she said quickly, in an excited voice. "Who are you marrying?"

"Michael Tomlin," I said.

There was a long pause on the line. Then she said, "Do you want to talk about this now, or when you get home?"

"I don't want to talk about it at all," I said. "I've made up my mind. I wanted you to hear it from me before word gets out in Nashville."

Two days later, after we'd moved the furniture into the Florida house and settled my girls there with my Aunt Athalene, Sheila and I returned to Nashville. I had to go out on the road right away, but first I called John Lentz to tell him my plans. He was surprised and didn't sound very enthusiastic when he learned I intended to marry Michael, but he said, "If that's what you want, I wish you happiness."

Then he added, "But there's a small problem we'd better take care of before you announce marriage plans. The *National Enquirer* is about to release a cover story on a romance between you and Burt Reynolds. They're using a picture of you two taken in Los Angeles, and they know all about the dates you've had out there and in Nashville. They also know you've bought a house close to his ranch and they're saying it will be a 'honeymoon house' for you and Burt."

"John, that isn't true," I said. "You've got to stop the story. Imagine how it will look if I announce my engagement a few days before a story like that comes out on the cover of the *Enquirer!* It will be terribly embarrassing for me, Michael, *and* Burt." He promised to do what he could to keep them from printing the story.

After a weekend on the road I flew back to Florida to finish putting the house in order and to spend a few days with the girls. Monday morning I went out to buy food, and when I returned from the grocery store there were five reporters waiting at the house. Jackie said, "Mom, when I opened the door they just walked right in to wait for you. They've been asking us a lot of questions, mostly about Burt, and I didn't know what to say."

I was furious that they would come to my house without an appointment, push their way in and ask questions of my family. I learned that two of the reporters were from the *Enquirer* and the rest were from local newspapers. The minute I walked into the living room where they were waiting they started firing questions at me. I told them I had no intention of giving an interview. The girl from the *Enquirer* said, "Well, okay, but will you just tell us this. Why did you buy a house here, so close to Burt Reynolds's ranch? It is true that you've been dating him, isn't it?"

I said, "I was looking for a house in Florida before I ever met Burt Reynolds. The girls and I wanted a place where we could get away from some of the things we have to contend with in Nashville—like reporters showing up at the house. Burt asked his attorney down here to look around for me and it just happened that he found this place."

"But this will make it more convenient for you to see Burt, won't it?" the girl asked.

"No, it won't," I said. "Because I'm getting married."

You could have heard a pin drop. Even my girls, who were sitting there listening, were stunned. I hadn't told them anything about my plans to marry Michael. The reporters all wanted to know who I was marrying so I answered questions about Michael for the next few minutes. Then the *Enquirer* reporter asked how this marriage would affect me and Burt. I said, "It has nothing to do with Burt." I hoped I was convincing. "You've got it all wrong about us anyway. We're just friends. We've had a few dinner dates, that's all. There has never been anything serious between us." They left, finally.

The next day articles ran in the local papers about my moving to Jupiter Beach and telling of my plans to marry. One paper ran a picture of my house along with the address. For the next two days people were constantly driving by and slowing down to look. A few aspiring songwriters even came to the door to pitch songs to me. Evidently it was too late for the *Enquirer* to kill their cover on me and Burt, so they changed it and divided the story between me and Lucie Arnaz, insisting he was having a romance with both of us.

When I returned to Nashville, Michael and I set our wedding date for July 18. Mary Ann McCready, who handled artist-press relations for CBS, Columbia, and Epic, had been receiving dozens of inquiries about me and Burt, so she arranged for a press conference to announce my marriage plans. The next day I left to go on the road. Michael went with me for the first three days of my Texas tour. My band tried to act happy for me, but it was exceptionally quiet on the bus that trip.

After I accepted his proposal Michael told me there would be people in Nashville who would criticize him and our marriage. "You'll probably even hear that I'm a fortune hunter out to marry you for money," he said.

"But don't you believe it. Rumors like that are started by people who are envious."

I did hear many rumors about Michael, but I refused to listen. John Lentz even tried to persuade me to let him draw up a premarital financial agreement; he used the Onassis-Jackie Kennedy document as an example. I was horrified. "John, you don't understand. We're in *love*. It's *real* this time! There's no need for any kind of legal agreement about money because this marriage is my last. And besides, it would hurt Michael's feelings terribly if I even suggested such a thing." Then when George Jones called to warn me about Michael, I told him straight out to mind his own business. Later I realized he was only telling me what others wanted to say but didn't have the guts. At the time, though, I thought he was prejudiced because he didn't want me to marry anybody else.

The only time I admitted to anyone that I might be making a mistake was at my last show the night before the wedding. The Hager Twins set it off; they were to appear on the same show. I hadn't seen them since months before in Los Angeles when I was with Burt. They came on my bus with a bottle of champagne.

"This is a wedding gift," Jon said. I thanked them and they sat down to talk. Jon said, "Have you seen Burt lately?" I shook my head. "He really likes you, you know," Jon went on.

Then Jim said, "Yeah, he has nothing but praise for you. He really admires you, not just as a singer, but as a person, too."

I said, "What has all this got to do with the champagne?"

"Well, nothing," Jim said. "We're really very happy for you." Then they got up to leave and gave me a hug. But as they were getting off the bus Jon turned around and said, "He really does, you know."

All of a sudden I felt I had to talk to Burt. I knew where he was staying in Mexico, so I tried to call on my bus's mobile phone. But the operator couldn't get through. We were playing a fair date, so there was no backstage dressing room where I could try to use a regular phone. Then I decided to write him a letter. I pulled some paper out of a drawer and started, "Dear Burt." But I couldn't think of anything to say. I didn't know exactly what it was I wanted to say to him. I just knew I needed to talk to him. I was alone on the bus, and I started crying from the frustration of not being able to get in touch with him.

Charlie Carter came in just then to tell me it was nearly time for me to go on. When he saw me crying he said, "What on earth is it?"

"Charlie," I said, "I don't know what's the matter with me. I can't get Burt off my mind. I've tried to call him and couldn't get through, and tried to write him and didn't know what to say, and it's driving me crazy."

Charlie sat down. "Now, let's talk about this," he said. "Don't you think maybe it's just last minute jitters?" Everybody goes through it, thinking, I'm not going to be single anymore. Am I doing the right thing?

I said, "I don't know, Charlie. I guess it's a good thing I couldn't get in touch with Burt. It's too late now anyway."

"Well, I'm going to ask you point-blank," Charlie looked me in the eye. "Do you love this Michael? Because if you don't it's *not* too late by a long shot."

I felt ashamed and lost. I wanted to be a little girl again and crawl up in my Daddy's lap and have him put his arms around me and tell me it was going to be all right. I was embarrassed to tell Charlie the stark truth—"No, no, NO, I don't love him"—so I said, "It doesn't matter because I couldn't call the wedding off now anyway. It's tomorrow! I couldn't do that to Michael. It would make him look like a fool. He loves me (I was convinced that he did), and I just couldn't treat him that way."

By then it was past time for me to go on, so Charlie and I left the bus. On the way to the stage we passed the Hagers again. Jon stopped me. "Have you been crying?" he asked.

"No," I lied.

"Yes, you have," he said. "I'm afraid we opened our mouths when we should have kept them shut. We should never have brought up Burt's name. I'm sorry." With that I started crying again.

"Oh, Lord," Jim moaned. "Now I *know* we should have kept quiet. Please, Tammy. We're so sorry."

I ran back to the bus to get myself together. My false eyelashes were falling off from crying, so I removed them, washed my face in cold water, dried my eyes, and put the eyelashes back on again. All the while I was talking to myself silently. I vowed I would *not* shed another tear over Burt Reynolds or my situation. I told myself I was lucky to have a man as attractive as Michael in love with me and that I was being a silly fool to pine over a movie star—a sex symbol who had women falling all over him. When the eyelashes were in place again I was ready to go on. I looked in the mirror. Tomorrow you will have a beautiful wedding, I told myself, and you *will* make it work.

Chapter 11

THE band and I arrived back in Nashville after midnight. They had flown in with me instead of riding on the bus because they were coming to my wedding. Michael met us at the airport. I joked about it being bad luck for the bridegroom to see the bride on the day of the wedding, which was set for 2 P.M. that afternoon. "That's just a silly superstition," he said. We drove to my apartment, then he kissed me goodnight and left. Although it was late and I was tired, I couldn't sleep. I was walking the floor when my fiddle player Charlie Justice called to ask who was driving me to the wedding. I said, "I don't know. I hadn't even thought about it." He said, "Then I'll pick up you and the girls tomorrow morning in my car."

He arrived about 11 so the girls and I would have time to dress at my house, where Nanette was meeting me to fix my hair. When I got in the car he said, "How do you feel? Are you happy?"

"Very happy." I didn't look at him when I answered.

"Then I'm happy for you," he said, reaching to turn on the car radio.

He tuned in just as a deejay was saying, "And now the number one song in Nashville this week—Tammy Wynette and George Jones singing 'Golden Rings.'" Charlie and I just looked at one another as if to say, Do you believe this? In the back seat my girls were suddenly very quiet. We all listened to the song in silence as we drove to my house.

I was overwhelmed by the way the florist and caterer had transformed the grounds into a perfect wedding setting. This was to be my first *real* wedding, and I wanted it to be a day I would remember for the rest of my life. (And I will, but for all the wrong reasons.) I had chosen the grounds of my Franklin Road house as the site of the ceremony because it has a serene, woodsy atmosphere. In one part of the yard the land forms a small, sunken bowl; the former owners put in a fountain there and planted dense foliage to make it look like a tropical garden, an ideal setting for an outdoor wedding. The florists had built an archway of orchids where Michael and I would stand to say our vows. They had hung hundreds more orchids from the trees and planted exotic tropical flowers all around the cleared area where white chairs had been set up for the guests; it was exquisite. It looked like the movie set of a Polynesian paradise. The reception was to be held at the pool area, and they had made huge arrangements of pineapple and other tropical fruits and flowers on a styrofoam platform to float in the pool, surrounded by hundreds of colorful hibiscus blossoms. The centerpiece on the refreshment table was made of flowers shaped to resemble a luau roasted pig, and the five-tiered wedding cake had a bride and groom standing on a little bridge in the center.

While I walked around the grounds admiring the artistic decorating job they'd done, Nanette was trailing along behind me with a drink in her hand. She kept repeating over and over, "It's not too late."

I begged, "Nanette, please, *don't*." Normally, she is not a daytime drinker. She will have a cocktail before dinner on occasion and maybe a glass or two of wine, but that's it. But she was so upset about my marrying Michael that she'd already had two drinks before I got to the house, and she was high enough to say exactly what she felt. So all the while I was inspecting the wedding site, trying to talk myself into feeling as romantic as the setting, my best friend was urgently trying to talk me out of my marriage!

When Nanette left to get herself another drink I thought, She's right. This isn't what I want, but I'm trapped. And I have no one to blame but myself. It's the stupidest thing I've ever done in my life, but I can't let Nan know how I feel or she'll lock me in a closet to keep me from going through with it. There was no doubt in my mind that I was making a mistake, but I felt powerless to do anything about it. It had gone so far I didn't have the guts to stop it. If I've ever hated myself, it was during those last few minutes just before I went outside to get married.

My dress was cream-colored lace with a matching picture hat. Michael wore a formal morning suit, dark gray jacket with tails, and black striped pants. His groomsmen wore the same style with black jackets. Foy, who was giving me away, also wore tails. It was a picture-book wedding party—pretty ladies and handsome men. Everything *looked* so right and felt so wrong.

As I was on my way out of the house, Nanette tugged at my dress. I turned around and tears were streaming down her face. "Please, please for the last time, *please* don't do it," she cried. "I know there are guards on the front gate, but we can take the golf cart and get out the back way. It's *not* too late. Please come with me!"

I just shook my head, "No." She broke down and ran back into the house where she proceeded to get higher than a Georgia pine.

Mother and Foy were standing by the back door

with Cliff and Maxine, whom I had invited up from Lakeland. Mother hadn't had one thing to do with the wedding; she hadn't said a word but her silence was a strong enough disapproval. I took PeePaw's arm and said, "Are you ready?"

"Yes," he answered, "but I'm awful nervous. If I forget what to say will you tell me?"

I said, "PeePaw all you have to say is '*I* do' when the preacher asks 'Who gives this woman in matrimony?' "

He said, "Yes, and it will be the hardest thing I've ever had to say in my life." Foy is a man of few words, and this was as close as he'd ever come to criticizing me in my whole life.

We walked down to the grotto area where the guests were already seated. The girls were carrying the hem of my dress so it wouldn't get dirty. I had prerecorded "Hawaiian Wedding Song" which was playing over speakers as we started down the aisle roped off with white satin ribbon. Just as we approached the altar and Michael was reaching for my hand, I heard my voice singing the lyric "I do . . . I do love you . . . love you," and I wanted to cry. Instead I looked up at my smiling bridegroom, and he winked back.

After we'd said our vows we went back to the pool area where a small combo was playing. We danced the traditional first dance alone with our guests watching us circle the pool area. I don't know if any of them recognized the melody being played. I learned later the combo had chosen it because it was the only song that I've recorded which they knew how to play. It was "I'll Keep On Falling in Love 'Til I Get It Right." The lyrics ran through my mind as we danced, knowing that it was Burt's favorite of all my records made it worse. I couldn't wait for the dance and the reception to be over so we could get out of there. I knew it would be easier if Michael and I were alone and my friends and family weren't watching me, because it was obvious what they were thinking.

Michael had suggested we hire a helicopter to land on the grounds and take us away from the wedding party. He knew his brothers had devious plans for him, and he wanted to outsmart them. But when the 'copter showed up, it almost took off with the wrong couple. Two of Michael's friends jumped in, and the pilot was lifting off before someone on the ground motioned frantically that he was taking off with the wrong pair.

I had agreed to perform a special show at the White House the next day, so we secretly planned to spend the first night of our honeymoon in Nashville at the Hyatt Regency, then fly on to Washington the next morning. But we'd left my limousine at the airport to make his friends think we'd already gone. The helicopter landed us at a private airfield where a car was waiting to drive us to the hotel. We'd been pre-registered under a false name.

We had just been settled in the suite and Michael had opened a bottle of champagne when the phone rang. It was Sheila. "Ha, ha. You didn't think I would find you, did you?" she teased.

Michael grabbed the phone and said, "Where are you?" She told him they were at home getting ready to go out to dinner with Deirdre and Kelly, Richey's children by a previous marriage, who were visiting from California. "Well, come on up and have dinner with us," he suggested.

Richey got on the phone and said, "That's really nice of you. It will thrill the kids to death."

A few minutes later the phone rang again. This time it was two of Michael's friends, David Blanton, the son of the governor of Tennessee, and Hap Hugley. They laughed about finding us, and David said, "Ya'll missed all the fun. After you left everybody got pushed into the swimming pool. We made a mess out of that pineapple float!"

Michael said, "Well, since you've found us, you might as well come on over and have dinner, too."

Before it was over we had about fifteen people in our suite for dinner. The party was still going strong at 2 A.M., but by that time Michael had had so much to drink he was about to pass out, and I was exhausted. We went into the bedroom and closed the door while they kept on partying. Michael was asleep the minute his head hit the pillow, but I lay there for a long time, too tired to sleep, listening to the laughter and music coming from the next room, wishing I felt as happy as they sounded. Well it's over, I thought. You've done it, so you'll have to live with it. You made the commitment, and now it's up to you to fulfill the obligations that go with it.

The next morning I awoke with a terrible stomach-ache. We flew to Washington and checked into the hotel. Mary Ann McCready was there to make sure things went smoothly. There had been a lot of publicity about "The First Lady of Country Music" performing for "The First Lady." She called to tell us my band and bus were already waiting at the White House; we had scheduled a rehearsal for that afternoon. By the time we got to the White House my stomach was hurting terribly. I told Michael that if I didn't get some medicine to ease the pain I didn't see how I would be able to work that night. I suspected it was my gallbladder because I'd had trouble before, so we called to get my prescription refilled. As soon as I saw my bus parked behind the White House, I got on it and lay down. I was to perform at a big banquet for the foreign ambassadors, along with Roger Miller and Ella Fitzgerald. I was a nervous wreck, but they both acted as though it were just another job.

President and Mrs. Ford were as nice as they could be, and I really enjoyed the evening in spite of the fact that my stomach pain had returned. I met so many important people I can't even remember them all. But I'll never forget meeting Elizabeth Taylor. I couldn't take my eyes off her. She had on a long lilac dress, exactly the color of her eyes, and she was breathtaking. Michael said, "My God, seeing her has made my week." When we were introduced to her I told her what he'd said. She knew we were on our honeymoon, and she laughed and said, "Oh, that's men for you. They say such foolish things they don't mean." She was so charming and *so* beautiful. Every man there turned into putty in her presence.

When I met the Russian Ambassador he said, "You must come to Russia, you *must*. Opryland came to Russia." Roy Clark had taken a group of performers from Opryland Park on a Russian tour the year before, and the Soviets had apparently loved the music. My drummer Freddie Haws overheard what the Ambassador said, so after we'd moved on he slipped up and said, "You VILL come to Russia!" We laughed and teased one another all night about being a bunch of hillbillys in the White House.

We walked into a room where an orchestra was playing, and I found myself standing beside President Ford. He asked me to dance and my knees started shaking. "I don't dance very well," I said.

He said, "Well, neither do I so we'll get along fine."

As we started to dance away I heard Michael ask Mrs. Ford to dance. When she accepted he said, "Since you're the expert at this, why don't you lead?"

She laughed and said, "Oh, I like you." (He did have a good sense of humor.) "Come on, we'll show them how it's done."

While we were dancing the President asked me where I was from in Mississippi. I was so nervous I stuttered trying to get out "Itawamba County." We talked about the South and he was so down-to-earth I almost forgot I was dancing with the President of the United States. After the party Secret Service men took us back to the hotel and the next day we left on our honeymoon.

We flew to San Francisco first, then to Honolulu to change planes, then on to the big island of Hawaii. We rented a car to drive across the craters of burnt-out lava to the famous Mona Kea Hotel, one of the most beautiful vacation spots in the world. But the romantic surroundings were lost on us, because by the time we arrived at the hotel Michael and I weren't speaking.

En route to the hotel he had asked if I'd ever been to the islands before. I said, "Yes, to Honolulu, but I've never been here."

Very sarcastically he said, "Oh, I suppose that was with Mr. George Jones."

"Yes, that's right," I answered. For miles after that we didn't speak. Finally he pulled off the road at a scenic spot where you could look out over miles of mountains, pineapple fields, and sugar cane. I said, "This is really beautiful, isn't it?"

He said, "Oh, now you've decided to talk to me?"

I touched his arm. "Michael, please. This is the first day of our honeymoon. Let's don't spoil it."

"That's up to you," he answered belligerently. So I got back in the car and we drove the rest of the way to the hotel in silence. My stomachache, which had never entirely left me since the attack in Washington, was coming on strong again, but I didn't want Michael to know I was hurting. After we checked into the hotel I took my medicine, and we went to bed early. No more was said about the words we'd had in the car.

The next day the hotel packed a picnic lunch for us of cold chicken, avocados, fresh fruit, and white wine. We drove to a secluded beach where we had a pleasant, quiet day. My stomach was better and Michael was nice, so I thought, Things are going to be all right. The following day we decided to lie on the beach in front of the hotel and enjoy the sun. When we got hungry we walked up to the Snack Shack nearby and took sandwiches back down to our beach chairs. My stomach was feeling very shaky and I was afraid to eat too much, so I wrapped what was left to save it for later. We both dozed off in the sun and when I awoke I was really in pain, but I was also hungry, so I thought it might help my stomach to finish the sandwich. But when I picked it up it was covered with ants. Michael said, "I'm hungry again, too."

"Do you want to go back up and get more sandwiches," I said, meaning did he want us to eat on the beach again or eat inside the hotel.

He turned around and snapped at me, "Let me tell you one thing right now. I'm not waiting on you hand and foot while we're over here. So far we've done everything you wanted to do—from a picnic to lying on the beach—and I haven't said a word. Now if you want another sandwich, go get it yourself."

I was stunned. First of all I hadn't expected him to go fetch my sandwich. Second, I thought the things we'd been doing were his choice too. I stood up and walked back to the food stand without a word, ordered my sandwich and sat there and ate it. When I came back to the chairs he said, "Where's my sandwich?"

I said, "I didn't bring you one."

He was furious. "You'd better not get smart with me," he fumed. "I won't put up with that."

I got up and went back to the room. He came up about two hours later, but he didn't say a word about what had happened. We ate at one of the hotel dining rooms, and after dinner my stomach started hurting so bad I thought I was going to die. It was the worst pain I'd had since the attack started four days earlier. I couldn't keep it from Michael any longer. He called downstairs for a doctor and was told the nearest one was thirty-five miles away at a tiny village hospital. The hotel arranged for one of their security guards to drive us there.

The hospital was a little green building sitting off by itself in the middle of a huge grove of palm trees. The building had no air conditioning so all the windows were open. The doctor examined me and took X rays; then he gave me a shot for pain and told me that I had to see a surgeon as soon as I got back to the mainland because there were serious problems with my gallbladder. He had already told Michael, who was waiting outside the room, that I would have to stay in the hospital overnight. I was lying there alone waiting for the shot to take effect when I looked up and saw a big lizard scoot across the ceiling. Then I glanced over to the open window where the edge of a palm frond was scraping against the sill and saw a snake wrapped around the branch. I thought, My God, what *is* this? Am I in the middle of a jungle? I knew it couldn't be the shot because it hadn't had time to work. A nurse came in then and I told her I wanted to see Michael.

When he came into the room he took my hand and said, "Tammy, I'm really sorry about today. I know you're sick. They want to keep you here tonight, so I'm going to stay with you."

I said, "Michael, there's a lizard on the ceiling and a snake right by the window." He patted my hand. "It's okay, Tammy. You get some rest." He thought I was hallucinating from the shot. But the nurse laughed and walked across the room to close the window. "Oh, that's a harmless snake," she said. "We get lizards and snakes in here all the time because it's too hot to close the windows. Sometimes when you turn on the light at night in the X ray room, they're crawling all over the place." I thought, Oh, that's wonderful. I'm really going to get a lot of sleep here. They brought another bed into the room for Michael, and both of us lay there all night watching the walls and ceiling. He'd be real quiet for a long time and I'd say, "Michael, are you asleep?"

"No, but I don't see any lizards, either," he'd answer. The shot never did put me to sleep, but I felt much better the next morning in spite of not having had any rest.

We had two more days before we had to return to San Francisco. Michael wanted to be in the Napa Valley to visit his brother on the day his little nephew was being christened. My stomach was just a dull ache until the morning we were packing to leave. Then the pain came back so sharply that Michael had to drive me by the hospital to get another shot on our way to the airport in Hilo.

After we landed in San Francisco we rented a car to drive to his brother's house. We hadn't had any conversation for miles when he said, "Let's buy a Rolls when we get home." I told him I didn't want or need a Rolls Royce.

"Okay, then we'll buy a Bentley," he said.

I said, *"You* may buy a Bentley, but I won't. I already have a limousine and a T-bird, and I don't need another car."

"Well, I'm certainly not going to drive that T-bird that George Jones gave you," he sneered. "And we're getting rid of that white limo. It looks like something Isaac Hayes would drive."

That made me even madder because I had recently worked a benefit with Isaac for Ivory Joe Hunter, who was dying of cancer, and I considered Isaac a friend. But I didn't say any more because there was no point in arguing with him. The whole rest of the trip went like that. He'd be nice for a little while, then he'd become hateful or wouldn't talk at all.

My stomach was still bothering me when we got back to Nashville, but I didn't go to the doctor because I didn't feel I could take the time off from my work to have surgery. I foolishly hoped that if I ignored it, it would go away. Michael wanted to take some of his friends down to the house in Florida, so he invited five couples and I asked my driver Steve Morse to drive us down on my bus. We stayed a week. During that time I did all the cooking, bought all the groceries, and picked up the check whenever we all went out to dinner. Michael and I were civil to one another, but there was an obvious coolness between us. We certainly didn't act like newlyweds.

I was back in Nashville only a few days when I had the worst stomach attack yet. I knew I couldn't put off going to the doctor any longer. After he examined me he sent me straight to the hospital and scheduled surgery for 7 the next morning. Michael didn't come to the hospital that night, but he did come the next day and stayed until after I came out of the anesthetic. When my mother came up to sit with me, he asked her to leave, explaining that he wanted me to have complete rest. Then he left, too.

Gallbladder surgery is worse than any operation I've ever had because it makes you so nauseated afterward. I was so sick the next day I couldn't hold my head up, and the floor nurses didn't have time to be running into my room every few minutes. Michael wasn't there, but he had left instructions for me to have no visitors, so I didn't have friends to help either. I asked the head nurse to call my doctor to order a private duty nurse.

I was released from the hospital eight days later. My doctor told me to get away somewhere and have complete rest for at least another week. I wanted to go to Florida, so Michael invited a couple who were friends of his to come along. Jackie wanted to come too, and she brought her girl friend Punkin. Michael and his friends started drinking the minute we got on the plane for Florida; during the layover in Atlanta they sat in the bar. By the time we landed in West Palm Beach, rented a car, and drove the half hour to my house, I felt very weak. I went straight to bed and Michael and the couple stayed up drinking.

I dozed off but I was awakened about an hour later by the sound of gunshots. It was after midnight. I got up and found Jackie and Punkin standing in the living room scared to death. "Mama, Michael's crazy," Jackie said. "He's down on the beach shooting off a pistol." I remembered that he had brought a pistol in his suitcase from Nashville, he said we should have one at the Florida house for protection. I opened the living room glass door and I could hear Michael and his friends laughing I was afraid the shots were going to attract the police, for the area is heavily patrolled all the time because it's a very quiet and exclusive residential neighborhood.

I was sure one of the neighbors would call to complain about someone shooting a gun on the beach. I walked down toward the beach to call Michael. When he came up I said, "I want you to give me the pistol right now. If you don't you'll have to explain what you've been doing to the police, because if this keeps up they're sure to come here." He gave me the gun and I put it away and went back to bed. He and his friends came in much later and started making a lot of noise in the living room, which is right next to the master bedroom. There is an open fireplace between the two rooms, so if you're in one you can hear everything that's said in the other. I couldn't sleep so I got up to go to the kitchen for a drink of water. As I passed through the living room Michael grabbed a bottle of rye off the table and said, "Where did this come from?"

"I don't know, why?" I said.

He said, "I just want to know if it was left here by Mr. Burt Reynolds." He knew he'd said the wrong thing before I even opened my mouth.

I stopped dead in my tracks, and if looks could kill he would have dropped to the floor. "Burt Reynolds has never been inside this house." I was so mad my voice was shaking. "And if you ever bring his name up to me again you won't be back inside of it either." His friends were sitting there listening.

He said, "Well, I'll drop it for now."

"You'll drop it, period." I went on to the kitchen then back to bed.

When he came to bed an hour later he said, "I don't like the way things are going with us."

"Neither do I," I said.

He told me he was going to drive his friends to the airport the next day so they could go to Tampa. "Then I'm going on back to Nashville and give you some time to think."

I said, "I don't need any time to think. Tonight has convinced me that this can never work. We may as well face it now. I made a terrible mistake and it's not going to get better."

He asked, "Do you still love Burt?"

"To be perfectly honest I don't know how I feel about him. I'm not sure I've ever really *loved* him. But he has nothing to do with the trouble between us. We couldn't make this work if I had never met Burt Reynolds."

The next morning when I got up Michael was sitting in the living room. He said, "I'm driving the rental car to the airport and I'll have someone there return it to you."

"Jackie will drive you and bring it back," I said.

"No, I don't want my friends to know I'm going on to Nashville after I put them on the plane."

A few minutes later they left. We waited all afternoon for someone to return the car but no one came. You're really isolated in Jupiter Beach without transportation because the nearest cab service is West Palm, fifteen miles away.

The next morning I heard the doorbell ring just as I got out of bed. I assumed it was the car being delivered. But it was a young man about nineteen. He said, "Is Michael here?"

I said, "No, he's in Nashville."

"Are you Tammy Wynette?"

I said, "Yes."

"Well I hate to bother you," he said, "but I didn't expect you to be here. I'm supposed to be meeting my family here this morning. We're friends of Michael's from Nashville, and he told us we could have the house for a week."

I remembered then that Michael had mentioned loaning the house to some friends of his, but I thought he'd said they were coming later that month. I invited the young man in and told him we'd go ahead and leave that day so he and his family could have the house. I called a cab right away because I knew it would take them a long time to get there. While we were waiting, Jackie, Punkin and I packed.

I was feeling rotten but I thought it was because I hadn't slept the night before. I knew I didn't have my strength back yet from the surgery. When we got to the airport we saw our rented car in the long-term parking lot with the trunk up. I assumed Michael had turned it in; three weeks later I learned he had not. I received a bill for over $400 for three weeks rent although the car was used only one day.

There was no direct flight from West Palm to Nashville so we had a layover in Atlanta. By the time we got there I knew there was something wrong with me that was a lot more serious than lack of sleep. I felt like I was going to pass out, and I was bent over from pain. I felt feverish and woozy. I went into the ladies room and when I looked at my incision I almost fainted. Pus was oozing out of one corner through a tiny opening where a stitch had been removed, and the whole area was red and swollen. I went back out into the waiting area and told Jackie I didn't know if I could make it back to Nashville. We still had more than an hour's wait before plane time, and I felt too weak to sit up.

Then I remembered that when I'd talked to Logan and Katherine at the ranch the day before, they said Burt was in Atlanta, still filming *Smokey and the Bandit*. I thought, At least he can recommend a doctor here. I knew where his film company had been staying when the picture started so I called there. They turned me over to a woman named Rosemary Schaefer, who handled the hotel's public relations. When she found out who I was she said, "You won't believe this and you won't remember me, but my father was your family's doctor back in Haleyville."

I was so relieved to hear a friendly voice I could have cried. I explained my problem and Rosemary immediately offered to send someone to the airport to pick me up. "Burt's out on location now," she told me, "but his manager Dick Clayton is here. I'll let him know you're coming." When we arrived at the hotel Rosemary and Dick Clayton met us at the door. She had already called her personal physician, Dr. May Lun Syn, to come examine me. Adjoining rooms had been arranged for me and Jackie and Punkin, so I went to bed. Dick told me that Burt wanted them to take good care of me and that he'd sent word he was very sorry to hear I was sick. I knew Dr. Syn couldn't get there until after his office hours so I tried to sleep.

About 7 P.M. I heard a light knock on the door and I said, "Come in," expecting to see Rosemary or the doctor. But it was Burt. He had on a black cowboy hat, a denim shirt, and levis. He looked like he'd just come from the set. The door was open into the room that Jackie and Punkin were sharing, so they came running in when they saw who was there. Jackie hugged Burt and thanked him for an Apaloosa mare he'd given her. (He had told Logan and Mr. Reynolds to make her a present of the horse the next time she came to the ranch, and this was the first opportunity she'd had to thank him for it.) After they talked for a few minutes Burt sat down on the edge of the bed, and the girls went back to watching television. We had said "hello," but that was about all. He just sat there looking at me, not saying a word; I looked at television, trying to avoid looking at him. Finally he said, "Do you want to tell me about it?"

It was the first time we'd talked since that day on the phone when he'd asked me to meet him in Florida after his Mexico trip. I hurt so bad I couldn't even think straight, much less talk about all that had happened, so I just shook my head. He said, "Okay, let me tell you what happened. You were upset by all that was going on at your house. The fire scared you half to death; you were worried about going on the road and leaving the girls; and you weren't happy with our relationship. So you thought this guy would offer you a stable home life and protection for the girls. Am I right?"

I just looked at him. I was about ready to cry and I wanted him to leave before that happened. He had no way of knowing Michael and I had separated, and I wasn't about to tell him that; I was too embarrassed.

"Well, is this guy going to be able to take care of you?" he said. "Can he support you if you get sick like this and can't work?"

I said, "I don't know."

"What do you mean you don't know? What you're saying, goddammit, is that you've married somebody you're going to have to support, is that right?" By this time I knew the tears were coming any second so I turned away.

"Well, I'm not going to give you a lecture." Burt's voice softened. "Just remember that if you ever need me for anything, anything at all, even a shoulder to cry on, you just call." He stood up and touched my forehead. When he reached the door Jackie saw that he was about to leave, so she came in from her room to say goodbye. "Take care of your Mama," he told her. "If you need anything tonight I'll be right across the hall." When he closed the door behind him, Jackie said, "Oh, Mama, he had tears in his eyes. He looked so pitiful." My own tears were spilling over by then.

I was still crying when Dr. Syn arrived. He was the sweetest man. He thought I was crying from pain, and he kept apologizing because it had taken him so long to get there. "You have a serious incisional infection," he said, "and you belong in a hospital." I begged him to let me stay there for the night, so I could try to get back to Nashville and my own doctor the next day. "All right," he said, "but you've got to have an I.V. tonight. I'll give you antibiotics and something for pain, and I'll rig up an I.V. so you can get some fluids in your system. But you have to get to a hospital tomorrow."

Burt stopped by at 6:30 the next morning on his way to the set. He said he would call later to see how I felt. Dr. Syn came at 8:30. When he examined my incision again he said, "You've got to go to the hospital right now. You're in no shape to make it back to Nashville." Pete Lacoccas rode with me in the ambulance. They kept me in the hospital five days, before I told them if they didn't release me I was going home anyway. Burt sent his sister Nancy Brown, whom I had never met, to keep me company some of the time. We hit it off right away. I liked her down-to-earth manner. She had recently gotten a divorce after twenty-five years of marriage, and she told me Burt kept nagging her to go out and meet people. "But the only place around here to meet a man is in a bar," she said, "and I'm not about to do that."

The day I left the hospital, I told Jackie, "Maybe I'd better call Michael and apologize for all that happened. I don't really feel that it was my fault, but I guess it would be the best thing to do."

She said, "Well, at least that way you'll know you've done your best, and that will make you feel better no matter what happens."

I made the phone call and told him I was sorry we'd gotten off to such a bad start. He said he was too. Then I said, "Your wife is coming home. Do you think you could meet her at the airport?" He laughed, "I can't get there quick enough." But when we arrived in Nashville it was Gwen who met us, not Michael. She said he had called her to pick us up because he was tied up and couldn't get away. I went home to wait, but before he arrived I was back in the hospital again. I had called my doctor for advice because the pain wouldn't go away; instead it seemed to be getting worse. The doctor said I couldn't be treated at home and told me to meet him at the hospital. I left my wedding ring in an envelope with Gwen and told her to give it to Michael when he showed up.

The next morning Dr. John Frist, an eminent Nashville plastic surgeon, who worked for six years in Rio with the world-famous Dr. Ivo Pitanguy (he's known as the plastic surgeon for the jet set), was called in to examine my incision. The infection had caused it to swell and stretch to nearly an inch in width, and it looked hideous. Dr. Frist is young and handsome, and when he walked into the room I thought, Well, here's a doctor I'm going to like! But he barely nodded in my direction, picking up my chart to read it in such a cold and indifferent way that I immediately changed my opinion. When he came over to examine me he didn't attempt to make conversation, and I thought, Some bedside manner he's got! Then he pulled the gauze aside and saw my incision. His expression didn't change, but he muttered something under his breath that sounded like, "My God!"

He left orders for medication and told me he would see me again that evening. When he came into my room the second time, he was like a different person. He stood at the foot of my bed with his hands behind his back and an embarrassed smile on his face. Then he brought his hand forward and gave me a single rose.

"This is by way of an apology," he said. "I have to confess that when I was called up here this morning, I had already made up my mind, before ever seeing you, that I was being asked to attend a spoiled star who was carrying on about pain when what she was really upset about was having a scarred stomach. But the minute I saw your incision I felt like a fool. If your pain has been half as bad as that thing looks, then I don't know how you've stood it this long. We have to clear up your infection before anything else can be done, but it's gone so far I don't know how much good surgery will do to improve that scar. We'll just have to do what we can and hope for the best. I hope you'll forgive me for judging you before we'd even met."

When the infection was finally cured I had to go right back on the road to work, so I wasn't able to have the corrective surgery for several months. But Dr. Frist was able to make a great improvement in the appearance of my scarred stomach. We've become good friends over the years and he still teases me about his first impression of a "spoiled celebrity" demanding more attention than her problem warranted.

I didn't see Michael again. By the time I got home from the hospital he had moved out. We had married on July 18 and he had left my house in Florida on August 30. We had been together a total of forty-four days. I asked for an annulment because there was no property settlement involved; Michael refused and insisted on a divorce. He started out by asking for a $300,000 settlement which was so absurd I couldn't even take it seriously. But it took John Lentz months of negotiation with Michael's attorneys before they finally settled for our filing a joint income tax return, dividing whatever refund might be due inasmuch as Michael had very little taxable income for that year.

While we were married I had paid for everything except our honeymoon trip to Hawaii, which he had financed on credit cards. Our wedding alone cost me more than $15,000. I even bought a dress for his mother to wear. While I was in the hospital for gall-bladder surgery, Michael had gone to my bank and told them he needed to borrow $8000 to get me out. They let him have the money, but the bank officer called John Lentz and discreetly suggested that he get me better medical insurance. John didn't know what he was talking about—there was no balance at all due on my hospital bill.

All in all, Michael Tomlin was an expensive lesson in my life. But our marriage cost me a lot more than money. My attitude toward men began to change after that and I hated what it did to me mentally. I had never before suspected the motives of people around me. Maybe I was naive but I thought my friends were there because they liked me, and I certainly assumed men were attracted to me for the same reason. I know I have money, but I was poor for so long that I guess I don't think of myself as *rich*. It seems to me that I'm always working to pay my bills. I know that if I wanted to take six months off from working on the road I couldn't, because I have too many financial obligations to meet, so from that viewpoint I'm not rich at all. Perhaps that's why it had never occurred to me to think a man would pursue me for my money. But after the experience with Michael I found myself becoming suspicious of all men. I was bitter, and that's not at all like me. Having Burt as a good friend probably helped me through that period more than anything else. He was the one man who, I could be certain, liked me for myself and not who I was, or what I had. He hadn't written any songs he wanted me to record, and he certainly didn't want or need my money. Michael had scarred my ego; Burt helped it to heal.

I didn't talk to Burt for about a month after I left the hospital in Atlanta, and by that time the news of my divorce from Michael had made all the papers. He wanted to know why I hadn't told him. I said, "It was a very bad time for me, and I was embarrassed about the whole situation. I hadn't told you I was getting married, so I didn't see any reason in Atlanta to tell you I had separated."

"Look, Tammy," he said, "we can't have a close friendship if we're going to play games and not be honest with one another. I want us to have the kind of relationship where you can tell me about any other man in your life, and I can tell you if I've met someone important to me. If I find I'm getting serious with someone you'll be the first to know, and I want that same assurance from you."

And we have had that kind of relationship ever since. We've dated in Nashville, Los Angeles, Dallas, Atlanta, Jupiter, and Miami, and we've had some great times together—as well as one or two that weren't so great. I'll never forget the day I thought he was drowning in my bathtub!

We spent Thanksgiving Day of 1976 at the Florida house with my family. A few days later Mother returned to Nashville with the girls, who had to go back to school. For the first time since we'd been dating, Burt and I had a vacation at the same time. He wasn't going back to work until the first of the year and neither was I. We had both planned on spending Christmas in Florida. After mother and the kids left, we had a couple of wonderful weeks at my house—just the two of us—not doing anything much but lying in the sun, walking on the beach, swimming. Then I had to go back to Nashville for a few days and he moved back over to his ranch.

When I returned he said he'd been sick, and he teased me about going off and leaving him when he needed a nurse. Burt hadn't felt right for over a year and

doctors were still insisting it was overwork, hyperten-
sion, nerves, etc. One night in the middle of December
I had fixed dinner at my house—including one of his
favorites, banana pudding—and we had both eaten
more than usual. We took a long walk on the beach
after dark, and when we came back Burt said he was
very tired. We went to bed long before midnight.

A few hours later I woke up to find him sitting on
the side of the bed. "I'm really sick," he said, "and I
don't know what to do. I'm *not* going back to that hospital in Jupiter." This was the first I'd heard that he'd
been in a hospital there.

"Do you have a doctor here that I can call?" I said.

He said, "No. He'll want me to go into the hospital
again, and I'm not going to do it. Why don't you just
run me a hot bath, and maybe if I sit in the tub a
while I'll feel better."

He stayed in the tub for a long time and felt a little
better for a few minutes. But then he started having
severe pains in his chest. He couldn't get comfortable
sitting or lying down, so we walked the floor. We walked
around my house for about an hour. I kept asking him
to let me call a doctor but he refused. He took another
hot bath and after that said he felt a little stronger. We
went back to bed and he slept until around 7 A.M.

When he awoke he looked tired and said he felt
weak. I offered to cook him breakfast, thinking that
food might give him some energy. He said he wanted
scrambled eggs, orange juice, and wheat toast, and after
he'd eaten he asked me to call his father and tell him
he'd be coming home later. I knew he didn't have the
energy to get up and drive to the ranch. I asked him
if he wanted me to drive him home and he said, "No,
but I do wish you'd do me a favor. Will you go get my
car filled up with gas for me so I won't have to stop
on the way home?" I should have known then how
sick he was because Burt had never asked me to run
an errand for him.

When I returned he was sitting in the living room
on the couch. But when he tried to stand up he fell to

his knees. He turned as white as a sheet and I could see that he was about to pass out. I helped him to the bed where he lay down. I said, "Burt you've *got* to let me call a doctor. This could be really dangerous and I'm worried."

"No, let's try the hot bath one more time. Maybe that will make me feel good enough to drive home and I'll call the doctor from there." I felt he was being protective of me, not wanting the doctor to know he'd spent the night at my house, and I appreciated his gentlemanly attitude. He asked me to fill the oversized sunken tub in my bathroom and add Vita-bath, his favorite bubble bath, and I teased him about wanting to be pampered. I helped him undress and into the tub; then I left the room, but I didn't close the door all the way. A few seconds later I thought I heard him call my name softly, so I pushed the bathroom door wide open and said, "Did you call me?"

There was no answer, and there was no Burt either! All I could see was a tub full of bubbles. There were bubbles everywhere, even spilling over the side of the marble tub onto the floor. Then I caught a glimpse of the top of his head under a mound of bubbles. I screamed, jumped in the tub with him—fully clothed, including my shoes—and desperately tried to pull him up out of the water. But his body was so slippery I couldn't get a good grip on him and he kept sliding out of my arms. At that time Burt weighed about 190 pounds and I weighed 110. I'm strong for my size, thanks to all those years in the cotton field, but he was dead weight and I couldn't get him out of that tub to save my life. To show how unnerved I was, it never occurred to me to pull the plug and let the water drain out!

All I could think of was keeping his head above the bubbles so he could breathe. I'd grip him and hoist him up for a second or two; he'd gasp for breath and inhale a big gulp of air; then he'd slip right back down into the water again. It must have looked like a scene from a slapstick comedy, but it was terrifying at the time. I had splashed water and bubbles from one end of that bathroom to the other; I was sopping wet all over with my clothes sticking to my body, and I just knew he was either going to drown or be suffocated by bubbles before I could get him out of there.

Then I spotted the phone lying a few feet away on the bathroom floor. I had just had the extension installed the day before. I tugged and pulled on Burt until I finally wedged him up against the wall behind the tub where I could hold him by pressing against him as hard as I could with my body. He had bubbles all over his head and shoulders, and his breathing was labored and irregular. I pushed against his chest with one hand while I made a quick grab for the phone with the other. I got the phone to my ear, but there wasn't a sound on it. It was deader than a doornail!

At that moment Burt started coming out of it long enough to squirm around. When he threw one arm up I lost my balance and my hold on him, and he slid right back down under the water again. Somehow I finally managed to slide half his body over the edge of the tub. His consciousness came and went, but I got the name of a doctor out of him before he passed out again. Then he came to long enough to gasp, "Oxygen, oxygen. There's a tank in my trunk. Get it."

I propped him over the side of the tub as best as I could, then ran like a mad woman out through my bedroom, around the pool, knocking my head on two of the hanging plants, down the steps to the courtyard where his car was parked, only to realize I didn't have his keys to open his trunk. I ran back in the house, found his pants on the bedroom floor, grabbed the keys, and ran back to the car. When I returned to the bathroom with the oxygen tank he had disappeared again. I climbed back in the tub, fished him out—by this time I was getting better at it so it didn't take quite so long—pulled him over the side of the tub and put the oxygen mask up to his face. He was conscious enough to tell me how to turn on the tank. He started trying to take deep breaths; then he threw the mask off his face and collapsed again. The tank was empty!

By this time I was absolutely panic-stricken, and it had *still* not dawned on me to let the damn water out of the tub! I knew I had to get him out of that tub so I could get help. I strained, struggled, and pulled on him until at last I had his whole torso over the side of the tub. His feet flopped out after him and I slipped down on the wet floor with him, falling half on top of him. I got up and checked to make sure he was still breathing. He was, but he was totally unconscious by then.

I found his doctor's number through information, but when I reached him he said, "Well, go ask him what the doctor at the hospital told him."

I said, "I don't think you understand, Dr. Lambert. I can't ask him anything; he's unconscious."

Then he said, "Well, keep checking him and call me back in ten minutes." And he hung up. I couldn't believe it!

I quickly dialed the Jupiter Chief of Police, who had been to my house several times since I'd lived there. I knew I could trust him and I knew he'd get there fast. Chief Shiffert arrived within minutes. He took one look at Burt, still lying unconscious on my bathroom floor, and said, "Call the emergency squad. He's not breathing right."

"Oh, dear. The *National Enquirer* will have their story now," I thought. Their offices are in Lantana, Florida, about seventeen miles down the road from my house, and I knew that they kept tabs on everything that went on in that community. They'd know if an ambulance was called to my house. I could just imagine the *Enquirer* cover with Burt Reynolds being carried out of my house on a stretcher, and I didn't even dare imagine what the headlines would read!

When the ambulance arrived the driver and the two attendants were all women. Chief Shiffert and I had managed to get Burt's levis up over his bottom, but he was still bare-chested and unzipped. At one point he came to enough to motion toward his feet. He wanted his boots on! Chief Shiffert laughed and said, "Boy, you better be glad we got your pants on!"

By the time we loaded Burt on the stretcher and walked out the front door, about twenty people had gathered in the driveway to see who was being put into an ambulance. One woman screamed, "Oh, look! It's Burt Reynolds. I've *got* to get his autograph!" She started to push her way forward, but a policeman stopped her. I rode in the ambulance with Burt. I had quickly put on dry clothes and changed shoes, but my hair was damp and sticky from bubbles. They began running tests on Burt immediately when they settled him into his room. It was then that one of the nurses asked me how I'd gotten him out of the tub by myself. She said, "What did you do, let all the water out?" That moment was the first time I'd even *thought* of letting the water out. I know my face turned red. I felt like an absolute fool!

I sat on a little wooden footstool outside Burt's door for the next few hours until I knew he was going to be all right. Then they let me wait in someone's office. I stayed eighteen hours before I went home to change clothes. I came back every day after that until he was released Christmas eve. He asked me to do part of his Christmas shopping for him so I occupied some of my time with that.

One day I was sitting in his room and he asked me for a piece of paper. All I had with me was some of my own stationery. He pondered and scribbled and pondered more and scribbled more for a few minutes, but he wouldn't tell me what he was writing. Finally, with a sheepish grin he handed me the piece of paper.

> I once knew a lady named Tammy
> Who had an old fashioned daddy and mammy
> At one time she had to pick cotton
> For which she has long since forgotten
> Now she's grown up with kids of her own
> Got a big shining bus, two houses, twelve phones
> She's pretty and smart, can even write charts

But what's best is this beauty's big heart
Sometimes she's sick and she stumbles
Sometimes she's mad and she grumbles
Nobody loves what's perfect ————————
This don't rhyme, but who gives a *shit*.

When I read it I laughed so hard he said, "Well, it's not *that* funny!" I told him it was probably the worst poem I had ever read, but also the sweetest.

A new doctor was brought in on his case and after all the testing his illness was diagnosed as hypoglycemia, which is low blood sugar. Eating sugar aggravates the condition, so my banana pudding may have brought on the attack! And we were told that taking a hot bath was the worst thing he could have done with his blood pressure so low. Between my feeding him banana pudding and his insisting on a bubble bath, it's a wonder we didn't kill him!

Thanks to Burt, 1976 ended on a high note even though it had been a traumatic year for me. In fifteen months I had had surgery three times—for a damaged kidney, for adhesions, for cystic mastitis, and for my gallbladder. I'd been hospitalized five other times for the gallbladder incision infection, an inner ear infection, and nodules on my vocal chords. At one point they thought they would have to strip my vocal chords, which is a horrifying thought for a singer. Mama (Mother's mother, who raised me) had died, and Daddy, my grandfather, was paralyzed from a stroke. I had lived with constant fear at home because of the threats and break-ins, then endured a terrifying fire that ruined my home, followed by harassment from authorities, whom I had expected to be considerate and concerned. I had made a foolish and costly mistake in marrying Michael and was still in the process of negotiating for a divorce.

Considering all this it's amazing that we were able to have a happy holiday, but we did. The girls came down to Florida as soon as school let out, and MeeMaw and PeePaw followed a few days later. Burt spent Christ-

mas morning with his family at the ranch, and the
afternoon with my family at our house. He gave me
three of the most beautiful original oil paintings I've
ever seen, and he also gave me a Pulsar watch engraved "To Tammy, With Love, Burt." I accused him
of buying me the watch just so he could get his back
(I still had the one he'd left in my hotel suite in Los
Angeles). I didn't have to go back to work until New
Year's Eve so we had almost a week together after
Christmas.

Burt and I continued to see one another whenever
we could through the next summer. Little by little our
relationship evolved to a warm, easy friendship I hope
will never change. Time, and another romance, helped
me get over the feeling that I had to run from him or
hold back for fear of falling in love. I still visit his
ranch when I'm in Florida to see Mr. and Mrs. Reynolds, Logan and Katherine, *and* our horses, which have
multiplied like rabbits. After Burt gave Jackie her
Apaloosa, "Sweetpea," I bought two more Apaloosas
for the other girls. Logan has since bred my mares to
some of Burt's championship studs, so we now have
eight horses boarded at the Burt Reynolds ranch.

I guess I will always see Burt as "Buddy," the name
he's known by at home, a proud man who has simple
tastes and great strength of character, a man who
hasn't lost his compassion or his perspective by being
the success he is. There are few men like Burt Reynolds.

Chapter 12

⚜

$\mathcal{T}$ HE 1977 tour season proved to be the most enjoyable time I have ever had on the road. Shorty Lavender and Dick Blake, who had gone into partnership in a booking agency, arranged a package tour featuring Ronnie Milsap, the Statler Brothers, and me.

Ronnie had won a Grammy the year before for "Best Male Country Performance." He had also won the Country Music Association's award for "Male Vocalist of the Year" twice, and "Album of the Year" once. In October 1977, just before our tour ended, Ronnie went on to win the "Album of the Year" award *again,* the "Male Vocalist" award for the *third* time, plus CMA's most coveted award, "Entertainer of the Year"! The Statlers had won three Grammys and five consecutive Country Music Association awards as "Vocal Group of the Year." That fall they won their *sixth* consecutive CMA award in that category, setting a record that will undoubtedly stand for years to come.

With my two Grammys (1967 and 1969 for "Best Country Performance, Female") and three consecutive

CMA "Female Vocalist of the Year" awards, we collectively represented eighteen major country music awards, a record no package on the road could match. But more important, we believed our show was the best too, and that made every appearance a special event.

Ronnie, a fantastic performer who plays and sings rock and rhythm and blues as great as he does country music, opened the show. He always left his audiences on their feet, fired up for more. Then I came on and did my segment, followed by the Statlers, who closed the show. In addition to being super singers with a unique sound, the Statlers are fabulous entertainers. They are always called back for at least two encores, so we not only played to capacity houses on that tour, we also received a tremendous response from the audiences. I'm afraid it spoiled us all. Standing ovations were the rule, not the exception.

There is always a thrill, a unique excitement, about being on a stage in front of a live audience, even when you're scared to death or the show isn't going the way you want it to. But when all the ingredients are right— when you're giving them the best you've got to offer and they're giving back enthusiasm, love, and approval —there's just no feeling like it in the world. To be standing on a stage before a thousand cheering, whistling, foot-stomping fans is the most intoxicating sensation I've ever experienced. There's really no way to describe what it does for a performer. A "force" comes rushing at you from a cheering audience that hits you like a physical experience, sometimes almost knocking your breath out, sending the adrenaline through your veins like a flash flood. The screaming and clapping and yelling may last for only a few minutes, but it keeps me high for hours after the auditorium is dark and the people have gone home. That's why it's impossible for a performer to go to sleep right after a show, no matter how worn out he is or how late the hour. Depending on the enthusiasm of my audience it can take me as much as two or three hours to come down after a good show. Sometimes, if we're driving on after a performance, we'll play tapes and sing and dance on the bus for a couple of hours, carrying on like kids at a party, just to work off the ecstatic energy we've gotten from the audience.

As a performer, the tour with Ronnie and the Statlers really kept me on my toes. Performing in between two acts as heavy as theirs made me more conscious than ever of working to put on the best possible show I could. Charlie Justice, my longtime friend and fiddle player, decided he wanted to retire from the road not long after the tour started, so instead of replacing him with another fiddle player, I switched Charlie Carter over to rhythm guitar and hired Buddy Church to play lead. Buddy was the first musician I had called two years earlier when I thought I was going to have to put my own band together after George and I split up. He added a sound all his own to the group, and having a musician of his talent join us gave the rest of my boys a lift that lasted throughout the entire tour.

But being a part of a great show that was making country music history—a package of this kind with three headlining acts had never been done before— wasn't the only reason the season was so great. After all, an artist is only on the stage for an hour, so if the rest of his time isn't spent happily he ends up living for those brief highs with nothing but long stretches of boredom in between. In this tour, however, our off-hours on the road were almost as much fun as the applause. From April until the middle of November our three buses caravanned across the United States, zig-zagging our way from New York to California, from Canada to Florida. We all hit it off so well that we became like one big gypsy family.

If it hadn't been for the companionship among the three groups, that season could have been the most grueling tour of my career. We were booked solid, with recording dates jammed in between. I was spending so little time at home that I bought a private plane just so I could fly back and forth to Nashville to see my kids.

When we had a couple of days off on the road, usually a Monday and Tuesday, the buses stayed out of Nashville, because even if we were only 500 or 600 miles from home it would have taken a day to drive in and a day to return again. Since we play more small towns than big cities, trying to make plane connections to travel back and forth within a couple of days is next to impossible. You end up with four- or five-hour lay-overs in places like Chicago and Atlanta, and by the time you arrive home you have to turn right around and go back again. Shorty and Dick encouraged me to buy the little Twin Engine Navajo Chieftain that came up for sale because the agency (I was still part owner) could use it for business, and it was tax deductible.

We immediately ran ads to hire a private pilot. One of the first applicants was a thirty-four-year-old former crop duster named Bernie Lentz (no relation to John Lentz). Bernie was the only pilot who applied who never asked about the salary or the hours. When he found out he would be flying me, he told the interviewer, "That's my job. You can't let anybody else have it!"

Bernie fit right into our road family like a long lost relative. He was a big, warm-hearted, curly-haired bear of a man who knew how to make his passengers feel safe and confident. Even members of my band who didn't like the idea of flying in a small plane felt okay with Bernie in the pilot's seat. I used to tease them that I was going to learn to fly the plane the way I drive the bus, and they all assured me if I did I'd be flying alone!

Even the Statlers loved Bernie, but not enough to go up in the plane with him. They dislike flying so much they'll turn down a booking just to avoid it. Their bass singer Harold Reid, whose deep voice and big build make him appear fearless, is terrified to fly, even in a 747.

Harold and Don Reid are the only real brothers in the Statlers' group. But the other two, Lew DeWitt and Phil Balsley, have known Harold and Don since junior high school, so they're all "family." You'd think they'd be sick of one another after all these years together on the road, as well as back home in Staunton, Virginia, where they still live. But, amazingly, they can still make each other fall out laughing as easily as they can someone they've just met. I've never known entertainers who were so consistently funny offstage. Whether we shared a table with them at a truck stop, or a press conference before a show, they always did something crazy that made the time pass easier.

Even backstage, that dismal place that usually looks like a men's locker room and smells like a public washroom, was fun with the Statlers around. Often we'd find Lew, their tenor and lead guitarist, and Buddy Church off in a corner together, jammin' on guitar. They did some of the best pickin' I've ever heard. Offstage Donnie played straight man to Harold's comedy just like he does in their show, and my band is convinced they spent half their childhood working out routines because we never saw the same one twice. Even Phil, the quietest member of the group, was warm and witty once we got to know him.

The last night of the tour was one I'll never forget. Most of us were crying and the ones who weren't kept trying to make silly jokes because it had been so good, and we knew we'd never share a long package tour like that one again. Jim Ebert, ole sweet "Ebe," my piano player, had chosen that night to say "goodbye" to the road. Like Justice, he felt it was time to leave the gypsy life and become a family man. There wasn't a dry eye on my bus! We all felt like we were losing a beloved big brother, which indeed we were (Milt Smith plays piano for me now and he's great).

Don and Harold and Lew write most of the Statlers' songs, and I have always admired their talent. Being around them made me more productive as a writer. I think one of the reasons was pure ego. I wanted to impress them that I could write, too! I wrote several songs I'm proud of while we were on that tour, including "We'll Talk About It Later" and "That's the Way It

Could Have Been," but my favorite is one that expresses exactly how I feel as a mother. It came about because of an incident that happened at home.

I had a weekend off unexpectedly, so I asked Bernie to fly me back to Nashville. All the way there I planned things the girls and I could do together during the two nights I had free. Something Jackie said to me when she was just a little girl has always stuck in my mind when I think of how much time I have to spend away from my children. She was once watching me pack to go out on the road and she asked, "Are you leaving?" in a sad little voice. I told her I had to go to work. Her little face drooped and she said, "But you just got home."

I said, "Honey, I was here all day yesterday."

She threw her arms around my legs and cried, "Oh, Mama, couldn't yesterday come again tomorrow?" That really got to me. Leaving my children has always been the hardest part of my work, so when I am at home I try to be with them as much as possible.

But this time when I got there and gathered them around the kitchen table to share my weekend plans, I could tell they weren't nearly as enthusiastic as I was. The expressions on their faces were more revealing than anything they could have said. It turned out they had already made plans of their own. Georgette was going to Mississippi to visit relatives with MeeMaw and PeePaw. Tina is a cheerleader and her school had a ball game Friday night; on Saturday she planned to spend the night with a girl friend. Jackie had tickets to a concert Friday night and Gwen had a date. They had both invited girls over to our house on Saturday for a slumber party.

Even though I realize kids their age have more fun with friends than they do with a parent, I was hurt that they didn't want to be with me as much as I wanted to be with them. I made some remark about how little time we have together. When Gwen saw that I was feeling sorry for myself she started teasing me. "What do you think we do when you're gone, sit around and miss Mama?" she asked. "When you're out there driving 500 and 600 miles a day to make a living, we're not hanging around here moping. We're over at Shakey's having a party!"

Jackie added, "Mama, we always keep busy when you're not here. If you were home all the time you'd drive us crazy and we'd get on your nerves, too. Don't ever worry about us adjusting to your being away so much because it's the only life we know."

I hadn't thought about it that way, but it *is* all they know. I decided then that since they had taken care of their weekend, I'd better take care of my own or I'd find myself wandering around that big house talking to the walls.

I wanted to get one of my cars down to the Florida house, so this seemed like a perfect time to drive it there. I could call Bernie to pick me up in Palm Beach instead of Nashville to fly back out to meet the bus. I like driving and I don't mind doing it alone, so I took off by myself about dusk, headed toward Atlanta, then on down Highway 75 to the Florida Turnpike, which takes you almost to my back door in Jupiter. It's a seven hundred mile trip, and since I planned to drive straight through I had a lot of time to think.

The conversation I'd had with the girls still weighed heavily on my mind, and I started jotting down thoughts about being an "absentee" mother on a pad I always keep on the front seat of the car. The lines began to fall into place before I hit Atlanta, and by the time I reached my beach house thirteen hours later I had a song. But instead of putting a melody to it, I decided to use it in my show as a recitation, with the band playing "Melody of Love" for the background. Now no matter where I perform—night club, open-air fair date, or auditorium—a hush comes over the audience when I start "talking" this song. When it's over I can always see women in the first few rows wiping away tears. It's called "Dear Daughters."

Dear daughters:
Gwen, you're my oldest.
You're quite a lady,
My only blue-eyed girl.
You turned sixteen in April
And you sure made a change in my world.
I'm sorry I missed the big evening,
Your first date, and I wasn't around.
Save all the secret things you did
And tell me when I get to town.
And on your graduation, I wanted pictures to look back on.
But I wasn't there to take them.
As usual, I was gone.
You've had to grow up much too quick, and you've done it
    on your own.
You did it without Mama
'Cause Mama wasn't home.

And Jackie you're quite a lady, too.
You're just one year younger than Gwen
And there's so much that I'm missing
By being Mommy now and then.
I remember the day you cooked your first meal.
You were just nine; you cooked biscuits and ham.
You called to tell me how good it was,
'Cause I was out of town.

And at the party for fathers and daughters
I know you felt out of place
Even the pretty dress I bought
Couldn't fill that empty space
And the time when you got sick
And the doctor turned you down
He said they couldn't treat you
With your Mama out of town

And Tina, you're such a pretty girl
With big almond eyes of brown.
They voted you homecoming queen
While I was out of town.

I know you were a beauty, 'cause your sisters dressed you
   right
And you said it didn't matter that I couldn't be there that
   night.
And the day you joined the cheerleading team
Nothing could hold you down
You yelled "Hip, Hip Hooray" over the phone
'Cause as usual, I was out of town.

And Tamala Georgette Jones,
You simply take my breath away
Born just six short years ago
And named for your Daddy and me;
Going to sleep on MeeMaw's arm, listening to her hum,
Drifting off to Fairyland
While sucking on your thumb.
Just yesterday you pulled a tooth
Boy, you sure are brave and strong.
I wish I could have been there,
But as usual, I was gone.

Even though I wrote it and have performed it count-
less times, the words still affect me as though I were
writing it for the first time. Once Dottie West, who
has also been a "road mother" for years, was sitting
in the first row of the audience when I recited "Dear
Daughters," and she cried so hard she had to leave
and go backstage! When I'm doing it so many little
scenes come to my mind involving my children. I remember things like the poem the girls wrote for my
birthday a few years ago. They gave it to me with a
note that read:

Dear Mama,
   We don't have anything to give you because we didn't
know what to give the lady who has everything.
   This poem is our way of thanking you for being the
mother you have been, and for giving us what we need
most—love.
   Happy Birthday!

We love you and hope you have the most fantastic birthday possible.

>   Your girls,
>   Gwen, Jackie,
>   Tina and Georgette

This is the poem:

Our Mother

> God made a wonderful mother
> A mother who never grows old
> He made her smile of sunshine
> And molded her heart of gold
> In her eyes he placed bright shining stars
> In her cheeks fair roses you see
> God made a wonderful mother
> And he gave that mother to me.

Needless to say, it was the most treasured birthday gift I've ever received.

As a mother who's away from home more than she's there, I can't help but worry about the girls at times and wonder if they're being cheated. But I won't let *anyone* make me feel guilty about being a working mother. *If I didn't work, we wouldn't eat.*

And I think it's lucky that my work happens to be music, because otherwise I'd still be a hairdresser, working long hours every day, coming home at night after being on my feet steadily, too tired to have fun with my kids and too poor to buy them nice things or take them to exciting places. I'd be making less in a year than I make in a night now.

We were still living in Florida with George when Tina came home from school one day with a note from her teacher. It said she was obviously suffering from parents who were out of town too much. "Tina apparently does not get enough attention at home because she causes disturbances in class," was the last line. The note really burned me up, and I went to school with Tina the next day. I told the teacher that George and I averaged only about ten days a month on the road, and when we were home we were there *all* day and *all* night, which meant we ended up spending more time with our children than parents who have nine-to-five jobs. I also explained that my mother, a certified school-teacher, stayed with the kids when we were gone, and that I knew for a fact Tina had never lacked for atten-tion; if anything, due to her premature birth and the aftereffects of the meningitis, she had had more than her share of attention. I told the teacher if she had taken the trouble to look at the records she would have seen that the meningitis had left Tina with a "hyper" personality, making it difficult for her to sit still or concentrate for more than short periods. At that time she was still on daily medication for her condi-tion. The thing that made me so mad about the teach-er's attitude was that she had just *assumed* Tina was somehow neglected because we were in show business.

I have never felt that my children have suffered be-cause of my work. In fact I'm convinced we have the best of one another because of it. Since we're not to-gether all the time we make a special effort to enjoy one another when we are. We don't take one another's presence for granted like most children and parents do, and we're never together long enough to get bored or irritated with each other.

I'm not a strict mother, but then I've never had to be. I have certain house rules, fitted to their ages, and except for a very few slipups they've always followed them just as closely when I'm not at home as they do when I am. My daughters know there are certain things I would never tolerate, and rudeness is at the top of the list. They don't talk back to me or to any adult. I would also be *very* upset if they ever acted as though they were special in some way because their mother happens to be in show business. But they've never done that. They're proud of me, but I'm just "Mama" to them and that makes *me* proud. I want very much to be known as a good singer, but it's just as important to me to be known as a good mother.

I don't doubt that Tina and Georgette will end up in the music business because they're both talented singers and they both like the spotlight, although Tina is going through a phase right now where she doesn't want to sing in public. But you'll never catch Gwen or Jackie on a stage. Gwen plans to go to the University of Colorado to study conservation and ecology. Jackie will probably get married and raise a family. She's very motherly with her little sisters and she likes the domestic life, which pleases me.

My own life is more calm and orderly now than it's ever been. As a woman, I feel that I am just coming into the best part of my life. The mid-thirties are wonderful because you've finally gotten to know yourself. I have a better understanding of who and what I am, and what I want from life, than I ever did in my twenties. I'm aware of my vulnerabilities and shortcomings—I'm still thin-skinned and easily hurt, and I'm just as stubborn as I ever was—but I know my strengths and abilities, too. I'm as capable of supporting a family as I am of running a home, and it's important to me to know I'm good at both. Maybe it's because I don't do much of it, but I actually enjoy housework, and I love cooking a good old-fashioned country meal almost as much as I love singing.

As for personal relationships, I've sure learned a few lessons there! I'm sorry my mistakes had to be so public, but I'm not sorry for the experience I gained making them. I hope I *never* become cynical about men or marriage. I know what it's like to wait for a man to come home at night, not knowing where he is or when he'll show up. And I know what it's like to be *alone*—waiting for no one because no one is coming. Neither situation is good, but I'd rather be waiting than wishing I had somebody to wait for.

I've met financially independent women who say, "Who needs a husband? They expect to be pampered and praised, and they're not worth the aggravation. I can get anything a husband can give me on my own, including sex, and not have to answer to anybody about anything."

Well, that's all right if that's how you feel, but it wouldn't work for me. I *enjoy* pampering and petting a man. And I don't like the kind of sex where somebody has to get up and go home. Since I'm still too old-fashioned to live with a man without marriage (maybe because I don't want to set that example for my daughters), I don't doubt that I will marry again. And I won't apologize for the fact that it will be my fifth either! Each of my husbands has taught me something about myself, and to be perfectly honest I don't even think of my relationships with Don and Michael as *marriages*. They were more like legalized, ill-fated affairs. My marriage to Euple seems so remote from anything I know today that it's almost like it happened in another life. So when I think of being "married," I think mostly of George. I don't know if I'll ever completely get over the disappointment of that breakup because I wanted that marriage to work more than I ever wanted anything in my life. But it didn't work . . . and brooding over the past is a waste of time, especially if you feel, as I do, that the best is yet to come.

Right now, I'm dating a very special man. I don't know where it will lead, but I do know that being with him makes me happy. And let's face it—it wouldn't be me if I wasn't in love!

Tammy Wynette
Nashville, Tennessee
January 1978

It was such a perfect fit that even the smallest were
were welcome. They stood already formed a figure, al

374

Epilogue

$\mathcal{I}$ LOOK from my bedroom patio out to the blue-green Atlantic beyond, sparkling brilliantly under a midday tropical sun, and a sense of calm I have seldom known settles over me.

There, on the beach fifty yards away behind a thicket of sea grape bushes that protect my house from high tides and winds, is the spot where I got married last month.

It's just an empty beach now, but it was transformed into a romantic setting that day. Three yellow striped tent-shaped awnings were erected, a large center one covering an astroturf-carpeted platform where the wedding party stood, and two others on either side above rows of white chairs for guests, friends, and relatives. It was such a perfect day that even the uninvited guests were welcome. They stood nearby behind a roped-off boundary—curious sunbathers with glistening oiled bodies who wandered down the beach, and determined paparazzi who came ashore by boat to push their way in front of the spectators, straining against the rope with cameras click, click, clicking throughout the ceremony.

The scene will be etched in my memory forever— 2 o'clock in the afternoon, July 6, 1978—the day that I became Mrs. George Richey.

Richey is the "special man" who came into my life just as I was finishing my autobiography. Actually, he had come into my life long before that. I've known him for ten years, first as a songwriter-producer, then as a trusted friend. He had written several George Jones hits, including "The Grand Tour," and "Picture of Me Without You." After George and I moved back to Nashville from Lakeland we saw Rich and Sheila often.

Then, after George and I split up, Richey and Sheila became my frequent companions and best friends. I often relied on Rich as a substitute father for my daughters. They adored him. I'd come in off the road to learn he'd been over in my absence to take them to a movie or out to dinner. It wasn't something I ever asked him to do, so it always impressed me as being a very kind and thoughtful way for a busy man to spend some of his limited spare time. When he heard Jackie didn't have anyone to escort her to the father-daughter dance at school, he called and told her to get dressed up in her prettiest outfit because she was going to be his date for the evening. Jackie was thrilled. When I got back to town she told me they had danced every dance together, and Richey had been the most popular "father" there. His own children, his son Kelly, twelve and a half, and Deirdre, his daughter, fourteen and a half, live with their mother (his first wife) Dottie in California. (But they spend a great deal of time with us, both at home and on the road.) I used to tell Nanette that I believed one of the reasons Richey spent so much time with my children was because he missed his own so much. He's a fantastic father.

Toward the end of my long tour with Ronnie Milsap and the Statlers, I came into Nashville to record. Richey stopped by my session. I hadn't seen him for nearly six months.

Since he's also a good friend of Billy Sherrill (they've written many hit songs together, and I've written a few with them, including one of my all-time favorites, " 'Til I Can Make It on My Own") I wasn't surprised to see him walk into the studio. But I was shocked when he told me that his three-year marriage to Sheila was ending.

Richey, who is one of the most dedicated family men I have ever known, was wrestling with the same kind of emotional upheaval I had suffered when I was forced to face the fact that it was over between George and me. Even when you *know* you can no longer live with a person you have loved, there's a sense of failure, if only because your best effort failed to make it work. Richey's unhappiness was written on his face; he looked worn out, and my heart ached for him. He had always been there when I needed a shoulder to cry on after George left, and I had turned to him often for advice and reassurance. He had become the best male friend I'd ever had, so it was only natural that I wanted to offer my shoulder when he needed one. After the session we talked the night away, and I actually hated to go back on the road and leave him because I felt like I was missing a chance to be as good a friend to him as he had been to me.

After that, whenever I got back in town for a day or two, he'd come over to the house and we'd talk. One time I sent Bernie to pick him up and fly him out to meet us on the road because Ebe was sick, and I knew no piano player in Nashville who could put on a better show than Richey.

Gradually, my feelings toward him began to change. Friendly love was evolving into romantic love. We both felt it happening, but we were a little afraid to admit it. When I realized I was in love with him it was the strangest sensation. It was like returning after a long journey and suddenly being able to see the warm lights of home beckoning through the dark night. He was so familiar and comfortable, yet at the same time "new," because during all the years I had known him I had never thought of him as anything other than a very dear friend.

We didn't make wedding plans until we were very sure of our own feelings and also of one another. We had both made enough mistakes to be wary of the full commitment marriage demands.

Now, I look back on the time we've had together as the most contented I've known since I was a little girl, when Daddy was always there to take care of me. Richey is like that. No man has ever done as much for me as he does. He gave up his job as musical director of "Hee Haw" to travel with me and manage my business affairs. He has private income from the sale of his successful publishing firm, so he didn't have to continue producing records to earn a living. He brought his sister and brother-in-law, Vi and Bill Whitlach, from California to manage our household and watch over the kids while we're away. His sister-in-law Sylvia Richey runs our office and takes care of the payroll. And Richey oversees it all.

He's like a one-man army. He's the only person I've ever seen who can do six things at once and do them all well. He can talk on an important business call on one line, have two others on hold, go back and forth among all three conversations, keeping straight in his head the purpose of each, while he's handing Sylvia notes about something totally unrelated, answering a question for one of the kids hovering nearby, and eating a sandwich, all at the same time! It makes me tired just to watch him!

There are people in Nashville who call George Richey a musical genius. I'm prejudiced, of course, but his vast knowledge of music constantly amazes me. Recently I played with the Dallas Symphony and he conducted the orchestra for me. He was brilliant, and afterward the musicians came to tell him he was one of the best guest conductors they'd ever had.

Richey has lifted so many responsibilities from my shoulders—both at home and in my work—that for the first time since I began my career I'm free to pour my full energy into my music and my show. He is also the most attentive and protective man I've ever known. Being the one receiving the pampering and petting instead of the one giving it is a new experience for me, and I *like* it! But what I appreciate the most is that he's always there when I need him. I've finally found a man I can lean on rather than one who leans on me.

And I've learned *hard* more than once since we've been together. Our happiness has been dimmed by two tragedies that I sincerely believe would have broken me apart if Richey hadn't been there to hold me together.

The first one took place in January. I had had surgery in December—another futile attempt to get rid of the floating adhesions that keep me in pain much of the time—and I was still recuperating at home. I didn't have to go back on the road until the middle of the month so I had been spending my time finishing this book. It had been sent to the publishers when we got a phone call from Ray Williams, the owner of the private airport in Springfield, Tennessee, where my plane was kept. He told us that Bernie had disappeared in a single-engine plane over Lake Pontchartrain just outside New Orleans.

I had never had anything hit me harder. I knew that Bernie, like most pilots, hated single-engine planes, and I couldn't understand why he was flying one. Knowing how cautious and confident he had been made me feel that if Bernie could crash, no one was safe in the air. I refused to believe that he was dead.

Search parties had been sent out over the lake immediately after they received his last communication at the New Orleans airport tower. It was a clear morning, not a cloud in the sky. When he was less than three miles out over the twenty-five-mile-wide lake, he had radioed that he was having engine trouble and didn't think he could make it back to the runway. He told them he was 150 feet above the water and turning in an easterly direction to get as close back in as he could. They remembered that he sounded as calm and confident as someone relaying a routine position. There was not a hint of panic in his voice. But helicopters and search boats arriving on the scene within nine minutes could find no trace of the plane or Bernie. I was certain he had escaped and swum to safety. I just *knew* he would turn up somewhere along the shore, exhausted but alive. My girls agreed. They worshiped Bernie. Gwen kept saying, "Mama, don't worry. Bernie's a *survivor*. He'll make it."

I insisted on flying to New Orleans immediately so we could be there when they found him. Richey didn't have the heart to discourage my optimism, even though he held out little hope for Bernie's survival.

We were met in New Orleans by the Coast Guard who took us to their headquarters where we were shown a map pinpointing the location Bernie had radioed back to the tower. Then they showed us how far they had extended the search around that location. They were puzzled that they hadn't even seen an oil slick on the water, but they weren't too surprised that the plane had not been found because the bottom of Lake Pontchartrain is covered in four to six feet of silt.

We learned that Bernie had flown to New Orleans to visit his girl friend, who had recently moved there from Springfield. He had told her he flew down in a single-engine plane because it belonged to a doctor in Springfield who owed him a favor. He didn't say what the favor was, but he did say the doctor had offered to lend his plane to repay it.

We hung around the New Orleans Coast Guard for two days while they continued their search; finally, they gave up. But I couldn't. I even made up fantasies about Bernie taking off in the doctor's plane to start a new life in the Bahamas. I couldn't think of any reason he would want to run away from his old life, but anything was better than believing him dead.

Fifty-one days later they found Bernie's body. It washed up on the banks of Little River, which empties into Lake Pontchartrain. They still have never found a trace of the plane.

Richey brought me the news of Bernie's death. I cried for days. I told him to sell the plane immediately. I never wanted to see it again. I knew I couldn't fly in it again because it held too many fond memories of being in the air with Bernie—haunting memories like the night we flew over Pittsburgh with a full, luminous moon hanging just ahead of us in a midnight blue sky. It was just me, Georgette, and Chris Schmitt, a little friend her age who had come out with us for the weekend. The children were awed by the enormous white moon that appeared to be no higher in the sky than we were. And they delighted in looking down on a city of lights below us, dazzling and twinkling like a brilliant Milky Way fallen to earth. It was an incredible sight, and Bernie banked over the city again and again so the children could "oooooh" and "aaaaaaah" and take it all in.

They buried Bernie the day after his body was found, in a family plot in Whitehouse, New Jersey. I couldn't go to the funeral because I was working, but I'm glad now that I didn't. I want to remember Bernie as I last saw him—happy, full of life and laughing at some silly joke we'd shared.

From the time we received the phone call that Bernie was missing, all through the days they were searching for him and afterward when we were told they had found his body, Richey was by my side, giving me his strength for support.

Later, last spring, I needed his support even more than I had in January. I still hadn't gotten over losing Bernie when Mother called in hysterics to tell me that Carolyn, my beloved "sister" who has been an inspiration to me all my life, had only a short time to live.

Terminal cancer! Mother could hardly bring herself to speak the words. Richey and I went down to be with her on the day of surgery. But when they operated, they found the cancer had spread so far throughout her body that surgery was useless. They closed her back up and sent her home to die.

I could *not* accept it! Not Carolyn, who had barely slipped out of death's grip when she was so young, only to go through months and months of excruciating pain following the automobile accident, and then to have to live with a disfigured face for the rest of her life. I knew I couldn't have adjusted in a million years the way she had. She learned to laugh and joke about it, never once complaining, always setting such an inspiring example for the rest of us that we felt ashamed to let our own petty problems get us down.

If ever an angel lived on this earth, it was Carolyn Jetton. She was always doing for others, thinking of others, never too tired or busy to offer a helping hand to a friend, neighbor, or relative. She spent the past two years taking care of Daddy, who lives next door to her in Mississippi, and has been incapacitated and unable to communicate since his first stroke shortly after Mama died. Carolyn has worked hard all her life, and she has always been to proud to accept any financial help from me. Her third child, Kris, who is now seven, was born with a number of physical defects, including no fingers or toes. The minute Kris was old enough to start undergoing plastic surgery, Carolyn stopped having any work done on her face. She couldn't afford both and she stubbornly refused to let me pay the bills. She would laugh and say, "Oh, Wynette, it isn't important. I'm used to this old face now anyway."

She was always a patient and loving mother to all three of her children (Kathy is now eighteen and Kerry is ten), but her wisdom and strength showed most with Kris. When he was a toddler, he'd try to pick up things in his little fists with no fingers for gripping. Invariably he would drop the object, whether it was a glass of milk or a toy. I would try to help him hold it, but Carolyn would say, *"No*, Wynette. Let him do it himself. I don't want him growing up dependent on others to do things for him. If we let him do it on his own, he'll eventually get the knack of it." And of course she was right. Kris can do almost anything for himself today. He goes to a regular school and he's happy and well adjusted. He's also exceptionally bright, so much so that we sometimes think God gave him extra intelligence to compensate for his physical defects.

The only time I have seen Carolyn break down since she learned she has terminal cancer was over her children. I was sitting on her bed holding her hand, and we were talking about our childhood when tears began streaming down her face. She was sobbing as I took her in my arms. "Oh, Wynette," she cried, "I don't *want* to leave without getting to see my children grow up. *Why* do I have to miss that?"

There are no words of comfort to ease a mother's pain when she knows she'll never see her children go to college or marry and have children of their own. All the reassurance in the world from me, and from Mother and Gerald, that her children will be loved and taken care of doesn't make it any easier for her to leave them.

But most of the time it is Carolyn who tries to comfort us. Even though she is in constant pain and has to take heavy medication to ease her agony, the cancer has not yet destroyed her brave spirit. She simply won't give in to self-pity. Rich says she is the bravest woman he's ever seen and Gerald the most courageous man. Gerald tells Mother and me that we *must* accept what is and cannot be changed. "All any of us can do is try to make her last months as easy as possible," he says.

Most of the time I've been able to put up a strong front in Carolyn's presence, but the minute I leave her bedside I break down. I've been flying to Mississippi instead of going home almost every time I have a day off, and I cannot imagine a horror worse than watching someone you love slip away little by little. Sometimes I feel so angry and hostile that I want to shake my fist at heaven and demand some sign that will justify this unbearable cruelty. I need to be told *why* someone who has been through so much pain and heartache already now has to suffer a horrible death at forty-one, an age when most people are just beginning to really live. But I know it's not for me to question.

There are other times when I cry as much for myself and Mother as for Carolyn. I know that as a Christian who sincerely believes in a life hereafter I should be able to comfort myself with the thought that Carolyn has earned a special place in Heaven. But my sorrow is inconsolable and it is with me every hour of every day. Thank God for Richey. Just having him near has been my one small comfort.

Carolyn has known Richey for years, and he was always one of her favorites among my friends. When I told her we had fallen in love and were going to marry, she hugged me tight and tears came into her eyes. "I know this time you've found a man who will look after you," she said. "I won't worry about you now."

I prayed Carolyn would be with us long enough to be at the wedding, and my prayer was answered. I wanted her to stand with me as my matron of honor, but I couldn't be sure she'd be up to that. By June 1, she was going downhill so fast we were just thankful to have her with us one day at a time. But when I told her the wedding date had been set for July 6, she seemed to perk up. "You've just *got* to stand up with me," I pleaded.

"Don't you worry," she squeezed my hand. "I'll be at that wedding if it kills me." When she realized what she'd said, she laughed as though it were a wonderful joke. "That didn't sound right," she said, "but you know what I mean. I wouldn't miss seeing you and Richey get married for anything. You can count on me."

On the day of the ceremony, when she walked down the long path from my living room to the platform on the beach, she was holding Gerald's arm securely, but she never faltered and she looked serenely happy. Even though she is now skeleton-thin and pain is reflected all over her face, she had a proud, victorious air about her that day as though she had conquered her fate, even if only for a little while.

The day before the ceremony she told me she was embarrassed about her hair. Even though she was wearing a navy blue picture hat to match her long gown, she was afraid people would notice that chemotherapy treatments had caused much of her hair to fall out. "I'll spoil your wedding pictures," she worried. I told her we'd take care of it. I drove to Palm Beach and bought her a wig, just the color and length of her own hair. That night I styled it, and when we tried it on her, she was as delighted as a young girl getting all fixed up for a date. "Why, it looks better than mine did even before I got sick," she said. "I'm going to wear it all the time."

All of Richey's large family showed up for the wedding: his children from California; his brother Paul with his wife Sylvia; Vi and Bill; three other sisters, Ginny Towery, Gladys Meier, and Violet Livingston; his brother Carl with his wife Beth; Violet's daughter Sandy, with her baby Christie, plus a house full of cousins.

My family made a good showing, too: Mother and Foy (who was happy about standing up with me this time!); my father's sisters, Earleen, Athalene and Princey; Hazel and Dan from Red Bay; and my good friends Cliff and Maxine, who drove over from Lakeland.

A number of our friends flew down from Nashville, including John Lentz, Ralph and Phyllis Gordon, Frances and E. J. Preston, Rover Sovine, Shirley Fleming, and Harry and Betty Bernow. Mr. and Mrs. Burt Reynolds Sr. and Logan and Katherine Fleming drove over from Burt's ranch. And Huell Howser, my favorite

Nashville television interviewer, came down to cover
the wedding as the only representative of the press
invited.

The ceremony was even more meaningful to me
because Richey's father, C. R. Richardson, a Baptist
minister from Malden, Missouri, performed the ceremony. Richey surprised me by inviting The Statesmen
quartet to fly down to sing at the ceremony. They have
been my favorite gospel group since I was a little girl,
and Mother's too; she was as thrilled to meet them as
I was. Richey also surprised me with the most beautiful
wedding-engagement ring I've ever seen in my life. It's
a four and a half carat solitaire mounted on a wide
gold band covered with diamonds.

After the ceremony on the beach, we all went by
motorcade to the Hilton in Jupiter for the reception.
The Statesmen really entertained us there, and Richey
joined them on several songs, singing bass. His exceptionally good voice didn't surprise me because he and
George and I, and whoever else wanted to join in,
have sat around our living room many a night, singing
old songs. But some of my guests weren't aware that
Richey sings almost as well as he plays piano.

One of them said, "Music just pours out of that
man, doesn't it?" It sure does, and it's one of the
things I love most about him. Our interests are so alike
it's as though we grew up in the same environment;
and actually our backgrounds aren't that different. He
grew up in Arkansas, the son of a preacher, spending
a good deal of his time playing and singing in church.
My Daddy wasn't a preacher, but I couldn't have spent
more time in church if he had been, because it was our
second home.

I remember reading somewhere once that the worst
thing about being an atheist is not having anyone to
thank when you're grateful for your blessings. That
alone would be enough to turn me to religion! When I
look back on the ups and downs, the highs and lows
of my life, I can't help but realize that at the worst of
times I was better off than most. God was generous

enough to give me a talent and the ambition to use it. If I hadn't had hurdles along the way, I wouldn't fully appreciate my success, anymore than I could appreciate Richey as much as I do if I'd never been married before.

When I was first asked to write my autobiography, I was not yet thirty-five. I protested that I was too young and still had too much living ahead of me. I said it would be like ending a song after the first verse, before I'd had time to sing the chorus. But it was pointed out to me that I had done more living in thirty-four years than many people do in a lifetime, and that it might be a good thing to pause and reflect at the halfway mark. This book represents the verse of my youth. Sometimes the notes were flat and the words didn't rhyme, but I have endured. Now I'm ready to sing my chorus. All the people I love—my family and friends—have contributed the notes. But the melody is mine. I sing it for them.

Index

351